by Wink Martindale

Winking at Life

Wink Martindale
5744 N. Newcastle Lane
Calabasas, CA 91302

Printed and bound in the United States of America

Winking At Life
Copyright 2000 by Wink Martindale
Library of Congress Catalog Card Number 00-90322
First Edition
ISBN 0-9677914-1-3
Published by:
    Century Hill Books

Cover, interior design and editing by Ernie and Patty Weckbaugh, Casa
Graphics, Inc., Burbank, CA 91504. Caricatures (for each chapter) by
Ernie Weckbaugh.

Dedication

Every word and picture in
this book is dedicated to
my wife Sandy, who
continually reminded me
that others had written
books before me.
It could be done!
Thanks Sandy, for
keeping me
on course.

On the Cover

Legendary
television
hosts with Wink
are left to right:
Jack Barry
Allen Ludden,
Bill Cullen,
Gary Moore,
and
Art Linkletter

Winking at Life

~ Contents ~

Acknowledgements

In writing this book I found myself recalling times, memories, events, and even people that in some way made an impact on either my life or career. It is virtually impossible to acknowledge each and every person that crossed my path in this continuing journey called life. So allow me to apologize to anybody who should have been mentioned here but were omitted. I would like to thank the following people, production companies, networks and photo services for helping me in various ways during my career, and for the pictures used in my book.

ABC Television, Art Alisi, Morey Amsterdam, Ralph Andrews, Bob Arrington, Gene Autry, Alfred Baker, Susan Bancroft, Chuck Barris Productions, Ken Berryhill, Richard Brockway, Leslie Brooks, Buena Vista Television, Al and Sally Burton, CBS Television, California State University - Northridge, Century Towers Productions, John Cleghorn, Cleveland Press, Dick Colbert, Bill and Shirley Cole, Dick Covington, Ann Cullen, Madelyn Dale, Michael Davies, Rev. Jimmy Elder, Susie Bancroft Elder, Dan Enright, Jimmy Exum, Mary Lou and Tony Ferra, Kerry and Tammy Fink, Homer and Joyce Formby, Dan Fox, Jean-Marc Gargiulo, Bill and Millie Goforth, Andrew Golder, Merv Griffin Productions, Merv Griffin, Bill Grumbles, Michael Gwartney, Al Ham, Christine Hamilton, Nancy and Dave Hannah, Heatter-Quigley Productions, Merrill Heatter, Bill and Meri Hillier, Charlie Hodge, Ron and Stephanie Hoffman, Jim Hoppers, Gary Hovey, Darrell and Dana Howe, Chuck Hurewitz, Barbara and Gordon Hyde, Mark Itkin, *The Jackson Sun*, Robert Johnson, Billy Johnston, KMPC - Golden West Broadcasters, Mary Kellogg, KingWorld Productions, Michael King, Roger King, George Klein, Darwin Lamm, Library of Congress, Gordon Lawhead, Art Linkletter, Ed and Nona Lojeski, Jack and Irma Longley, Jesse Martin, Memphis Commercial Appeal, Memphis Press Scimitar, *MEMPHIS Magazine*, Maria Melin, Ann Miller, Linda Mintz, Art Moore, Dick Murgatroyd, Bob Murphy, Hope Murray, Museum of Television & Radio, Tom Naud, NBC Television, Bob Neal, Wayne and Kathleen Newton, Bob Noah, D.A. Noel, Jerry Osborne, Col. Tom

Parker, Personality Photos, Inc., Stuart Phelps, Mike Phelps, Regis Philbin, Dewey Phillips, Stan Porter, Elvis Presley Enterprises, Catherine Price - TV Guide, Frank Proctor, Bob Quigley, Rick Quintana, Larry Reed, Jack Reeves, Tim Robertson, Aaron B. Robinson, Gene Roper, Noel Rubaloff, Lance Russell, Kermit Schafer, Jerry Schilling, Murray Schwartz, Arnold Shapiro, Jerry Shaw, Martha Sherman, Bill and Karen Smith, Jack Soden, Syracuse University, Vince Tapler, Dr. Ivan C. Tiholiz, Lois and Fred Travalena, University of California - Los Angeles, United Press International, University of Southern California Archives, Ernie Weckbaugh, Patty Weckbaugh, Betty White, Chick Wingate, Bill Winsett, Randy Wood, Lois Wood, Fred Wostbrock, Bill Yaggeman — and a *special thanks* to my wife Sandy.

Winking at Life

INTRODUCTION

Wink Martindale and I have been friends for longer than either of us care to mention. Our friendship started when he announced on radio that my new record was being sung by Margaret Whiting, recording under a different name.

He is one of those special people who define loyalty and commitment to his family and friends, and throughout all aspects of his life. Wink embodies those rare qualities of morals and honor in his personal and professional life that so many strive for and so few achieve in the entertainment world, or any other business — a dedication to his audiences, uncompromising integrity and an incredible enthusiasm for his work. His longevity in the radio and television industry, chronicled in this new book, is a testament to a man who has provided his viewers with years of entertainment and a rare opportunity to see greatness, as he is one of the best in the world at what he does. A true professional at work, Wink Martindale is a unique icon in the entertainment industry.

It has been said that no matter how rare true love, true friendship is even more rare. I am honored to tell you what I think of Wink Martindale, for to say these things in person makes him blush. I am truly blessed to call him friend.

P.S. Whoever wrote "Behind every great man is a great woman" had Wink and Sandy in mind.

Winking at Life

FOREWORD

"Here's the star of our show . . . Wink Martindale."

America's television audiences have been hearing those eight magical words for close to forty years. Wink Martindale has set the standard for style and excellence in an industry where he's accumulated countless awards, a gold record and graced the cover of the national TV Guide.

Today, Wink Martindale's name has become synonymous with game shows.

Since 1964, when the Winker was known as Win Martindale, until today he's almost never been off the small screen, either in first-run syndication, network, cable or in re-runs on the Game Show Network. In total, Wink has hosted 19 different game shows, one of a few select group of emcees who have hosted game shows on three networks (CBS, NBC and ABC). In fact, it's interesting to note that Wink has a couple of "firsts" in the game show genre.

In 1970, only two game shows premiered and Wink hosted both — *Words and Music* for NBC, and in syndication, *Can You Top This?*

Wink, in 1993, became the first emcee (as well as executive producer) to host television's first interactive game show *Trivial Pursuit.* This show allowed home viewers to play along, live with Wink, by calling a 900 number.

In addition to his game show successes, Wink has been a success in radio — as well as being a million-selling recording star. In 1959 Wink scored a top-ten record, selling over one-million copies of "Deck of Cards." Each year his recording returns as a favorite during the Christmas holidays.

Long before television came his way, Wink's first love was radio. In fact, while as the top-rated disc-jockey at WHBQ in Memphis, Wink had the chance to see and to hear the very first Elvis Presley record ever played on the radio. It was that magical night when both Wink and Elvis became life-long friends, from 1956 until Elvis' untimely death. Wink was so moved by his friend's death that, in 1978, he recorded a 15-hour radio tribute to the memory of his Memphis friend, Elvis Presley.

To this day, some 25 years later, Elvis' fans around the world consider Wink's tribute the best ever on the life and times of Elvis Presley.

If you're asking how I know all this information on Wink, I'll tell you . . . I'm his agent.

I first knew of Wink Martindale when I was 10 years old, in 1970, while watching *Can You Top This?* in New Jersey on WOR-TV. He was my Mickey Mantle . . . my hero.

I first spoke to Wink in 1976 when I called KMPC Radio in Hollywood where he was one of the stations top paid radio superstars. He took my call and we chatted on his career. Over the years we kept in touch and, in 1982, when I moved to Los Angeles after college at Syracuse University, I was employed by Wink until the late '80s . . . and, I might add, he was a terrific boss who paid well!

So you see, first I was a fan, then a friend, then an employee, and finally I became Wink's agent in the spring of 1992. It's been a delight every step of the way. I'm proud to be his friend, and proud that he trusted me with his multi-faceted career.

You see, dreams do come true! So sit back, butter the fat-free popcorn, and enjoy the Winker's book. I know *I* will.

—Fred Wostbrock, Hollywood, CA

Chapter One

A BOY'S DREAM

Fulfilled . . . and Surpassed

"**W**hat do you want to be when you get big?" Hasn't that always been the adult's favorite question of the little kid? And to this day, aren't these some of the most popular answers to that age-old question:

1. Policeman
2. Fireman
3. Doctor

Okay, granted we might hear an occasional baseball, football, basketball, or hockey player in this modern age of professional athletes and monumental salaries. But for the most part, when I was growing up, those listed above ranked as the top three. *But not for me!* I was among the lucky kids on my block, the 400 block of Burkett Avenue in Jackson, Tennessee. Just as sure as I was born in the front bedroom of my parents' house December 4th, 1933, I was born to be a radio announcer.

With the exception of one brief period during junior high school when I had visions of becoming a candy mogul, I was constantly fascinated by radio. The fact that one could talk into a piece of metal and that person's voice could then be heard coming out of a radio speaker miles away literally blew me away. I didn't have the first clue about what made radio work. I only knew that I wanted to be one of those guys sitting behind a microphone talking, reading the news, and playing records. Where this strong desire originally came from or precisely when it began, I have no idea to this day. I have a couple of logical theories. I spent a lot of my youth playing alone. And many of those hours found my ears glued to the radio speaker. So eventually I began to "play like" I, too, was one of those radio announcers. I quickly discovered at a very early age that if you cupped your hand over your ear you could hear yourself. What a kick that was!

I also noticed early on that the better radio announcers had pleasant voices and could read very well. So I was determined to become a good

All the Martindale kids, except oldest brother Kenneth, were born in the front bedroom of this house on Burkett Street in Jackson, Tennessee.

reader. My mother was the first in my family of three other boys and one girl to know for sure that radio was in my future. As a kid of six or seven, I became an avid reader of *Life* magazine. My dad was a lumber inspector, and his boss, Mr. W.C. Hanafee, would give us an annual subscription to *Life* every Christmas. I developed my reading skills by tirelessly cutting out full-page advertisements from *Life* magazine, then reading the content of those ads as if they were radio commercial announcements. This not only helped to improve my reading, but this practice required a certain amount of ad libbing, or improvisation as we might call it today. Little did I know back then that I was laying the groundwork for becoming a deejay, and subsequently a game show host, both specialties in the business of radio and television that require the ability to ad lib and think on your feet.

Wink (far right) pictured here with brothers Leo and Kenneth, and sis Geraldine (Gerry). The youngest brother David (not pictured) was deceased.

"Doing Radio"

Time and time again my Mom would find me sequestered in the back bedroom with the door tightly shut pretending to be selling everything from Carnation milk to DeSoto automobiles. To her credit I don't recall that she ever made fun of me. The fact is she encouraged me, unless she caught me "doing radio" when I was supposed to be cutting firewood or helping wash and dry the dishes. Some of my fondest memories are of rushing home from West Jackson Grammar School in the afternoon so I wouldn't miss hearing mother's favorite soaps. I practically grew up on "Stella Dallas," "Young Widow Brown," "When a Girl Marries," "Just Plain Bill" and "Lorenzo Jones." While the story lines of those vintage radio dramas pale when compared to the steamy plots of television's "The Young and the Restless" or "As the World Turns," they reflected the simple life of post-war America. As a youngster I could become immersed in the trials and tribulations of Stella Dallas and her daughter Lollie without wor-

Wink's Mom was Frances Mae Mitchell before her marriage to James Auzie Martindale. This might well have been taken the day of their marriage.

rying whether or not parental guidance was required.

Radio, as I knew it growing up in the Forties, provided not only a source of interest and entertainment but also a training ground of sorts for what was to come. Many were the nights I buried my head in a pillow next to the radio speaker in my darkened bedroom to live the adventures of Jack, Doc and Reggie (*I Love a Mystery*) on the old Mutual Network. It was as if they were my personal friends. They were in my room five nights a week! I had friends in the neighborhood I didn't see that often. There was the mystique of *The Shadow* around which I planned Sunday afternoon. At four o'clock, Lamont Cranston asking, "Who knows what evil lurks in the hearts of men?" never failed to send a shiver up my young spine. But then everybody's favorite cowboy Gene Autry would invite us into his *Melody Ranch* to sing a song or two, and prove once again that the good guys always win! And how fun it was to be able to picture Gene and Champion after just seeing them in a double feature the day before. Ironically, later in my career, The Singing Cowboy would be my radio boss for 13 years at KMPC in Los Angeles.

The Cat's Whiskers

The very first radio that was all mine I bought through a mail order catalogue for the astounding sum of $3.99. It wasn't rea*lly* a radio as such. It was a crystal set, and if you gently placed the "cat's whisker," a small wire pickup device, on the surface of the crystal in precisely the right spot, you might (if you were lucky) pick up the sound of a local radio station by wearing headphones. It also required a ground wire to the outside, which I accomplished through the use of a coathanger. As crude and unreliable as it was, that little crystal set gave me some of my earliest and most exciting radio memories. When, after tireless attempts, I luckily found a hot spot on the crystal and picked up the signal of Jackson's only station WTJS, I was the happiest kid in the world.

Wink worked 13 years at KMPC Radio for his boyhood idol Gene Autry.

My next most exciting foray into the wonderful world of radio announcing came when I sent off for a small palm-sized ribbon microphone. Cost? $7.95. I was advancing rapidly. With this device called a beginner's mike, the trick was to place the two small metal prongs at the end of two wires under two separate tubes in the back of your radio...or, in this case, my Dad's console radio in the living room! If you followed directions correctly, you could then speak into the little mike while holding your ear close to the radio's speaker and in theory, hear yourself in the speaker. Unfortunately for me, two things went wrong. The manufacturer's theory was flawed! And tragically, the mike blew out two tubes in the living room radio, and my use of it in playing announcer!

MOTHER—Mom and Mr. Woody

A lot could be said for growing up in a small West Tennessee town of 25,000 people in the thirties and forties. Everybody seemed to know everybody else . . . *and their business as well.* Times were so simple then. Trust seemed a given. For example, Mother carried a running charge account at Mr. Woody's neighborhood grocery on Campbell Street. Though she tried to pay it in full each Saturday, that wasn't always possible. But Mr. Woody didn't seem to mind. Many of his regular customers had, what we might term today, cash-flow problems. Imagine trying to check out at your favorite supermarket today by saying, "Pay you Saturday!" Good luck! Yet the manner by which Mother did her grocery shopping for our large family was also a sign of the times. She would pencil out a list, phone the store with her needs and within a couple of hours a delivery boy would come riding up on his bicycle with the wire basket attached to the handlebars overflowing with sacks of groceries. My brothers Leo and Kenneth and

Ironically, Wink had to walk past his church, Lambuth Memorial Methodist, on his after-school visits to Woody's grocery store where he pocketed candy.

I all delivered groceries for Mr. Woody at different times in our sub-teens, daily during summer vacation and on Saturdays during the school year.

One of the nicest and most pleasant employees of Woody's Grocery was a gentleman named Mr. Bishop. He stands out in my mind because of his many kindnesses to my mom and his understanding of her frequent financial woes. And he was such a fan of Leo's and Kenneth's athletic careers during both high school and college. Mr. Bishop later followed my career with great interest, to the point where he called me on at least two occasions during visits home from California. The two of us had shared an unspoken secret ever since I was a fifth and sixth grader at West Jackson Elementary School. Woody's was just a stone's throw from the school. So it became quite convenient for me to include a stop by the grocery store on my walk home each day. I became as much a regular as the owner and Mr. Bishop! I would walk in the front door to the welcome tinkling of the ever-present bell. Ah, what a sweet sound that was after a long, hard day at school — **in more ways than one!**

Just Hangin' Around

After my usual greetings to Mr. Bishop I would just hang around — and hang around — and hang around, while all the time edging closer and closer to the candy counter. It is with no pride at all that I admit for the first time through this writing that day after day in some mysterious way some gum balls or a Snickers Bar or a Goo Goo Cluster would find their way into my overall pants pocket. Which would have been fine if that pocket had held the proper change with which to pay Mr. Bishop and thereby complete our transaction. Such was seldom the case, however, since spare change was in short supply at our house. And we kids knew never to put *anything* on Mother's charge account. That was a very big no-no! In any event, as wrong as I knew this habit I had acquired was, it continued until I entered the seventh grade in junior high on Dederick Street, a much different path home and far too inconvenient to Mr. Woody's Grocery Store.

Now it's years later and I'm having a nice little chat with my long time friend and fan, Mr. Bishop, from Woody's. Wouldn't you know? It was then I discovered that Mr. Woody and Mr. Bishop weren't so dumb after all! Right in the midst of congratulating me on my niche of

Could this be the same innocent looking Winkie Martindale who loved visiting Woody's Grocery Store?

success with the game show *Tic-Tac-Dough*, he says, "Now maybe you can afford to repay your Mom for some of that candy!" After we both stopped laughing, he confessed that most times they simply added the nickel or dime to Mother's bill. And other times they just "forgot" to write it down. He even said they used to make bets on which candy selection I would make on a given day. Did my Mom ever notice any of the strange and sweet excess charges? Well, if she did, she never let me know about it. My instinct tells me that had she noticed, my rear end would have felt the wrath of a weeping willow switch, ever-present and hanging from the giant tree in our back yard.

The Doctor is in . . . Trouble!

My butt still remembers to this day one particular whipping Mother gave me with one of those branches. I told her a fib (no, it was more like a full-blown lie) in answer to a question to which she already knew the answer! No Mother who ever lived was more devoted to her kids than ours. But she taught us early in life not to tell "stories." She assured us that God always knew when we were lying, and most of the time s*he did, too*!

Well this time I must have forgotten her admonition not to fib. It was about eight o'oclock at night, but that didn't matter. She took me out to the backyard, broke off a willow limb, and in the same motion, stripped it of its bright green leaves, then proceeded to teach me a lesson I've never forgotten. Thus this recollection. I can honestly say I cannot recall *EVER* lying to my Mom again.

Well, maybe that's stretching the truth a bit. There was this *one other time*. An elderly widow lady lived next door to us. Mrs. Crawford had a cute little granddaughter my age named Maquita Replogle, a name she later changed to Connie (the Maquita part, not Replogle). Maquita was my very first girl-friend at a time when neither of us really knew why boys were attracted to girls. I only knew that when she made one of her frequent visits next door, I always found it necessary to go over and say hello to Mrs. Crawford.

As time went by, Maquita and little Winkie (a nickname

A young left-handed Wink hones his skills as a future passer for Jackson High School, a dream that never quite materialized.

given me by a playmate across the street, Jimmy McCord, who always came out with "Winkie" when he tried to say my real name, Winston), discovered that instead of playing cars under the house or hide-and-go-seek with the other kids in the neighborhood, it was much more fun to play doctor and nurse. I don't remember how or when this realization hit us. It just sort of did. We chose the Martindale yard instead of the Crawford yard, thanks to a very young but full-foliaged peach tree just under Mother's kitchen window. The area under the tree apparently made the perfect emergency room for our imaginary hospital.

Jimmy McCord (right), who gave Wink his nickname as a childhood playmate, renews their friendship at a 1998 high school reunion.

Show and Tell

Finally one day, it came time for Maquita and me to graduate to the game of *Show and Tell*. Up until this day Mother had left us alone to our own devices in running our hospital in the backyard. Dr. Winkie

Wink's three daughters (left to right), Lisa, Lyn and Laura, enjoy their grandmother's front porch swing during a visit to their Dad's homeplace in Jackson.

and head nurse Maquita were doing just fine by themselves while Mother was going about her less important tasks in the house.

For reasons unknown to me till this day I drew the short straw in our game. It fell upon me to drop my pants first. And wouldn't you know that just about the time Maquita was discovering there was a distinct difference between boys and girls, Mother chose that particular moment to peek under the tree just to be sure all was well in the emergency room! Needless to say, that ended *Show and Tell*, closed down the ER, and essentially ended what could have been a wonderful relationship. Destiny dictated that I was never to view Maquita's private parts. When Mother asked me if we had played that game before I assured her we had not. Did she believe me? I never knew. I was more concerned that she didn't take a switch to me for my childish experimentation. She didn't! Incidentally, I never saw much of Connie in later years. But one Sunday in the late seventies, all the Martindale kids *and their kids* were at Mother and Dad's house bummin' a free meal (as we kids will do), when suddenly there was a knock at the front door. Guess who? Yep! Connie Replogle. And I must say she was a knockout! Just happened to be next door and wanted to say hello. Sadly, that's the last time I ever laid eyes on my favorite nurse.

The Neighborhood

From time to time something will occur in our present neighborhood that will be reminiscent of Burkett Street. But those times are rare indeed. A couple of those rare exceptions would be Halloween and the Christmas holidays. For example, my wife Sandy answered the doorbell

Wink, even then surrounded by lovely neighborhood girls, Mary Nell Jones and Carole Stewart!

this past Halloween over three hundred times, each time to the sound of munchkins large and small yelling "Trick or treat?" Of course, the silver bells, the holly and mistletoe, the carolers, the holiday lights and the manger scene on front lawns are as familiar today on our Calabasas, California streets as they were during Christmases past in Tennessee. Some things never change regardless of passing time or location.

But for the most part, age notwithstanding, how different our neighborhoods of today seem to be when compared to our old neighborhoods. Today we hardly know anybody on our block. Yesterday we not only *knew* our neighbors; it wasn't at all uncommon to know the Dads' occupations and the Mothers' first names! Let's see, next door to us was Mary Elizabeth Owens (who later married and became a Medical Technician at the hospital). Her mom was a homemaker and Mr. Owens worked for the GM&O Railroad. Of course you rememebr Maquita Replogle's grandmother, Mrs. Crawford. She lived in the house on the other side of us. Every street, no matter where, has its very own know-it-all. Burkett street was no exception. Across from us was Gene Stewart and his wife, Katherine. Gene was a former Jackson High School football hero and he lived the part twenty-four hours a day. The Conners, with only daughter Kathleen, lived on one side of the Stewarts', and Mr. and Mrs. Jones lived on the other. What made *these* Joneses different, however — nobody tried to "keep up with 'em"! Their son Gene was several years older than I, but

he was one of my earliest buddies. He delivered groceries for Williamson's Grocery down on Poplar (later changed to Hollywood Drive), but unlike the Martindale boys, his *bicycle* was a Chevrolet truck. Every now and then Gene would let me ride with him during his deliveries. And when he was in a really good mood, he'd let me feed the accelerator pedal on the truck. Compare that for kicks with the thrills some kids need today. Like the song said, "Give me the simple life." Hard to beat.

Up on the hill in the next block lived the Walkers and

The Burkett Street "Six"; (front) Jimmy McKissack, (second row) Billy McKissack, Neville Stewart (head down), Wink, (third row) Wink's sister Gerry, Mary Elizabeth Owens.

their infamous son Gerald. Everybody for miles around knew when it was time for Gerald to come home, because Mrs. Walker literally screamed at the top of her voice, "G-g-g-e-e-e-r-r-r-a-a-a-l-l-l-d Walker, you get in here this minute!" making a five-syllable word out of his first name in the best Southern tradition. Gerald was the first one on the block to learn (and teach) everybody to curse and swear. He was also the first person I ever saw who carried a comb in his back pocket, no matter where he was or what he was doing. It was never clean. But it was a comb. Gerald would have been perfectly cast in *GREASE*, but he was born too soon.

Later into that same house on the hill came the Kirks. Billy and Carl Dean Kirk were two of the good guys, well mannered and just plain nice. Billy was my age, while Carl Dean was two or three years younger. For some reason we "older" boys felt the need to pick on and slap around the younger ones. Carl Dean got picked on a lot!

Great Friends

Rounding out our lively group were Charles and Robert "Beans" Beasley down on Robbins Street; the Neil Gilberts and their son Russell, who worked as an undertaker for Smith Funeral Home; and aside from my first cousin Tommy Marcom (who lived with us after the death of his parents), my very best friends were Billy and Jimmy McKissack. They lived two doors down at the

The soda jerk at Baker's drug store only *dreamed* of being a sports star.

corner of Burkett and Williams Streets. I think I spent more time at their house than my own. Mr. McKissack worked for National Harvester and got to drive a company pickup truck home every day. Plus, they already had a car! Being from a family that either walked, rode bikes or took the bus, I viewed the McKissacks as having it all. A car AND a truck — and their *house* was really special. You know why? It was a two-story house. It actually had an upstairs. And, wouldn't you know, Billy and Jimmy both had bunk beds. I would have given anything to have a bunk bed. Sometimes, when I stayed overnight, one of them would let me sleep in the top bunk. The greatest! Bunk beds, a car and a truck, all in the same family. Go figure.

Almost every one of the pals I've mentioned worked with me as a soda jerk at Baker's Drug Store downtown. And almost every Sunday night, after we got off work, we'd congregate at Billy and Jimmy's house. There were usually ten or twelve of us making just enough noise that Mr. McKissack would have to make a dozen trips a night up the stairs to quiet us down. But he was a gentle, soft-spoken man with that ever-present pipe hanging from one side of his mouth. Although innocent as it seemed, we actually were running our own version of a casino up there. We played various card games, including poker and blackjack. An occasional pair of dice even found their way into our den of iniquity. We even played odd-man-out with quarters, depending on how tips had been that day. Yes folks — there was trouble brewin' in River City (. . . *er* Jackson). This phase of our life eventually passed with none of us, to my knowledge, suffering permanent damage, thanks to our amateur guide to Las Vegas.

Common Sense . . . *Not* So Common

Early on, in part thanks to the McKissacks', I learned that whatever radio and television skills God had blessed me with far exceeded my entrepreneurial talents. Unfortunately, however, I didn't always allow my brain to listen to what common sense dictated to me. This personal flaw would later lead me to some real estate, restaurant and television production losses amounting to over a million dollars.

Frank McKissack was a man who could have tutored Tim Allen in the art of home improvement. As one who represents the antithesis of do-it-yourself skills, I marveled at the fact that he never had to hire anybody to do anything for him at 422 Burkett Street. He could do it all. So one summer when Billy, Jimmy and I decided to partner in a lemonade and soft drink stand, Mr. McKissack wouldn't stand still for your typical table on the sidewalk with a sign reading "Cold Drinks & Lemonade, 5 Cents." Oh no! He proceeded to build a very large wooden structure in their backyard complete with counters on all four sides, two used professional soft drink boxes, electric lights, and finally a gas grill just in case we wanted to expand our summer enterprise into serving hamburgers and hotdogs.

I haven't seen a better fast-food setup at Ram games than what we ended up with. We had it all! Except customers. When there was a lull in business, though, we had the perfect solution. As Andy Griffith put it in his hit soliloquy "What It Was Was Football," we each "had a big orange drink." Once our parents and friends had come by to check out our digs and make their obligatory purchase, we might as well have closed down. But hope springs eternal when you're young. So we hung in there — *for three weeks!* By then the local swimming hole looked much better than days spent watching cars speeding by us on Williams Street without even catching a glimpse of Mr. McKissack's *custom-made neon sign.*

> ICE COLD DRINKS
> HOT DOGS AND HAMBURGERS

For years when I would come back home to visit Mother and Daddy, my trip wouldn't be complete unless I walked two houses down and once again sat on one of the supposed customer benches that surrounded the

stand. By now, the once sparkling white paint that Mr. McKissack had so carefully brushed on the new wood had long since begun to peel. And that new grill that might have been a precursor to perhaps a fast-food chain somewhere down the road, was now hardly recognizable through the rust. If I listened very carefully, I could almost hear a seven-year-old Jimmy suggest, "Hey, anybody thirsty? Why don't we all have a big orange drink 'til a customer comes?"

The Near Miss

As youngsters we all have one thing in common. We view ourselves as in- vincible — immortal. Until something occurs inour life that wakes us up from the dream. One such event happened to

Wink and his Mom during a Christmas dinner at "The Hut" circa 1979.

me during my Jackson Sun paper route one cold winter day. I was reaching the half-way mark of my route, which always meant a brief stop at Mr. Fred Michie's Used Cars on Poplar for a chance to warm myself around the cozy pot-bellied stove in his office. He also sold candy bars, and I looked forward each day to sinking my teeth into either a Hershey Bar or a Snickers. It was my mid-route energy boost! On this day I must have been daydreaming about one or both, the warm fire or the sweet candy. As I was turning my bike across the busy street, I failed to see an oncoming car over my right shoulder.

"Is my bike okay?" Those were the first words out of my mouth as Mr. Michie was raising my head off the pavement. He assured me the bicycle was not beyond repair, but that I couldn't ride it 'til it was fixed.

As the accident began to draw a crowd, I wondered just how hurt I was, and how hurt my bike was. Is Mama gonna be mad at me for not being careful crossing the street? I had begged her to let me carry a paper route. Plus, the bicycle really belonged to my brother Leo. He was letting me use it each day to deliver my papers. He's gonna kill me! These concerns bothered me so much I really didn't think to worry about any broken bones, a concussion or worse. The only other time I had ever been hurt was when I broke my collarbone (clavicle) playing touch football at Gerald Walker's house. Mother was furious, mainly because she had told me *not* to play, in no uncertain terms. Plus, the doctor bill at that time was a headache she didn't need, and a bill not covered by insurance.

Luckily, I wasn't seriously hurt. Just a few scratches and a couple of bruised ribs. But I was old enough to have this accident put the fear of God into me when it came to safety on my bike. This time I was lucky; might not be the same next time. That is, if Mother would allow a *next time*. Actually, to no one's surprise, she was very understanding and just happy that for the most part, my "parts" were unhurt. I paid for having Leo's bike repaired and, as they say, all's well that end's well.

Delivering *The Jackson Sun* and working as a paper boy was my first real job, as Dad would say. When I first began I was too young to have my own route, so my older first cousin Tommy Marcom and I shared a route. Each Wednesday we were handed a small white envelope with $4.70 inside, i.e. $2.35 apiece. Later Tommy gave up the route and my friend Jimmy McKissack shared it with me. Though an afternoon daily, The Sun also published a big Sunday morning edition. Sunday deliveries were particularly fun because Mr. McKissack would drive us in his truck, no bicycles! But even better, at the break of dawn he would take Jimmy and me downtown to Joe's Poolroom and Restaurant for pancakes and eggs that were to die for. Yes indeed, Sundays were very special.

Childhood Fantasy . . .

The three story building on Baltimore Street which housed the *Jackson Sun* presses in its basement was also home on the third floor to the city's only radio station at that time, WTJS, an owned subsidary of the

Ken Berryhill, host of "Ken Calling" on Jackson station WTJS in 1948. Ken's show was Wink's first visit to a radio station's studio.

newpaper publishing company (TJS in the call letters stood for *The Jackson Sun*). As an avid radio junkie, this provided a perfect opportunity for me. Almost every day before picking up my papers downstairs, I would nervously climb the well-beaten stairs of this old building to the third floor, and there above the double-glass doors were the four neon letters that never failed to send an excited chill through my body: WTJS! Remember, this was 1945. I was a very impressionable twelve-year-old kid who had to share a paper route, because I was too young to have my own. Television was still a far-off dream. But those four call letters to me represented the most immediate chance to one day fulfill my fantasy of talking on the radio.

For an hour or two I would just sit there in the cramped foyer, my eyes glued to the oversized Jensen speaker and mesmerized by the realization that every word, every commercial, every jingle I heard in that room, from that speaker, were the same words, jingles, and commercials that people could also hear outside that room in their homes and cars for miles and miles. Eventually the station's staff began to recognize me and call me by name. My two older brothers were athletes of some renown in town, so I was Leo and Kenneth Martindale's little brother Winkie.

Country superstar Eddy Arnold began his career at Jackson's WTJS.

Didn't matter. By now staff announcers Sam Lollar, Vince Tapler, Larry O'Brien or Glen Johnson would occasionally say hello to me . . . *in the same voice I had heard them use on the radio for so long!* I couldn't get over it. I idolized these men much like a kid today might idolize Green Bay quarterback Bret Favre. They were saying things like, "Hi Winkie. How are you today?" In today's parlance I might describe my reaction as surreal, like my feelings fourteen years later when Ed Sullivan would be talking to me about my recording of "Deck of Cards" on CBS Television.

. . . Comes True!

There was no way for me to know that just a scant seven years later, in 1952, I would be welcomed as the newest member of the WTJS announcing staff by managers Frank Proctor and Leslie

Brooks. They would hire me away from rival station WPLI after just a few months on my first job in radio. That was another red-letter day early in my career, for I remember that another unknown had received his initial break, though as a singer, on radio station WTJS. That singer would become the country superstar we know as Eddy Arnold.

DADDY . . . and Simpler Times

Growing up in Jackson was much like it was depicted in the feature film *Breaking Away*. The times seemed simpler . . . slower paced . . . less stressful . . . and perhaps, even happier. As an adult *today* reflecting on my boyhood *then*, maybe those descriptive words are more convenient than accurate. Webster's New World Dictionary defines "nostalgia" as *a longing to go back to one's home, hometown, or homeland; a longing for something far away or long ago, or for former happy circumstances.*

Wink's Mom and Dad. Francis was a homemaker while James was a lumber inspector.

Why is that what we had yesterday often seems so much better than what we have today? It surely didn't seem so special at the time, did it? But when we're very young we view everything from a completely different perspective: I can't wait to reach thirteen! If I **ever** hit sixteen I can get my driver's license! . . . God, will I **ever** reach twenty-one? We all walked that walk and talked that talk at one time. And suddenly — where did the time go? I can recall so clearly thinking how elderly I thought my Dad was when he hit forty. **FORTY!** Now two of my daughters have eclipsed that mark! It's a cliche to say everything is relative. But it really is true, isn't it?

All five of the Martindale kids, with the exception of the first born, Kenneth, were born at home on Burkett Street. Ken was born in my folks' first little apartment on Linden Street when they were still newlyweds. The stork came to our house with amazing regularity, delivering babies given the names Edward Leo, Frances Geraldine, Winston Conrad, and David Lynn. All four delivered on the same bed by the same doctor in the same front bedroom. Home births were not so un-usual in those days — and far easier on a very tight budget. Dad had only two employers as a lumber inspector for all of his adult life; the Wood Mosaic Company, and The Jackson Sawmill. His job was to grade large stacks of lumber from the time it arrived as logs, until the time the sawmill cut the logs into planks, which were stacked, graded and loaded into boxcars for the trip by rail to the buyer.

Dad's Diligence

Dad was always a hard and diligent worker. He never had a car 'til much later in his life, so he walked to work every day—no short dis-tance. Then he would walk back home for a hot dinner (we called lunch dinner), listen to Paul Harvey's noon news on the radio, take a short nap, then walk back to work in time for the one o'clock whistle. Such was his routine every day, Monday through Friday from 7AM till 5PM. He worked only a half day on Saturday. His wages were adequate for our family of seven, but we had none of the frills of life. We were anything but rich in terms of material things. But we certainly were not poor by any means.

While Dad was the breadwinner, Mother was the weaver of a certain Martindale magic when it came to making ends meet. In his younger years as a husband and father, Dad's Saturday routine would include a walk down-town for several hours, and many beers at Joe's poolroom and cafe. More often than not, by the time he stumbled up the front steps at ten or eleven o'clock that night, he had been separated from most of that week's paycheck. Which meant that Mother was left with little or no funds for the next week with which to buy groceries and pay bills. But someway, somehow, she al-ways seem to pull off her magic means of making a dollar go just far enough to get by.

One of Wink's early dreams was realized when he won the job as morning host of *Clockwatchers* on Memphis station WHBQ.

Older and Wiser

In all fairness, as Daddy grew older he grew wiser. By his mid-fifties he had said goodbye to that smoking and drinking habit and was the kind of father we all knew he could be. Though he was not the man to apologize or admit any short-comings during our formative years, he nonetheless showed us in many different ways his love for us, and more importantly for his wife, our mother.

A caricature of Wink by artist Jack Lane.

Dad's love manifested itself in many ways in later years. Early on, he had not really looked with favor on my desire for a career in radio. He felt that those who worked as radio announcers chose that profession out of laziness, or just a lack of desire to hold down a legitimate nine-to-five job. He could cite several announcers who had worked in Jackson just long enough to run up some substantial bills before running out of town. And that was his perception of anyone who worked in the radio business. It wasn't a *real job*.

Co-Signer

I was able to change the way he viewed radio as a possible career in the best possible way. I began to prove, first in Jackson, then in Memphis, that I could make a living wage sitting behind a microphone doing what I loved to do. The sure-fire indication that he approved of my vocation in radio was when I asked if he would sign a note at the bank for my first car, a green 1948 four-door Plymouth. I was only seventeen and just out of high school, but already in my first year of radio I was making $45.00 a week. I had seen this like-new used car at the Newsom Bros. lot on Poplar Street, and I just had to

Big brother Kenneth dares to lean on Wink's first car, a 1948 Plymouth!

have it. But I couldn't get the loan without Daddy's signature. And he was . . . let's just say he was frugal and leave it at that! I was prepared to offer interest if I had to. But he would have none of that. To my delight he couldn't have been nicer. He went on my note, I drove my first car off Mr. Newsom's gravel lot that day, and I knew two things for sure. One, he was convinced his radio announcer son could handle the monthly car payments, and two, he'd forgiven me for blowin' out those two tubes on the console radio so many years before!

Sister Gerry, here with husband Jack King, helped Wink negotiate Memphis' one way streets on his first visit to WHBQ in 1953.

Dad died suddenly and unexpectedly from a brain tumor in 1969. At his funeral, there seemed to be a thousand and one memories swirling around my brain; memories of a tow-headed son growing up with a loving father. But not one single memory outshone that memorable day Daddy "took a chance"— and said "okay" to going on my note for that first car.

It was in that '48 Plymouth on a day in 1953 that my sis Gerry rode with me on a joyous ride to Memphis. Joyous because I had auditioned and won the job I had coveted so much, that of morning host of *Clockwatchers* on WHBQ, arguably the most popular wake-up radio show in the midsouth. Now I was to come face-to-face with my new employers, President John Cleghorn, General Manager William H. (Bill) Grumbles (who would become my mentor), and station Program Director Gordon Lawhead.

Our destination was the mezzanine floor of the old Chisa Hotel on South Main Street, a rather unusual neighborhood for this radio facility owned by the religious school, Harding College in Searcy, Arkansas. Anyone watching us wind our way to downtown Memphis might well have wondered if this redneck from Jackson and his sister would make it in one piece. As one who seldom ventured outside the city limits of home, I was immune to such foreign street signs as ONE WAY! But, thanks to the excellent navigational and directional skills of my sister, we made it on time and in one piece. Gerry was no dummy, thank God! She wasn't named valedictorian of her senior class for nothing.

The rest of the day went very well with just one exception. I was to begin work in two weeks as "morning man" and assistant record librarian to Jill Bishop, the lady in charge of record selection for each music show on the station. The afternoon show was *Covington's Corner,* presided over by Dick Covington, whose stentorian tones could be compared to those of my current colleague on *Music of Your Life,* Gary Owens. Dick's seniority and his knowledge of music gave him the right to assemble his own play list each day. I had remembered listening to Dick for years while a teen in Jackson, and I was in total awe of

The venerable Art Linkletter was one of Wink's show business idols. Today he's privileged to call Art a friend.

his deep, baritone voice. Now I would find myself on the same staff with this man I admired so much. It was like another unreachable dream — that suddenly was within reach.

Close Call

Art Linkletter, another of my show business heroes, once wrote a book entitled *Kids Say The Darndest Things.* Well, I can assure you that **older** kids—like me—have that ability as well. It's been termed foot-in-mouth disease at times. My budding career, such as it was around 1952, could well have ended as quickly as it had begun. I was in my first weeks as the kid announcer at WTJS, and proud as punch of myself with new-found ego to match! I had always known what I wanted to do with my life and now *I was on my way, BIGTIME!* I was playing the music I loved, playing newscaster for real, doing real, live commercials, and calling football and basketball games play-by-play. I was living my dream and loving it.

Friday evening: Time for me to read the Ten O'Clock News, a nightly fifteen-minute summary of the day's events. As noted earlier, I always took great pride in my reading ability, a skill that I worked on diligently as a boy. But this night, for whatever reasons, my reading skills deserted me. The harder I tried to concentrate the more mistakes I made. It was real disconcerting! To make matters worse, when I played the recording on disc of the sponsor's commercial, I played it at 78RPM rather than 33 1/3! Not once, but twice. The Budweiser people would have loved that.

The situation didn't improve during the ten-fifteen sports report either. It was September 23rd, the night that Rocky Marciano defeated

Jersey Joe Walcott in the 13th round for the heavyweight boxing championship. I'll never forget that fight . . . or the way I reported it in Jackson, Tennessee. You see, the bout was actually televised in a closed circuit to 125,000 paying spectators in 50 motion picture theatres across the country. In my eagerness, or whatever, to right my reading ship, my report had Rocky Walcott defeating Jersey Joe Marciano in the 13th round for the heavyweight boxing championship! And, I had the bout televised to 50 paying spectators in 125,000 motion picture theatres. Now Dick Enberg I'm not. But to verbalize such a gross misstatement while having more than a passing knowledge of boxing was almost more than I could handle.

Oops!

Then I inadvertently left the microphone open while I was thinking out an appropriate response to my stupid reading. "Dammit! What the s _ _ _'s gonna happen next"!

In light of an already unbearable situation, I had succeeded in making matters worse. I was beside myself. Mortified might be the right word. While it's true that what I said might be rated on the big screen today as PG, or "so what" on *The Howard Stern* radio show, in the Forties and Fifties we were living under a more stringent set of rules, personally and professionally (thanks to the ever-watchful eye of the FCC).

Somehow I made it through the sportscast and joined the ABC Network program, *Dream Harbor* at 10:30. I called my engineer at the transmitter and asked him if he had heard what I said. Perhaps I was looking for some assurance that what I said was not all that bad, knowing full well how bad it must have sounded coming out of a radio speaker. Surprisingly, Marvin Pyles assured me he hadn't heard any profanity! Marvin should have been a politician.

Then my phone rang. Was it Mr. Brooks or Mr. Proctor? Was tonight the beginning of my end in radio? How would my firing look on my future resumé? Would the headline in Sunday morning's *Jackson Sun* read:

Martindale Arrested!
WTJS Announcer Fired
<u>Profanity Cited</u>

What would my parents think? How could I explain this away! All manner of thoughts went through my mind as I picked up the phone in a cold sweat and said, "Good evening, WTJS." A lady on the other end responded, "I would suggest you tell your announcer he's swearing on the air." With a small measure of relief and without skipping a beat I simply said, "Yes, Ma'am. I sure will tell him. This minute!"

I later met that lady, and we had some laughs about that awful night for me.

She was Ruth O'Neill, the mother of a longtime friend and school buddy Jimmy O'Neill. But more importantly, and in a touch of irony, she was Executive Secretary to Mr. Aaron Robinson, who owned WDXI, the newest and largest station in town — and whose Program Director, Jim Hoppers, would be offering me my next radio job in a matter of months.

Ethel and Alfred Baker, pictured here, were Wink's first legitimate employers when Wink was a soda jerk at Baker's Drug Store in Jackson.

Oddly, no one at WTJS including my bosses, ever breathed a word to me of my unfortunate news and sportscast. As far as I could determine only one other person had heard my verbal outburst. She had been out driving with her date Gene Bond that evening.

It was my sister Gerry! And she didn't seem awfully shocked by what she heard her brother say. Case closed.

The Drugstore Connection

"Can't you pack that in there a little harder? When I get home I don't want to find air holes in there!" Her name was Ms. Walker Nance. I had waited on her several times before, but she was never like this. She would never accept the ready packed ice cream in the pint bricks. Hers had to be hand packed, by the quart. This particular Sunday afternoon we were overflowing with customers. The few tables we had were filled. Customers were backed up to the front door waiting their turn for a soda, shake, malt, sandwich, ice cream cone, you name it. The curb service customers were impatiently honkin' their horns on both sides of the store, Main Street as well as Shannon Street!

And Mrs. Nance is all over me like a wet suit. She won't let up. Finally, enough was enough. I threw my scoop down and almost in tears walked to the back of the store .

I said, "Mr. Baker, that lady is so rude. I'm packing her ice cream just like you taught us to pack it. She thinks I should try to put two quarts in one! If my job depends on waiting on Ms. Walker Nance, I'll just have to quit." Mr. Baker understood. She was a difficult customer under any circumstance. He didn't say a word, but quietly walked to the soda fountain, placed the tops on her two quarts of ice cream, gave them to her at no charge, and amid all the hustle and bustle of the moment chided her for being so rude. Every time I saw her after that day she was as nice as could be. Even when I packed her ice cream.

Friendship and Admiration

It was a moment indelibly etched in my memory. Not because of its importance in the big picture, but it was a moment that forever bonded my friendship and admiration for Mr. Baker. He had been a friend of the Martindales long before I came along. If we played the name game, or word association, and the name of Alfred Baker was mentioned, my immediate reaction would call up words such as gentleman, honest, fair, good husband and father, and integrity. He would easily be in the top ten of the most influential people in my life during the formative years.

Baker's Drug Store at Main and Shannon Streets in downtown Jackson was your stereotypical corner drugstore during the Thirties, Forties and Fifties. Prescriptions, sundries, ice cream, sandwiches, candy, cigarettes and cigars — you name it, chances are Baker's had it. One had only to assist in taking an inventory to be convinced that among the thousands of *things* in that rather small store, chances are they would have what you needed.

Alfred Baker was one of several Baker brothers. He and his brother H.F. (as he was called) were the most adept in the entrepreneurial sense; Alfred's business was running a drug store with H. F. next door in the service station, tire and storage business.

It is very strange to think back today at the way it was then. The most remarkable memory is that of segregation. If you were black, you were not allowed to be served any food or ice cream unless you waited in the back of the store — and, naturally, no curb service. This was true even if you were an affluent doctor doing a great deal of prescription business with the store. This seems so unfair and wrong in retrospect, but having grown up amid

Wink's first real job was as a dishwasher at Baker's.

the segregationist rules and attitudes of a time that seems so long ago, I knew that was the way it was. As a Caucasion kid then, I can tell you we didn't know any better because that's just the way it was.

First Job

It was another one of those typically hot, muggy summer Sundays when I received my first chance to work at Baker's. Both my brothers, Leo and Kenneth, were soda jerk veterans by now . . . having worked there for well over a year. Leo called and told Mother that the dishwasher (the live type) had gotten sick, had to go home and wondered if Winkie wanted to wash dishes that afternoon. I jumped at the chance for a couple of reasons: I would get to work behind the counter with my brothers, *and* I'd be getting paid for it. Not much! But something.

When Leo and Kenneth came home for lunch, I went back with them and dug into what all Martindales learned to do at an early age when there was no automatic dishwasher in the kitchen. But I never saw *this* many dishes! The customers and dishes continued non-stop that afternoon until Mr. Baker mercifully locked the front door at eight o'clock. He asked if I wanted to work again next Sunday. I couldn't say yes fast enough. Though I was exhausted I kept reminding myself that heck, **I do the same thing at home for nothing!** So why not?

I could hardly wait for next Sunday! Besides, one of Mr. Baker's long-standing rules was that during your shift you could eat anything you wanted without paying for it. In the beginning I definitely tried to turn myself into an extra thick, creamy chocolate malt — to the tune of no less than five or six per shift — without ever getting sick or gaining a single pound. Truly, those were times I thought I'd died and gone to heaven.

Well, the newly crowned "king of the dirty dishes" must have passed the beginner's test for it wasn't long before I was promoted to car hopping on Sunday. If that expression leaves you cold, it means you are far too young for us to be friends! A car hop took the food and drink orders curbside, then delivered those orders on a metal tray that attached to the window on the driver's side of the car. You might call curb service the pioneer of the drive-thru fast-food restaurants. I loved car hopping 'cause being the little *kid* (we were all kids once) I got the biggest tips. And during the hot summer months I really cleaned up. Between five and ten dollars was possible on the best of days, if I really hustled. With that added to my paper route on weekdays and Sunday mornings and my Sunday afternoon job at the drug store, I soon decided to open my first Christmas Club account at The First National Bank just a block up the street from Baker's.

Promoted to Jerk

As I gained experience in dealing with the public and in handling money, within a year I had given up the paper route and was working at the drug store after school and on weekends. I always disliked the term *soda jerk* as much as I would later learn to dislike the term *disc jockey*. But now I was a full-fledged soda jerk — and proud of it. What made the job so neat was the fact that practically all my best friends eventually got hired there as well. Leo and Kenneth had long since moved on to greener pastures as lifeguards at Mr. Long's West End *Beach*, the local swimming hole. But through the doors of Baker's Drug Store passed cousin Tommy Marcom, Billy and Jimmy McKissack, "Beans" Beasley, Bobby Knox and "Fats" Oliver, among others. Even my sister Gerry became our Sunday cashier for a while. All us Martindales got our retail initiation at Baker's, with the exception of David.

I consider the experience gained at Baker's invaluable. It taught me how to meet people and how to get along with people. Well, *most* people (I momentarily forgot about Mrs. Walker Nance). But I finally learned what Mr. Baker preached, that the customer is always right. I learned the meaning of teamwork, and how to accept responsibility. I learned the value of money, and how to handle another person's money. I learned the basics of sales — what to do, what not to do — what to say, what not to say. Most importantly, I learned early on that it wasn't as important what you *EARNED* as how much you *SAVED!*

For years after I moved from Memphis to Los Angeles, Mr. Baker made it his business to know when I was coming home to Jackson for a visit. He never failed to call the house, say hello and offer me one of his cars to drive while there. I never took him up on his offer, but I always took a few minutes to drop by the drug store to say hello.

His wife Ethel was a lovely lady, too. She was always smiling when she dropped by the store, and had a nice greeting for every employee there. She still lives in the family home at Beech Bluff, just outside Jackson. Mr. Baker died several years ago, but his memory, and the mark he made on a young group of Martindales will never be forgotten.

Family Pride

By the same token, the mark my two older brothers made on me in those days could only be termed extraordinary. In retrospect, my boyish admiration for Kenneth and Leo bordered on idolatry. I wasn't aware of it at the time. I hadn't even heard of the word. But in my eyes they could do no wrong. Both excelled in athletics, in both high school and college.

Ken could kick a football so high and so far he was dubbed "The Toe" at Union University. Leo could do it all. Run, pass, kick, block and tackle. At Jackson High School in the forties, if you had the talent, it was not uncommon to play both offense *and* defense. From the opening kickoff to

Wink's oldest of three brothers, Kenneth could kick a football so high and hard he was nicknamed "The Toe."

the final play, Leo Martindale was in the game. Never a big player, what he lacked in size he more than made up for with the heart and desire of a man ten times his size. To this day I can still see that banner headline streaming across the Jackson Sun sports page following one of Leo's super Friday night exploits at Rothrock Field . . .

Leo Martindale was a triple-threat athlete who was naturally gifted in all sports. He was a brotherly hero to Wink.

Martindale Leads Bears To Victory

He cut a mean path on the basketball court, too! Always a first stringer at a time when Jackson was blessed with athletes almost twice his size competing for the same position. And baseball? I think he played every position except catcher. And was outstanding at every one. He was a veritable vacuum cleaner on the infield, and had an arm like a slingshot. He could throw a 90-mile-per-hour fastball at seventeen. Just out of high school Leo served 18 months in the army, and in 1948 was signed to a professional baseball contract by the Pittsburgh

A regular on the suicide squad, Wink runs the plays of the following week's Golden Bear opponent.

Pirates. He was that good. But after a few weeks of being away from home, playing third base for class "D" Dothan, Alabama (and missing the love of his life Cokey), he said goodbye to a life of uncertainty in baseball and returned home. Baseball's loss was Jackson's gain. He later signed a contract to play for the hometown Jackson Generals in the Class D Kitty League. I loved to go see him play at the old Fairgrounds Park on South Royal Street. Sometimes he'd pitch, and other times he'd play shortstop or second base. I'd be on the edge of my seat with his every pitch, infield chance or time at bat.

The Unkindest Cut

I can remember crying shamelessly when the club's general manager and local attorney Russell Rice cut Leo from the roster. It was a heartbreaking event to this kid. And Daddy never stopped talking about the unfairness of it all till the day he died. Personally, my only possible comparison to that feeling would come on several occasions years later, *EVERY TIME ONE OF MY SHOWS WAS CANCELLED!*

Leo married his high school sweetheart, Mary Courtenay Hutcheson. He and Cokey wasted no time in raising their own triple-threat team of athletes — George, Edward, and Michael — and one lovely daughter, Courtenay. Leo retired a few years ago from Southern Bell, for whom he worked all of his adult life. He served as a city commissioner for several years while, at the same time, traveling the South as an NCAA official for both football and basketball. In 1995, Leo was inducted into the Jackson-Madison County Sports Hall of Fame. Kenneth is now a retired lumber inspector and still lives in the old Martindale home on Burkett Street.

As if it weren't enough to have two brothers who were teriffic athletes, Gerry was a mainstay on the high school *girl's* basketball team. So our family didn't lack for athletic prowess. That was nice in one sense because the Martindale name became somewhat synonymous with a degree of excellence in athletics. On the other hand, in my view, they were a tough act to follow. Following my brothers and sister through junior high and high school, I felt that I was given a mandate to continue the legacy they left behind, and God knows I did try. Unfortunately, I never possessed the athletic abilities of my siblings.

Frankly, on an athleticism scale of 1 to 100, I would be generous in giving myself a 35 or 40! I did what most kids do — as a left-hander I tried to play first base on the Lambuth Memorial Church softball team. There was the church basketball league at the YMCA. When I reached Jackson Junior High School, I weighed only 117 pounds.

Cheers!

I took a shot at playing quarterback in the ninth grade. But, instead of calling *plays*, I ended up yelling *cheers*. After watching me get creamed day after day in practice, Coach "Tubby" Taylor advised me to wait till my sophomore year to go out for football. I would have another year of growth behind me and, hopefully, I would put on some weight.

Wink and sister Gerry take their annual picture in the saddle atop a tired pony.

But didn't Coach Taylor know I was a Martindale? Martindales don't cheer players on. Martindales play! It was a rude awakening.

A friend suggested I would be a cinch to be elected one of six cheerleaders. At least I would be nearer the playing field than sitting in the stands. But what would my brothers think? "You're a what, a cheerleader?" I dreaded telling the family after I was elected. Only because I wanted so badly to enjoy the same kind of reputation my brothers had enjoyed in school. Deep down I knew that was impossible. But during my years of eligibility I never brought myself to admit that truth. Leo, especially, accepted my cheerleader role quite easily. I am sure he knew I was making the right decision.

Though I always knew what I wanted to do professionally, even as a kid, I am equally sure that I was somewhat driven to be successful in my chosen profession because of my inadequacy as an athlete. Did I have something to prove to somebody? Not really.

But maybe, just maybe, I longed for some of the adulation I saw the other Martindales receive during those school years. Perhaps.

School Daze!

"School days, school days, dear old golden rule days"— the first day of school.

September, 1939: I can still remember walking hand in hand with Mother to West Jackson Elementery School and being very frightened as she left me there to face my new world alone. There were new friends with whom I would share classrooms through all twelve grades, some for the rest of my life. Memories — some were good, some you'd like to forget.

First girlfriends: *lost* girlfriends. Valentines Day, when you wanted to be the one who received the greatest number of them. (I never got even close). Holidays. How about the holiday in 1943 when everybody had

Wink, at the tender age of twelve, seemed even then to be dreaming of a career in radio.

to bring a piece of scrap metal to assist in the war effort? That was special! Or the day in 1945 when the war was over. That was even more special! Also that was the year a motion picture photographer took all our pictures as we filed out the front door of school, then showed them at the Malco Theatre between pictures. If you had 40-40 vision and didn't blink, you could see yourself on the big screen.

Fifth grade disaster: Miss Roberts discovers a friend and me thumbing through a Kotex booklet and trying to figure why the word **period** was the most often used word!

Restroom breaks: when you hold up your hand denoting one finger for "number one," and two fingers for "number two." In the eighth grade, Senorita Heiskell enjoying my presence so much she allows me to repeat Spanish I three times!

Best day: Ninth grade—Mrs. Bennett citing my recitation of "The Rhyme of the Ancient Mariner" the best in her class!

Worst day: Ninth grade—Being expelled for three days for putting tacks in girls seats in study hall. Mother had to meet with Miss Lellie Fletcher, the principal, in order to get me readmitted. Neither lady let me forget it. Ah-h-h yes, those memories.

Young Love

How many times did you *think* it was true love when you were young? Four, five, six, seven times — or more? It's part of the fun of growing up, on the road to finding that perfect soul mate. They tell us there is a perfect match for each of us out there somewhere, and each of us sets out on that search very early in life — some earlier than others. I submit that my search began early on with my little friend Maquita (Connie) Replogle, under a peach tree in my backyard at the tender age of six.

After Mother closed down our doctor/nurse *Show & Tell*, somehow we didn't play together quite as often. However, one street over on Fairground lived the McKelvy family, and their grandaughter Evelyn Hooker. She was the apple of my nine-year-old eye, with her unusually long pigtail. Had she not been more interested in the horse housed in a backyard stable, I *might* have had a chance. But the romance was doomed from the start!

In the eighth grade, I was smitten like never before. Mona Murray was the daughter of one of Jackson's most prominent attorneys, Roger Murray — while her uncle was U.S. Congressman Tom Murray. While I considered Mona "my girlfriend," I was more than aware I was out of my league. She came from a prominent family on Westmoreland Place. I was a soda jerk at Baker's Drug Store. But we had some fun times together. I held her hand once. Perhaps a telling clue about where my head was at fourteen! By tenth grade Mona had fallen in love with Jerry Ward, to whom she is happily married to this day. I couldn't be happier for them.

The "Grandmother" Connection

During the summer of 1950, my junior year, fourteen-year-old Nancy Dugger came to town from Montgomery, Alabama, to visit her grandmother, Mrs. Merle Holmes. (I don't know what this is between grandmothers and me.) As puppy love goes, this was the kind of which Paul Anka wrote in his later hit song dedicated to Annette Funicello. First class puppy love. We were inseparable. Then her mom and dad left to go back home,

I begged her dad to let her stay longer. Mr. Dugger knew better, but gave in. I remember that summer being quite warm. No, make that *hot*!

Even after she left, Nancy and I continued to write a letter a day to each other. Plus, on more than one occasion, I drove with her Grandmother to Montgomery and visited with her and her family. Like I said, this was serious puppy love, big time — but a love that came, and went. After all, in everyone's life there is a summer of '50.

By that fall my young and wandering eye was focusing on a very cute and pert cheerleader, Jean Ann Scott. This was another example of Winkie getting in over his head. Jean Ann's Mom and Dad were wonderful people. They lived in a gorgeous two-story home on Arlington Avenue. L.W. Scott was the Gulf Oil distributor for that area.

High-Energy Affair

The marvelous thing about Jean Ann was that she was a human dynamo with more energy than should be lawful for one person. If one looked up "cheerleader" in the dictionary, there you would find her smiling picture. That Christmas she gave me a soft cotton eggshell-colored longsleeve shirt with a forest green sleeveless sweater. With it came the admonition not to roll up the shirtsleeves, as was a high school fad at the time. I **don't** recall rolling up my sleeves. I **do** recall that shortly after Christmas, we were no longer going steady. Jean Ann has been happily married to a prominent Jackson physician for a number of years. By coincidence, her brother Charlie and I later briefly shared an apartment in Memphis while we were attending Memphis State University (now the University of Memphis).

My final "Preppie" true love was a pre/post high school affair. But this girlfriend took me to foreign soil for the first time. Gail Wingo lived in far off Trenton, Tennessee, roughly 30 miles from Jackson—which made the long distance difficult since I didn't own a car. Fortunately I had a good buddy whose *understanding Daddy* owned a gorgeous new Buick! Jimmy Gleaves and I had struck up a friendship when both of us were on the school football team. Jimmy was a terrific running back. I was a sometimes third-string quarterback. So I *watched* Jimmy play a lot. He was good, with good wheels.

Conveniently, he was dating Gail's best friend Jean Barker, so Jimmy and I would double date. A lot! There wasn't a great deal to do in Trenton unless you like to watch grass grow or paint dry — or "park," which we opted to do most of the time. Our routine made for a pretty simple date — movie, go to Mac's Drive-In for a "brown cow" (a Coke with ice cream), then find a suitable place to *talk.* We found ourselves talking a great deal! But as we all know, when you're in love you discover the most unusual points to converse about.

Stop!

However one hot, muggy summer night there was one parking episode we would still like to forget about. God only knows where we were, we certainly didn't. That was one of the interesting challenges to a date in Trenton—finding yet another new and original place to park. I just remember it was pitch dark this night. The radio was on, the windows were steamed up pretty good, and about the only sound was lips smackin' and birds chirpin'!

Suddenly Jimmy heard a sound of leaves crunching against the ground. Somebody was approaching the car. Jimmy jumped up, yelled an expletive and tried to find the key in the ignition. Gail, Jean and I were frozen still — and scared beyond belief!

It seemed an eternity before we heard the engine fire up, but by the time it did we were hearing a strange male voice yelling at the top of his lungs, *"STOP! STOP!"* As Jimmy put the car in gear and hit the accelerator in one motion, the tires dug into the dirt. As we jettisoned from there we could see the flash and hear the sound of pistol fire. My God — he was shooting at us! I remember thinking this was a dream and I'd wake up any minute now. But when we heard a second shot I knew this was for real.

There was no way of knowing who that person was or his intentions. We were only left to surmise. But it was the last time we parked on a lover's lane! I was always too embarrassed to tell the others, (but I'll tell you) — I peed in my pants that night. A lot!

The Times of Our Lives

Certain events in our lives are etched indelibly in our minds.
One such time for me was a Saturday afternoon in 1949 when it
seemed the entire population of Jackson turned out for a parade
honoring hometown baseball hero Ellis Kinder. He had enjoyed a
"career" year as a star pitcher for the Boston Red Sox, winning
twenty-three games while losing only six. He finished fifth in the
most-valuable-player voting. In fact the Red Sox lost the American League championship to the New York Yankees on the final
day of the season. Ellis Kinder Day was marked by dozens of
wonderful gifts given by his friends and fans, topped off by a
shiny, new Pontiac convertible. After having spent twelve seasons in the major leagues, Kinder was now receiving the acco-
lades of his hometown.

To a youngster who had followed his year, pitch-by-pitch, and
proud as a peacock that Ellis was a fellow Jacksonian, that October
day was a day to remember. Sadly, Ellis Kinder, who lived in Jackson 30 years, died in 1968 at age 54 following open heart surgery.
Kinder played sandlot and semi-professional baseball around West
Tennessee all of his adult life. An enormously gifted athlete, his
greatest nemesis was not the opposing team, but himself and his
lifestyle.

Barnstormers

While never an outstanding athlete, I have always considered myself a "jock" due to my love, particularly, of football,
basketball, tennis and baseball. Another hometown memory of
note to me—before baseball games were as regular on television as station breaks—many players would "barnstorm" around
the country visiting small cities and towns that would never have
the opportunity to see major league players. It was a good way
for players to pick up some additional bucks in an era prior to
the multi-million dollar contracts of today.

The Philadelphia Phillies had won the National League pen-
nant that season thanks to the strong right arm of Ken Meyer,
complemented on the left side by crafty Ken Heintzleman.

Both of these players were part of a group of players from various
teams to visit Jackson's small Lakeview Park. It might seem strange today, but in 1950 for this young baseball fanatic to be within a few yards of
a real major leaguer and to get his autograph was quite special indeed!

From little Winkie's "hard-to-understand" file: For years our house on Burkett Street had only *one bathroom, and one bathtub.* A shower was a figment of the imagination. When hot water was needed for cooking — or a bath, it was heated in pans on the wood-burning kitchen stove. Perhaps economy of water was the reason my sister Gerry and I always took baths together while growing up. Then one day, I found myself in the tub alone, without Sis to wash my back. I must have been about eight years old — Gerry perhaps ten or eleven. Mother never did answer my question about why Sis and I no longer shared a bathtub. Come to think of it — I never did find out!

A Whole New Meaning

In my potpourri of unforgettables, there was "Mom and Dad"! (No, not the two teriffic parents who raised us.) In the Forties, Hollywood made a low-budget movie on the verboten (at the time) subject of teenage pregnancies and the terrible results of the so-cially-transmitted venereal diseases of the day, syphilis and gonor-rhea. The movie had what we might term today "underground sta-tus," playing every nook and cranny in the country. As well in-tended as the movie might have been, it was viewed by many over-protective parents as going "over the line." But word spread quickly among Jackson's kids — "Have you seen *Mom and Dad?* " "Did you see what they showed?" "I can't believe they said that!" Pre-ceding the movie in each town were the headlines and pictures of the registered nurses stationed inside the theaters to administer aid to those who became ill and/or fainted at what they saw on the screen! By today's accepted standards on the big screen, even tele-vision, time has proven that *Mom and Dad* was simply Pablum for the pubescent set. And only a precursor for what was to come in just a few years.

The Memory File

Indelible memories? My brother Kenneth home on furlough, and he and Leo letting me go with them to see Rita Haworth and Glenn Ford in *Gilda.* It was the first time in my young memory that a movie song made an impression on me — Gilda reclining on that piano and singing "Put the Blame on Mame."

P.S. Even better than the song *or* the movie was me overhearing Ken tell Leo, as we walked to the movie, all about something called "rubbers" the Army made them use. I didn't know what they were. I just knew they made a circle in his wallet. Later, when I got my job at the drugstore, I giggled every time a customer asked me for what I *thought* they were calling "condrums"!

Talk of the Town

During my formative and impressionable teen years in Jackson, a young student at Lambuth College became the talk-of-the-town because of a Saturday night radio show he hosted on WTJS. It was 1948. Television's stranglehold for our attention span was still years away. And Ken Berryhill's "Ken Calling," with his quick wit and hit records of the day, were just what the high school and college crowd needed to make their weekend complete.

As an aspiring radio star myself, I was in luck! By now my sister Gerry was not only a student at Lambuth, but was a *personal friend* of Ken Berryhill. So, thanks to Gerry, I got to actually *see* Ken conduct his deejay show in the studio — live no less! Thinking back, it is truly difficult to imagine the impact that Saturday night visit to WTJS (the station that would be my second radio home just four years later) would have on my future career. Without question, that young Lambuth College student deejay named Ken Berryhill unwittingly helped chart the future course for a teen named Winkie Martindale.

It Begins!

Finally, a *defining* moment in my life. I was 17. It was April, 1951. The military operations in Korea continued. The Rosenbergs were sentenced to death for treason. Truman fired MacArthur. Nat "King" Cole was singing "Too Young" . . . Eddie Fisher, "Anytime" . . . Jo Stafford's "Shrimp Boats" was a smash . . . and Patti Page was making a state song outa "Tennessee Waltz"! Classmates and football teammates, Charlie Pate, Dickie Beare and I, were hanging our tails over the metal railing outside The First National Bank, killing time and probably solving the major problems of the world.

Suddenly up drives Chick Wingate in his little 1950 Henry J. automobile. He parks in one of the spots smack dab in front of us. "Hey Chick, when are you gonna give me a job?" That was the same question I posed to my Sunday School teacher and WPLI station manager every time I saw him! His reply had always been the same: "Soon!" But tonight, I must have caught him right. (Either that, or he was growing tired of answering "Soon!") "Come on up," he said, motioning for me to join him for the four-floor elevator ride to the WPLI studios. Jumping at the chance, it was "See you later" to Charlie and Dickie.

This was my big chance, and I was determined not to blow it.

Jackson now had *three* radio stations: the oldest, and the station considered by most to be number one, WTJS (an ABC affiliate); WDXI, 5000 watts and with the fanciest studios (a Mutual affilliate); then there was the smallest station with 250 watts of power—independent WPLI. This station was owned by Mayor George Smith. To me, that made it very special. And tonight was *more* than special because Charles J. (Chick) Wingate was going to give me an audition. He was going to sit me down in front of a real microphone for the first time in my life, give me some news copy and a few commercials to read, and determine once and for all whether he was going to continue to ward me off with his stock "soon" answer to my incessant question about a job. *Or,* be forced to say, "Winkie, I want you to meet the Mayor!" I knew that would mean I was hired.

Well, luckily, I cut through all the copy like Grant going through Richmond! In all humility I can honestly say Chick was truly impressed. Much later he told me had he known I was ready at such a young age he would have hired me much sooner. Next day after school I could hardly wait till three o'clock, and my appointment with the Mayor.

I Would Have Paid *Them*

He listened to me read some copy, and immediately made it official. *I was hired!* I would begin immediately, first learning the ropes — then taking over the night air shift from four till eleven. My starting pay was $25 per week. Little did they know I would have paid *them*! Thank God!

"Mother! Guess what? I got the job at WPLI! I start today. I'm going to get to read my first commercial at 6 o'clock." My Mom was the first to know. At first she didn't believe me. When I assured her it was for real, I said, "Listen for the Nolen's Kiddie Shop commercial at six. That'll be *me*."

I read and re-read the commercial, practicing and practicing, rehearsing and rehearsing just as I had done so many times in the back bedroom at home. Now it was for real. I could hardly stand the wait. As the hour grew closer I was so nervous I thought I was going to vomit. I tried to think about all those *Life* magazine ads I had cut out and read, *pretending* to be on the radio. What was so different?

At six o'clock, the announcer on duty in the control room, Ted Roney, flipped the switch turning on my mike in the adjacent studio and pointed at me. That commercial for Nolen's Kidde Shop went off without a hitch, and officially kicked off a career in radio and television that has spanned the better part of five decades.

Walking on Air

By the way, my Nolen's commercial really made an impact on Mother. "I thought you were going to be on the radio at six o'clock," she said to me when I got home. I said, "What do you mean Mother. I *was* on at six!" She had raised me for seventeen years, but didn't recognize my voice on the radio! When I finally convinced her it was me, she gave me a big hug. She, more than anybody else, knew what I was feeling. I was less than two months from graduating at Jackson High School. I was walking on air.

WPLI's large neon call letters in the fourth floor window of the bank building went dark not too many years later. The little station at 1490 on the dial just couldn't compete with her stronger, more powerful competition. After only a few months at WPLI, I received a call from Leslie Brooks, Sales Manager and Program Director at WTJS. He and Station Manager Frank Proctor liked my work "across the street," and offered me a job with a $25.00 increase in pay—to $50.00 per week!

More importantly, in addition to my announcing chores, I would get the opportunity to do play-by-play broadcasts of the high school

Abby Dalton and Jack Jones try to prove who's "tops" on "Win" Martindale's first network game show, NBC's *What's This Song?*

football and basketball games. I remember thinking, "How can this get any better?"

I was in a dream world. Those well-worn steps in the Sun Building that I had climbed so many times as a paper boy, just to sit in the station lobby and watch the announcers work. I would now be climbing to "go to work." Who knows, perhaps I might even see a young boy sitting in the lobby one day, dreaming the same dreams I had dreamed not so long ago.

Musical Chairs

My radio days in Jackson seemed much like a cross between a rollercoaster ride and a game of musical chairs. I certainly didn't plan it as such. It just turned out that way.

It was very flattering to be hired away from WPLI to WTJS in less than a year. But then to have Jim Hoppers, Program Director of the new 5,000 watt WDXI call me in short order with *another* job offer, convinced me that I must be doing something right. By now I was feeling stronger than ever that my choice of radio as a vocation was not just a shot-in-the-dark. I was a year out of high school, and everywhere I went in town, people knew who I was. I was no longer the high school quarterback with two left feet. I was no longer referred to as Leo and Kenneth's little brother. And I wasn't the kid soda jerk at Baker's Drug Store. I was Winkie Martindale, radio announcer. ("Winkie" wouldn't be shortened to "Wink" until I began on-the-air at WHBQ.)

It was the idea of my future mentor and WHBQ boss Bill Grumbles, who felt Wink was a better-suited name for radio and television. While certainly unusual, it *was* catchy. People seemed to remember it after hearing it. Johnny Carson used my name countless times on The Tonight Show, almost as a non-sequitur. Same for Jay Leno and David Letterman. They just seemed to like saying "Wink Martindale." I have always taken these mentions as a compliment . . . as long as they pronounced it right!

There was only one period in my career when I was not *Wink*. My very first game show was for NBC in 1964, *What's This Song?* Bob Aaron was Vice-President of Daytime Programs, New York. His view was that *Wink* had a somewhat youthful, even juvenile ring to it. "Why don't we just drop the 'k' and call him *Win Martindale?*" Which is precisely what happened. For the one-year run of *What's This Song?* announcer Steve Dunne introduced,

" . . . The star of our show, WIN MARTINDALE!"

What, Me Worry?

What did I care? I was on network television thirty minutes a day, five days a week. They could have called me Joe Blow! (The only person offended? Naturally, my mother. She always felt my name should have remained WINSTON! Not Wink, not Winkie, not Win.) Incidentally, after that show the name thing never surfaced again. For better or worse, it's been Wink ever since.

A Boy's Dreams

THE DREAM CONTINUES . . .

The year-plus at WDXI was my most rewarding in the sense that it gave me the opportunity to expand on my desire to learn play-by-play sports, specifically football and basketball. I had begun calling the high school games while at WTJS, then when sportscaster Jay Black left Dixie (as WDXI was called) to join WHHM in Memphis, I joined Dixie as their combination sports and staff announcer. It was the best of all worlds for me at the time. My daily air shift began at noon, and ended at seven. I could stay up late, sleep until eleven o'clock in the morning and still get to the station from Mother's house in less than ten minutes. Such a deal! I was now making $60 bucks a week, and driving my first car, that shiny, used green 1948 four-door Plymouth my Dad had signed for.

Every evening I ended my shift with the 6:15 *Sports Final*, followed by the long running *At Your Request* program, thirty minutes of the most requested pop hits of the day by phone, sponsored by the Black & White Stores, a local clothing chain. This was the most popular music show on the air. Kids could call in and not only request their favorite song but dedicate it to their best guy or gal. There was something special, in 1952, about hearing your name on the radio. Keep in mind, we are talking pre-TV! *At Your Request* had been hosted by station manager Bill Winsett ever since WDXI had gone on the air. It was his baby. But Bill was in his forties and Mr. Horner, the sponsor, had been hinting for someone younger to take over. So at 18, still on a first-name basis with the kids in high school, I seemed the logical choice.

They called *ME!*

I was more than thrilled! As a kid myself I had listened night after night, for years, as Bill followed the show's familiar theme "Because Of You," saying, "Because of you, your friendly Black And White Stores present *At Your Request*." Now I would get to say those words, experience my *first* job as a sponsor spokesman (spokes*person* today), and continue to live my lifelong dream! Almost immediately I noticed a sort of metamorphosis taking place, the likes of which I had never experienced in my teenage years. Instead of me *calling* girls, I was getting calls *from* girls. How strange! And how absolutely wonderful! I still recall a first for me. Bonnie was at least four or five years my senior. She began a habit of waiting for me outside the Williams Building when I got off the air. She was cute, and looked even more alluring sitting behind the wheel of the new, fire-engine red 1952 Ford Fairlane convertible her Dad had bought her. "Forward" would be the word used then in describing Bonnie's actions toward me. Today's parlance would preclude me from using an acceptable word for my family-rated book! Though certainly not a prude, I knew from my first few chats with her that I was in *way* over my head. Then, when I learned her Dad owned the infamous Blue Moon Motel on the Humboldt Highway, I began taking the alternate exit from the station! I guess Bonnie got the hint. She stopped showing up, or calling. (But what a neat set of wheels — *WHEELS!)*

From the time I started hosting *At Your Request,* to the many Jackson High football and basketball games I called with my good friend and color-man Lance Russell, I began to sense that with the territory went not only a responsibility as a role model of sorts, but a certain celebrity status, even in a town the size of Jackson. Initially it was so much fun to be on the radio one minute, then five minutes later be playing the jukebox and enjoying a Pronto Pup at Hicksville, or a pig sandwich (barbeque) at The Hut across the street, with your friends. But I discovered early on that notoriety, or celebrity status, really meant very little in the big picture. While it takes from your privacy at times, the best upside, in my view, is that you can almost always get a good table in a restaurant!

Mac MacFarlin, with his deep, mellifluous tones, and far too advanced to be an announcer in Jackson, was my hero at WDXI. And I must say that he looked upon me as one with an uncanny promise for my age. He wished for me what he dreamed for himself, a staff job with CBS in New York! He revered the call letters CBS, and everything Edward R. Murrow and their award winning news organization stood for. Quality and depth in news journalism. I do not know what ever happened to Mac and his wife "Jigger." One loses track of his friends of the moment in this ever transient business. Another such talent who, like me, was a Jackson native, with a natural, God-given voice,was a man named Al West. But like baseball's Ellis Kinder, Al was his own worst enemy. He dropped by the wayside, somewhere along the road.

I would be remiss if I failed, at this point, to mention two fellow Jacksonians who went on to fame and fortune. Bud Dancy and I went to school together, and also worked side by side for awhile at WDXI. With a great deal of natural ability and an innate desire to succeed, Bud Dancy cast his nickname aside and went on to become a mainstay with NBC News. *John* Dancy went on to travel the globe for NBC. He knew what he wanted. And he got it.

Well it's one for the money, two for the show,
three to get ready now go cat go
but don't you step on my Blue Suede Shoes.
You can do anything, but stay off of my Blue Suede Shoes!

One of the most famous sets of lyrics in the early history of rock 'n roll. And written by another Jackson native, Carl Perkins. Like his longtime friend Elvis Presley, Carl came from humble beginnings to cut quite a swath in the music industry. His body of work left its mark on everybody from the Beatles to Bob Dylan. I was proud to call him friend. Jackson lost a legend when Carl died of a stroke at age 65 in January of 1998. His legacy is the Exchange Club—Carl

Carl and Wink smile for the camera at Carl's museum in Jackson.

Perkins Center for the Prevention of Child Abuse, for which he worked tirelessly.

Madelyn

It was during my tenure at WDXI that I met the girl I would marry. No, not Bonnie. She had long since driven her Ford Fairlane into the Blue Moon sunset! I had heard the name of Madelyn Leech long before I met her. She was very popular in high school, and though she didn't take part in athletics like friends Jane Marie Thompson or Lynne Spraggins (who played girls basketball), she was highly thought of by her friends and classmates, many of whom I'd met while working at Baker's Drug Store.

The first planned "meeting" that I remember with Madelyn, was with her mother, Erin. I had mentioned that I thought I was going to a mid-week football game at Rothrock Stadium. Madelyn said she and her mom were thinking about going as well. So we three conveniently ran into each other that night at the game. Didn't see much of the game, and I'm not sure I knew what teams were playing. We just did a lot of talking, and getting better aquainted.

Madelyn would occasionally call and request a song on my 6:30 to 7:00 show. And since I answered all the calls myself we came to know each other better through the telephone. Then there were times we'd see each other at The Hut in Hicksville, or at The Supper Club, a popular dance joint on the outskirts of town we all frequented on weekends.

In any event, we started dating pretty regularly. I came to know her mom and dad real well, and liked both of them very much. We all became very good friends. William E. (Bill) Leech was a longtime Jackson resident and a well respected lawyer. Madelyn was an only child who was the apple of her parents' eye, especially her mom's! Erin Leech was a homemaker who kept a very neat house at the corner of Wisdom and Lambuth Streets. But it was clear to me at the outset of our relationship that her daughter was Erin's number one priority. It was obvious both parents had done an excellent job of instilling the kinds of

A Sixties picture showing Madelyn (right rear) with her dad Bill Leech and stepmom Aileen, plus Laura, Wink, Jr., (first row), Lyn and Lisa (second row).

high morals and values Madelyn would later pass on to our own children.

More than Erin, Bill was thinking long range. After a dozen or so dates he let me know that he was delighted that I knew the direction I wanted my life to take at such an early age. But early on, he was free with this advice: *get into sales*, if I wanted to pursue a radio/television career. "That's where the good money is," he would tell me.

But I had tunnel vision. My sights were set on performing. Not selling advertising. I was so certain of my goals that I determined after two quarters of attending Lambuth College, a Methodist school in Jackson, that more formal education should be the least of my concerns. After all, I had a pleasant and maturing voice. I could read well. My commercials were better than average. I already had a high school education. In short, what else was there for me to learn about radio that I didn't already know? Isn't it amazing how we think we know it all when we're still only babes?

Hello Memphis!

It was with this attitude and stern will that after just twenty months in radio, I went to WDXI one Sunday afternoon, grabbed some appropriate news and commercial copy and proceeded to make an audition tape to send to WHBQ in Memphis, the station for which I dreamed of working. It seemed everybody in Jackson listened to WHBQ. In fact it seemed eveybody within the station's powerful Mid-South signal listened. I only knew that was where I wanted to be. I sat down and began to compose the letter that would soon change the course of my life. I have reproduced that letter, just as it was written, *mistakes notwithstanding.*

Program Director
Radio Station WHBQ
Hotel Chisca
Memphis, Tennessee

Dear Sir:

I would like to place my application for a job in your station as staff announcer. At the present time I am employed by WDXI here in Jackson.

I am ninteen years of age, single, a high school graduate and attended Lambuth College a year. I worked previously at WPLI, the small 250kw station in Jackson. After two months at WPLI I moved to WTJS, a 1kw ABC affiliate here. I have a total of 20 months experience in radio.

I came to WDXI as a Sports and staff man when Jay Black, with whom you are probably aquainted, left WDXI and went to WHHM in Memphis. I did football for Coca-Cola last fall and currently am doing basketball, plus, of course, everyday staff work.

I am perfectly happy at WDXI, but would like to come to Memphis to a larger market. I was called by Mr. George Faulner last September and offered a job at WMPS in Memphis, but because of the on-coming sports season, I decided to stay at "Dixie" and get experience in this field. I am experienced in sports and other phases of radio, but prefer to do popular D.J. shows and sports. To me radio is very interesting and I enjoy my work very much. I can furnish references if necessary.

I am enclosing an audition tape. If you do have an opening or anticipate one in the future, I would be grateful for any information you might give me.

Sincerely,

Winston Martindale
418 Burkett Avenue
Jackson, Tennessee

WM/pm*

(* I am sure I typed the letter sent that day, and simply added the letters "pm" at the bottom to make it appear more businesslike, or as if I had a secretary type it.)

Bingo!

Well, either they had a quick opening or PD Gordon Lawhead was impressed with my tape and letter. (He later confided that they had been planning a change in their morning show host and I happened to be the right person at precisely the right time). In any event, within weeks he called me at home suggesting I drive over to Memphis for an interview. I put down the phone completely transfixed. It was a phone conversation that I still remember to this day almost verbatim. I could hardly get through my radio shift that day. I felt so smug!

It was the last day of March 1953, when my sister Gerry drove with me the 86 miles via the old winding Highway 70 to Memphis. (There was no speedy Interstate as yet). We would meet the gentlemen who would prove to be my employers for the next seven years, two of whom would have a profound impact upon me, personally and professionally.

Operations Manager William H. (Bill) Grumbles would become my personal mentor from that day forward, for he seemed to take a liking to me from the moment we met. *Seven years later* he would hear me say to him, "Mr. Grumbles, I would like to try my wings in a larger market. Will you help me?" Instinctively, not wanting to stand in my way or try to talk me out of what he knew had been a gut wrenching decision for me, he would pick up the phone and place a call to his counterpart at KHJ in Los Angeles, Norm Boggs.

"Norm, I have a young man in my office who has been with me for seven years. He now has visions of palm trees and Malibu. His name is Wink Martindale. I know he can be an asset to you on both the TV *and* radio side. Think you might have an interest in talking to him?"

WHBQ station manager Bill Grumbles (circled) was Wink's mentor who first hired him, put him on TV, and arranged his transfer from Memphis to Holly-wood in 1959. (Wink is front right)

Due to our personal friendship this was not an easy call for Bill to make. He had seen me grow in every way in both radio and television. I had become somewhat of a fixture in Memphis. A very saleable personality. He would hate to lose me. But friendship was superseded by his knowledge that this was the right time for me to move on to greener pastures. To leave the womb, as it were.

As long as I live I shall never forget my now silly, but inquiring question of him when he placed the phone back in its cradle. "Mr. Grumbles, forgive me — but what is *malibu?*" As one who would later buy a home there, perhaps my question proved beyond a shadow of a doubt that it was time for me to venture beyond the city limits of Memphis. We had many laughs about that conversation in later years.

John Cleghorn, WHBQ Radio and Television General Manager, was the other gentleman in my introductory meeting that day in 1953. He was a man with strong spiritual beliefs, and as such had been selected to guide the fortunes of WHBQ by its owners, Harding College, a religious school in Searcy, Arkansas. Mr. Cleghorn became another guiding anchor to me. One that would become increasingly needed as I began to experience increasing popularity, leading to personal pitfalls that seem to shadow one in show biz.

It was Mr. Cleghorn, along with my future father-in-law Bill Leech, who convinced me to return to college and finish my education, regardless of any measure of success I might enjoy. He assured me he would see to it that my station schedule would be compatible with my college courses at Memphis State, if that was where I chose to go. It was. I enrolled in 1954 and was graduated in 1957, receiving a Bachelor of Science degree, with a major in Speech and Drama, and a minor in Journalism.

Notorious

It was during my Sophomore year that I was elected Mr. Fabulous! Obviously a semi-popularity contest on campus, I most certainly won because of my growing notoriety as a radio and television performer. Miss Fabulous was classmate Janelle Brower, editor of *The Scholar*, the campus literary magazine. While perhaps a silly "honor," it was an occurrence that led John Cleghorn to intuitively write me this memorandum:

To: *Winston Martindale*   Date: *March 28, 1955*
From: *John Cleghorn*

Dear Winston:

I make it a practice to congratulate other people when they receive extraordinary honor and I think I should do the same with you.

Accordingly, my hearty and sincere congratulations on your being named "Mr. Fabulous" at Memphis State. I can remember from my college days that popularity on the campus is deserved. Consequently, I think you should feel as if a signal honor has been conferred upon you.

If you don't mind taking advice from an old man, the secret of continuation of that popularity is to remember two things:

1. If you want people to like you, you have to have a genuine and sincere love for the human race.

2. The only way to avoid arrogance that comes with outstanding success is to remember that you are God's creature and what you have achieved is due to Him and not due to your own accomplishments. If you can remain a humble and surrendered instrument in His hands, there's no limit to the good you can do.

If you forget that you are God's creature, you can fall a lot further and a lot faster than you can ever climb.
It's a pleasure to have you on the station.
Sincerely,

John Cleghorn
JC:d

In all honesty, I would have been better served to follow those words of advice and encouragement. There would be far too many times when I let my moral upbringing be overcome by the worldly passions associated with show business. But John Cleghorn would prove to be one of the five most influential persons in my career.

It wouldn't be until March 1959, that I would board that American Airlines plane for Los Angeles. But in those seven years with WHBQ I would get married, father three children, host two local television series, and take sixteen hours per quarter in an attempt to graduate from college in four years. I would be a busy boy. Uh, *Man!* You might call it "required adulthood." As

THEY'RE FABULOUS—Sophomores at Memphis State College named Mr. and Miss Fabulous at the class dance last night. Miss Fabulous in Miss Janelle Brower of 957 Circle Road, editor of *The Scholar*, campus literary magazine and college correspondent for *The Commercial Appeal*. Mr. Fabulous is Winston Martindale of Jackson, Tenn., vice president of the class and better known as Wink Martindale, star of *Mars Patrol* on WHBQ-TV.

I had never really spent any extended time away from home, my first few months in Memphis were marked by homesickness, bigtime! In all candor, it was as much lovesickness as anything else. There was a point when I even entertained the idea of giving up my latest dream and going home. Fortunately, my mind ruled my heart. For after awhile I controlled my feelings enough, thanks to a letter a day from Madelyn, so that I could make it through the week. But when I finished my air shift on Saturday, I wasted no time hitting the highway to Jackson!

By now I had traded the Plymouth for my second car, another good, clean used car — a '51 Chevrolet. The weekend routine seldom varied. Get to Jackson, drop off my bag and say hello to my folks, freshen up a bit, then to the Leech house. Most dates called for doubling with Art Buehler and Lynn Spraggins. They were as much an item as Madelyn and I, so we did most everything together. Saturday nights usually meant The Supper Club for dancing and listening to a teriffic local singer, Frank Ballard. Then to either Fox Cafe downtown or to Hicksville for something to eat.

The Martindales gather for David's wedding to Lynn Freeman in Bells, Tennessee. (Left to right) David, Kenneth, Gerry, Mom and Dad, Leo and Wink.

Close-Knit Families

Sunday morning meant church, depending on the lateness of the night before. Sometimes I would go with Madelyn and her folks to First Methodist, and other times with my family to Lambuth Memorial Methodist. Sunday dinner was a fun time when Mother would cook a huge fried chicken dinner with all the trimmings. Usually the entire family was there—Leo, Cokey and their first child Courtenay, then Edward, their second little one, came along. There was Kenneth, his wife Evelyn (later divorced), their son little Scott; Sis Geraldine, her husband Jack King and their baby Kevin, plus little brother David, and me. Ours was a close-knit family in those days and Sunday dinner, like holidays, especially Christmas, were super warm and special for us.

After dinner and some time with the family, naturally it was back to 431 Wisdom for me to spend what was left of a short weekend with Madelyn. I never seemed to hit the road back to Memphis before midnight, or later. I'd pull in to Aunt Susie and Uncle Pat's driveway (I roomed with them) usually around two or two-thirty, just enough time to grab a few winks before signing on the radio station at five o'clock. We do crazy and wonderful things when we're young. There were so many nights I would hit the Memphis city limits not even remembering much of the 86 mile winding drive. How I made it all those times only God knows. He must have been holding my hand.

Marriage/Family

As the months wore on our long-range romance was wearing thin. Not our love for each other. The weekend trips were becoming harder and harder. And I was becoming insanely jealous at times. Every night during the week I would wonder where Madelyn was, who she was with and what they were doing. I was now a student at Memphis State and sharing a small apartment above Bill and Joy Webb's photography studio near the campus. Though Madelyn and I did very little dating of others between weekends, we did leave the option open. Her parents liked that better, too. Regardless, there was one occasion when I learned that an admirer of hers was getting a bit *too* close His name was "Coonie" Phelan, from nearby Trenton (remember Gail Wingo? Same Trenton!).

I didn't really think Madelyn felt strongly about him. Just the nickname "Coonie" was a turnoff to me! But one of our biggest pre-marital arguments was over this live-wire from Trenton, Tennessee. We were successful in smoothing over that disagreement. But it convinced me that I wanted no more of that kind of confrontation. I saw us as lovers, not fighters! Plus I had been thinking how we might be able to spend more time together, short of giving up school and the career inroads I was making in Memphis.

Another strong consideration was her parents' decision to send her off to Mary Baldwin College in Virginia that Fall. Nothing could change their minds. The distance from Memphis to Jackson was nothing compared to this new, looming certainty.

The answer, in our minds, was to get married immediately. We decided that Madelyn would drive over under the guise of a shopping trip, which she did anyway from time to time. And we would drive just over the Mississippi line to a little town called Hernando. As in Las Vegas, there was no month-long waiting period in Mississippi. Beginning that July day in 1954, we signed our checks and received our mail under the names Madelyn and Wink Martindale! Had a good ring to it. We were happy.

Not the same could be said, initially, about Bill and Erin Leech. Though as days and weeks passed they warmed to the idea of having a son-in-law named "Wink." It sure beat "Coonie"! They planned a beautiful reception for us at The New Southern Hotel in Jackson and invited, seemingly, half the city, and practically ALL of the population of Tiptonville, Tennessee. This was a little soybean farming community north of Jackson on Reelfoot Lake, where Erin's Mother and Dad and her entire family of Vaughns lived. (There was almost as many Vaughns as Martindales.)

Our first of several homes was an apartment on Union Avenue, a main artery of Memphis. We had no sooner moved in and started playing house and decorating the place, when we discovered that some space would have to be set aside for a nursery!

So much for the best laid plans. Lisa Dawn Martindale, our first of four children, was born April 10th, 1955. We learned quickly, as do all first time parents, just how radically your lifestyle changes. But Lisa was a wonderfully sweet baby. Cried a lot. But what babies don't? So

Could Wink Martindale of the *Mars Patrol* be the same Wink later on *Tic-Tac-Dough?*

what if I *did* have to get up at three-thirty in the morning to do a radio show at five? Our new Lisa Dawn taught me it would be more convenient for me to just not sleep at all! That way you never have to set a clock.

Just about the time we worked out schedules amenable to all three of us, we discovered that our three was now going to be four! Madelyn Lizbeth Martindale drew her first breath the 17th of July, 1956. In the midst of one of the hottest summer's Memphis had seen in years. The heat was sweltering, which didn't make carrying little Lyn easy for Mama! We were now a family of four. Our apartment on Union Avenue was beginning to seem a wee bit small. So we began to go house hunting in our spare time. Did I say spare time?

Madelyn and Wink's first born Lisa, with her young children (left to right) Blake, Emilee and Stephen.

Wink & The Mars Patrol

In addition to my attempt at filling my role as a full-time father, I was running to keep up with my daily schedule. For since WHBQ Television, Channel 13 had recently gone on the air as Memphis' second station, there was much local programming being produced to compliment those programs on affiliate CBS. I had been approached by Bill Grumbles, newly appointed Station Manager, and his Program Director Mark Forrester, about hosting an idea they had for a daily kids half hour using space travel as its theme. Naturally I was overwhelmed at the idea of being on television. My dream initially was to be on radio. It went no further. Now here was the chance to continue my *Clockwatcher's* show on radio and do a daily television show in the afternoon. And they would *pay me* too? Apparently!

"WINK MARTINDALE AND THE MARS PATROL" was a hit from the very first day it went on the air. The format was simple, and

Wink's first TV show *Mars Patrol* was a hit with kids from day one.

relatively inexpensive to produce. Build a set made up of six old metal army surplus seats, with cushions in each, three on each side of the space ship's "interior." Paint appropriate futuristic designs on the walls, and construct for Wink a "spacy" control panel for "blast-offs." Then fill up those seats each afternoon between 5 and 5:30 P.M. with a half dozen kids, ages six to eight. Interview each kid, give him or her a super beam signal ray as a gift to take home, mix and serve the sponsor's Bosco and milk to each Mars Guard on board. *THEN*, fasten those seat belts as we hear the exciting sounds of our space vehicle slowly beginning its rise into outer space! Then BLAST OFF!

To where you ask? We slowly dissolve from *our* space ship in studio to an episode of *Flash Gordon,* the old Saturday afternoon space adventure series starring Buster Crabbe as Flash Gordon, in an ever-lasting battle with the evil Emperor Ming on the planet Mongo! After six or seven minutes (we must save that precious footage) our space ship lands once again with appropriate sound effects; the little Mars Guards are thrilled by what they saw and heard and are now ready to hear Wink talk intelligently about the planets in space, their size, how far they are from Earth, etc. (these helpful and educational facts con-veniently placed on readable cue cards for Captain Wink on the walls of the studio!). Now kids, let's do a commercial for Hasbro's "Mr. Potato Head"!

This was Mark Forrester's creation and the show took off immedi-

Mars Patrol sponsor Goldsmiths Department Store hosted Wink's first ever public appearance, this autograph signing.

ately. *And me with it!* I was suddenly this local space hero to the kids, wearing a turtle-neck sweater complete with lightning bolt emblazoned across my chest and gold epaulets on each shoulder. Suddenly I was recognized everywhere I went, by parents and kids alike. It was a new experience. My first public appearance for *MARS PATROL* was on a Saturday morning at Goldsmith's Department Store downtown. I'll never forget the lines and lines of kids waiting to recieve an autographed picture. As I think back on that adventure, my little Mars Guards and I were blasting off into space on a daily basis! *Before* it became com-monplace at Cape Kennedy.

Memphians lining downtown Memphis streets for the 1954 Thanksgiving Day Parade saw Wink atop his new-found mode of transportation.

A Star is Born

This was yet another life-altering experience for me. I came to the somewhat shocking realization that I was a "star"—albeit small, and strictly local, it was my first taste of legitimate public recognition. It was one thing to have your name recognized from the radio, but to have your mug on TV thirty minutes a day, five days a week? Wow! I recall game show host and friend Tom Kennedy telling me long before *Tic-Tac-Dough* made me nationally well-known, "You think the *daytime* audience knows who you are? Wait 'til you get a show on at night!" And he was right, just as *Mars Patrol* had done for me in Memphis.

Mars Patrol gave Wink a "free ride," plus a career boost—big time.

Spare time? My feet would hit the floor about three-thirty in the morning in order to get the station on the air at five. (Unlike today it was not common for a station to be on the air 24-hours a day. WHBQ hours were sign-on at 5 a.m., sign-off at midnight).

My *Clockwatcher's* show lasted from six till nine. I then jumped in my car and drove to Memphis State for classes, which began at ten. I probably held the record for speeding tickets recieved on Central Avenue on my way to school. The last class ended at three, then it was a beeline to the television studio to don my "space suit," bone up on any space talk we planned during the show, and rehearse any live commercials for that day.

Everthing was live, except the serial episodes. There was no videotape. There was one shot at everything. So it had to be as right as we could make it the first time. One day one of my little six-year-old Mars Guards had to go to the bathroom right in the middle of our Bosco and milk. He wouldn't take wait for an answer either! Another day we were "returning" from our space trip, and a rather skeptical and unbelieving Mars Guard said, "We didn't go anywhere!" I just pinched his head off and pretended he wasn't there. (Just kidding!) Didn't go anywhere? The very idea!

After each day's show we would try to plan something special for the next day. And thanks to my play-by-play sports broadcasting in Jackson, I had inherited calling the schedule of weeknight high school football games on WHBQ Radio during the Fall. What do they say? *NEVER* a dull moment!

Too much of the time, when I finally got home I was ready to *CRASH*! But I also wanted to spend some quality time with my three girls, Madelyn, Lisa and little Lyn. Oh, there was also the subject of homework which was never in short supply. All this left little time for a social life in those days. Most every weekend we would pack up the car and head for Jackson!

But we were young then. Every day provided a new experience, a new mountain to climb. Life was good. Challenges came from the right, then the left. Compared to today's pace, we were walking—not running. Life was simple — and so uncomplicated.

On the Move

"Dad, why do you feel you have to move every five years?" That was an almost comical but fairly accurate question the kids would pose to me as we moved from house to house in California. I would use the old line "'Cause the rent's due," or whatever. But the truth was, on the

Wink reviews his cue cards with gal Saturday, Martha Sherman.

average, about every five years I got the urge to move on. I would simply get tired of a house. Madelyn could almost gauge the time she should call our real estate agent to start lining up new houses to look at.

But our first house was special. Perhaps because it was the first one. The address was 4270 Chickasaw Road in East Memphis. A very nice neighborhood. Our next door neighbors were our dearest friends during this period. Mary Ann and Jack Farris, with their daughter Jill, were the first to come knocking on our door, even before the moving vans had pulled away. I had always envisioned owning a one story home, with ranch type architecture, very popular with builders in the fifties. With roughly 3,000 square feet, a big kitchen, den, four bedrooms and a large back yard for the kids, it was a steal at $28,000. Can you imagine that today? But everything's relative. That sum of money seemed much larger to me then.

Television: Second Shot

"The higher they fly, the harder they fall!" As suddenly as it had blasted off, as with all shows eventually, time took its toll after three successful years and *Mars Patrol* hit the Neilsen ground with a resounding thud! Sure enough, my mentor Bill Grumbles was waiting in the wings with a new assignment for me.

With the amazing success of ABC's *American Bandstand*, practically every city in the country had its local version of the teen dance show, with its own "Dick Clark" to match. WHBQ-TV's *Top Ten Dance Party*, Saturdays from 5 'til 6:30, was sponsored in full by Coca Cola and an immediate hit with its first airing.

Wink and Dance Party co-host Susie Bancroft receive the Hamilton Time Award for outstanding public service.

With the demise of *Mars Patrol*, and with my deejay profile on radio, I seemed a natural to host the show. But Bill felt the show needed a co-host as well. I certainly had no problem with sharing the spotlight with Susan Bancroft. She was a dynamic gal with personality to match. A college grad and not that long out of Bartlett High School herself, she fit like a glove in her new role. Part of her duties, aside from on-air work, was to visit a different school each week and line up the dancers to be featured the following Saturday. It was a great opportunity for the schools of Memphis and surrounding cities to be spotlighted. Combined with the hits of the day and live performers when available, it was a winning combination. A natural extension for what I had been doing on television.

Dance Party was one of the first regularly produced shows in the station's new studios on Madison Avenue, after leaving the inadequate and confining space on the mezzanine of the Chisca Hotel. From the outset everybody involved with the show, from directors Stan Porter and Bob Lewis, to cameramen Durrell Durham, Noel Clarkson and

Chuck Staley, among others, took a personal pride in the look of the show that went above and beyond the ordinary. It was treated almost like the WHBQ "jewel"— with ratings to match!

Nobody took more pride in *Dance Party* than Martha Sherman. She was a full-time executive secretary during the week, then she would be there for us on Saturday as well. Martha did whatever needed to be done. From writing Coke commercials to printing cue cards. She was a dream, who bailed us out of many tough times!

The three years I hosted *Dance Party* were the best and most rewarding of my seven years in Memphis. For many reasons. Along with a couple of long-time news anchors, Trent Wood and Dick Hawley on WMCT Channel Five, by now my combined radio and television exposure made my name a household word. My popularity was mirrored by my rising income. I very much appreciated my new-found celebrity status and worked very hard to wear it well. I can honestly say that I never took it for granted. I appeared at as many high school events and charity fundraisers as my tight schedule would permit. But without question, my job brought with it many perks, which admittedly, I enjoyed!

I was the morning *Clockwatchers* host and assistant program director at WHBQ Radio. As such, I conducted the telephone survey of the leading retail record outlets each week, compiling the top forty best-selling single records. The station then published the weekly "Big 56 Record Survey," a station promotion sheet. So with these chores combined with hosting *Top Ten Dance Party*, it's easy to see how much music I was responsible for playing each week on radio and television. I found that I was receiving countless calls from local and national record company executives and promotional personnel. I was being deluged with offers of breakfasts, lunches and dinners! Realizing these perks were not being offered because I was just

IN PERSON

★ *Elvis* ★

PRESLEY

SCOTTY and BILL

The "Blue Moon" Boys

For Dates—Write—Wire—Call

BOB NEAL

Exclusive Personal Management

160 Union Ave.   Memphis, Tenn.

a nice guy. I had to be very careful not to allow their sometimes high-pressure tactics to sway my better judgment when determining my record selection, or in compiling a truly accurate list of Memphis' best-selling records. For a spot on the survey, either as a "hitbound extra" or as one of the top 40, meant a certain amount of extra airplay on radio. Sensing the importance of my job, I can also say I knew how vital it was to maintain my integrity. No matter where I worked in radio, I always played the records I felt were the best, most commercially popular at that given time. Whether in Jackson, Memphis or Los

Memphis deejay Bob Neal was the "King's" first manager—prior to Col. Tom Parker.

Angeles, station competition for the listener was much too keen to play Russian Roulette with records.

The Malco Fiasco

As *Dance Party* co-host with Susie Bancroft, I was approached by longtime Memphis radio personality, then artist personal manager Bob Neal, about an idea he had, putting together his fast-growing roster of Sun Record stars on the *same* show, on the *same* stage. Bob was an extremely nice man who had briefly served as Elvis' first manager at the beginning of The King's rise to popularity. In short order, Bob would give way to the man who would guide the Presley fortunes during the glory years, Col. Tom Parker. But in the late Forties and early Fifties Bob Neal was one of Memphis' and the Mid-South's most popular morning radio personalities on powerful WMPS.

A very young Texan, Roy Orbison, talks with Wink and Susie about his first Sun Records hit, "Ooby Dooby."

When he decided on a change in careers, artist management was the natural segue. With his friend Sam Phillips' fast-rising reputation as the prime discoverer of raw Southern singing talent for the independent Sun label, the two melded very nicely. Sam recorded the hits. Bob booked the artists who made the hits. It was a good combination. So when he approached Susie and me about emceeing a summertime, week-long *Rockabilly Revue* on the stage of the downtown Malco Theatre, we were thrilled with the idea! I think I had visions of a local version of Sinatra on stage at New York's Paramount Theatre in 1941! Wow! Summertime. Kids out of school. This new "rockabilly" sound had begun with Elvis and now everybody from Capitol Record's Gene Vincent ("Be-Bop-A-Lula") to balladeer Andy Williams ("Butterfly") had been bitten by the bug. I was even approached by Memphis society band leader Bill Justis (who shortly would take his composition "Raunchy" to the top of the charts) to make a recording of a pastiche he had written called "The Bug-A-Bop"! We made the record all right. But, needless to say, "The Bug-A-Bop"! got squashed quickly (and my record career with it).

The Malco Revue was set! Four hours a day. Five consecutive days. The Cha-Cha was all the musical rage. Warren Covington's "Tea for Two Cha-Cha" was climbing the charts. Bob Neal saw to it that a low-budget "B" movie featuring Latin-American music was booked for the week. Following the movie, Susie and I would run out on stage and emcee a live hour-and-a-half stage show, headlined by an up-and-coming singer from Texas named Roy Orbison (plugging his first Sun record, "Ooby Dooby"); Carl Perkins ("Blue Suede Shoes"); and a couple of additional Sun singers with new recordings, Warren Smith and Billy Riley. For whatever reason, the entire week was a disaster. The kids stayed away in droves! It was an eye-opener for me and an ego-leveler for all concerned. I came away from that experience with a couple of visions burned into my memory. One was of the half-gallon jugs of vodka that Carl Perkins and his band consumed that week between shows, without it ever affecting their performance! (Carl would later give up booze altogether). The other vision was that so called *MOVIE*! By week's end I felt that if I *ever* heard another Cha-Cha I would scream bloody murder. I never knew why that week turned out the way it did. Nor did Bob Neal. Obviously the featured stars went on to bigger and better things. I wonder what ever happened to the joker who produced that movie? I was so disappointed and heartsick over the failure of that week at the Malco, that I told myself I would never again attempt such a venture, or be part of such a live stage show.

Let's Play Radio!

The best laid plans! My father-in-law Bill Leech, and his brother, veterinarian Alexander Leech, decided they would apply for an available radio station license at 1460 on the AM band. A lawyer and a vet wanted to start a radio station! In Jackson, Tennessee! Well, they were awarded the license. Their first manager was my former Sunday School teacher who gave me my first job in radio, "Chick" Wingate. They hired a local electrician with engineering skills, Henry Lesh, to act as chief engineer. Guess who was hired to PROGRAM the daytime-only station. If you guessed your author, you would be right on the mark! I was thrust into the task of helping devise a format for the station that would be different from the other stations in town, yet saleable to the advertiser. Since Jackson's population was made up of a large number of Afro-Americans, we decided we would appeal to that unserved black audience. After all, the radio station in Memphis that enjoyed the highest ratings and the largest audience year in and year out was WDIA, programmed solely for the black listeners of Memphis. Thus WJAK, "Big Jack Radio" was born — and that's all I needed. Something else to keep me busy!

Madelyn, the girls and I would pack up the car on weekends, drive to Jackson and almost every minute of my time would be spent taking care of radio station activities. I would see very little of my family. Truly, it was all work and no play! We found our announcing staff by auditioning Lane College students (a Black liberal arts college in town). I was proud of the staff I put together: Roland Porter, Johnny Diggs, A.C. McFadden, and Memphian Frances Burnette. I persuaded WHBQ's Dewey Phillips to record a daily show for WJAK, for a very minimal amount of money. I recorded stationbreaks and various production features during the week at WHBQ, and put them on the Greyhound bus to Jackson. I was totally dedicated to that little Jackson station. Don't know why, really. Perhaps it was me trying to prove something again. Since it was being programmed for the black audience we took a lot of kidding, and many made fun of the station. Even in the Fifties. Oh yes! Our studios? In the attic of Dr. Leech's veterinary clinic! No kidding. I even tried selling some advertising during the week to some Memphis accounts. I remember one product in particular. Royal Crown Men's Pomade. They were big advertisers on WDIA in Memphis. So I tried for months to sell this little man on the idea of spreading some of his ad budget to include a black station in Jackson that he'd never heard of! He finally gave in and gave me a six week contract amounting to about $1,000. You would have thought it was more like a $100,000 deal! But was I proud? I could hardly wait to get to the phone to tell Madelyn's dad about my victory.

Never Say Never

Remember my promise to myself? NEVER get involved in *any* kind of live stage show after the Malco debacle! Well fortunately, *I didn't keep that promise!* Bill and Alex Leech had decided early on that when the time came, their form of repayment to me for all my time and work on WJAK would materialize in the form of — that's right, a live stage show. With all the profit, after expenses, going to me. But the best part was the calibre of talent they had in mind. Where we had featured the Sun Record roster at the Malco, for the "WJAK Rhythm & Blues Revue," a one-nighter at the Jackson National Guard Armory, we booked a top flight road show featuring several of Atlantic Records biggest acts at that time: Laverne Baker, Clyde McPhatter & The Drifters, The Bobbettes, plus Faye Adams, Roy Hamilton and several others. It so happened every act was red hot when they came through town. The advance sale was as strong with the white kids as with the Black population. Many of the tried and true Caucasian singers, such as Perry Como and Frankie Laine, were beginning to be phased out by rock and roll and rhythm and blues, much to the parents' dismay.

The day of the show arrived, it was a Wednesday. Midweek, but the show was a sellout! Standing room only! Susie Bancroft had agreed to come over to Jackson and help me introduce the acts, with help from all the WJAK personalities. Perfect station promotion. And it looked like I was going to hit the proverbial jackpot! All my time and effort will have been worth it tomorrow when I deliver my dollars to the bank. But during the drive over from Memphis, it started to rain lightly. Then the rain turned to sleet. I began to pray. "Oh please dear God, don't let this happen. Give us some good weather. I've worked hard for this night"! I no sooner said my "Amen," than the sleet turned to lightly falling flakes of snow. By the time we hit the Jackson city limits it was all I could do to see the road. I made it to Madelyn's parents' house, but by showtime six inches of snow had fallen. I just couldn't believe it. Memories of Memphis and The Malco began to flood my mind. Hadn't I said I would never do this again?

The snow kept falling. Deeper and deeper. The show was to begin at eight o'clock. We jumped in the car around five-thirty and started our drive downtown to the Armory. We expected the worse. After all, who in their right mind would venture from the comfort of their home on a Wednesday night to brave these temperatures, and the snow, to watch some people sing? As the car turned the final corner onto Balti-more Street toward the direction of the Armory (where I used to attend National Guard meetings on Monday nights), I couldn't believe my eyes. It was two hours before curtain time and the crowds were al-ready lined up two deep around the block waiting for the ticket win-dows to open. It was absolutely unbelievable!

The show went off without a hitch. Once inside the cavernous building we called the Armory, everybody had a ball. The show was sensational. It was truly one of those nights you didn't want to end. It was such fun. For everyone. And financially, it was everything I had hoped for. And more. From the radio station's standpoint, it was quite a victory. The only advertising for the show had been on WJAK. It seemed the station had made its mark. Everybody involved was over-joyed! We tried on at least two other occasions to duplicate that night. And while the follow-up shows were moderately successful, they never even came *close* to that cold night in January 1954.

The Hayloft Frolic

That aging National Guard Armory was demolished during the Sixties in favor of urban development. As Jackson's only facility large enough to handle events from a country concert to the annual high school prom, it rekindled many memories for me.

Long before country music became the billion dollar industry it is today, when the term for the music was "hillbilly" rather than "country and western" or "countrypolitan," I was a boy of nine when it became my regular Saturday night date to attend *The Hayloft Frolic*, Jackson's small-town version of Nashville's *Grand Ole Opry* or Shreveport's *Louisiana Hayride*.

The show was a weekly production of some enterprising country music lovers who saw a desire on the part of the citizenry to bring their music to town on a regular basis, providing a showcase for young, aspiring talent.

A young entrepreneur in his thirties, Aaron B. Robinson was the driving force behind this idea. A Jacksonian from birth, Robinson was circulation manager of *The Jackson Sun* newpaper. This position gave him ample opportunity to learn the basics of the radio business with the Sun station, WTJS, located just two floors above him. He would not only make a success of *The Hayloft Frolic*, but he would use the profits from this stage show to help lay the financial groundwork for creating a chain of radio stations known as The Dixie Broadcasting Company (The Dixie Network), for which his Jackson affiliate, WDXI, served as anchor.

No Love of "Country"

Even as a young boy, I harbored no love of country music. So much so that, frankly, I was embarrassed when any of my friends found out I was going to hear "that rural music" on Saturday nights. In truth, it was not the music that was drawing me to the Armory, it was the fact that WTJS was *broadcasting* two hours of the show each week, from 8 'til 10 P.M. I had made friends with the engineer who set up the mikes and equipment, and he allowed me to sit next to him during the broadcast. Billy Johnston was a wonderful young man in his early twenties who had been crippled since birth. He was a friendly and compassionate human being who seemed to sense my interest in radio and what made it work. It went a lot further than simply a boy who wanted to sit with him at a small table right at the base of the stage just to enable him to view the performers better. If I arrived by seven o'clock, Billy would even let me set up the microphones on the stage. I would stand up there, look out at the arriving audience and dream of introducing a singer. Or, if I allowed my imagination to really run amuck, I could imagine *myself* singing a song.

Again, I was living the earliest stages of a young boy's dream — that of a radio announcer. My fantasy hit a new high every time I walked into the Armory on Saturday night, sat down next to my buddy Billy, and watched him do his thing — send a live radio program from that building, through mikes, some wires and a metal box to anybody outside who happened to have their home or car radio tuned to 1390 AM, WTJS.

As Billy Johnston's "assistant," I eventually was given the okay to actually ride gain on the singers as they performed. That is, see to it that their voices did not get too loud on the air by riding (controlling) the volume of their voice. I was told that this was most important in assuring the sound heard on the radio was perfect for the listener. Therefore, in my youthful mind, this was my first *job* in radio! I learned just a few years ago that my dear friend Billy Johnston died at a young age, certainly never knowing the difference he had made in my life.

That same Armory building would be home to countless fraternity, sorority, junior high and high school dances I would attend in the next six or seven years. Though the place resembled an oversized barn, when festooned with an ample amount of crepe paper and balloons, and bathed with soft lights to cover a multitude of decorator deficiencies due to an undersized prom budget, the joint didn't look all that bad.

Fellow Jacksonian, Dave "Flat Git It" Gardner began on a small Memphis label, O. J. Records . . . Then he went on to record for RCA.

Plus, when you're wearing your best rented tuxedo, and that tux is wrapped around your best girl while dancing the last dance of the night, "Goodnight Sweetheart," who cared what the dance hall looked like. You were more concerned that it was dark enough in there so that none of the parent chaperones could tell how close you really were to her — and what you really had on your mind! As far as I was concerned, our own Charlie Baker Band (who played for 99% of the dances) was Glenn Miller incarnate!

Whoever said, "The more things change, the more they remain the same," never attended a Fifties high school prom. No matter how you cut it, the music was better. The lyrics meant something. When Nat

"King" Cole sang, "They try to tell us we're too young, too young to really be in love, they say that love's a word, a word we've only heard, but can't begin to know the meaning of," the lyrics painted a picture. How many of us, for example, can still recall a song that was "our song"? Chances are you can. But can kids today look back on a song by Boyz II Men or Hootie & the Blowfish, and honestly say, "That was the song we fell in love to"? Perhaps. But I think not.

"Moonlove"

"The Bug-A-Bop," though a miserable failure, served one purpose, for better of worse. It led me to a recording contract with a small Memphis label, O. J. Records. A gentleman named C. G. ("Red") Matthews had been in the record business for years with no real measure of success. Now with the success of Elvis, Johnny Cash, Roy Orbison, Carl Perkins and The Prisonaires ("Crying in the Chapel") on Sun Records, Memphis was becoming a small Nashville in the eyes of the record world. Sam Phillips had singlehandedly caused a recording reformation. Small labels began to spring up almost daily. One of those was O. J. Records. First there was a singing group called The Escorts, who caused a minor stir with a so-so effort. But then Red Matthews made the decision to record a Jackson, Tennessee native on a song Red had co-written years before, titled "White Silver Sands." Dave "Flat Git It" Gardner was a popular Southern comedian and sometimes singer whose recording of this song took the radio stations of Memphis, then the Mid-South, then the country, by storm! Though the much larger and well established Jubilee Records covered the song with their own Don Rondo, and took the lion's share of record sales, O. J. made enough of a splash to get immediate airplay on their next several releases. One of those was "Thought It Was Moonlove," by Wink Martindale. I know. You're saying "Thought It Was *WHAT*?" That was what most radio stations and the audience in general asked!

Red Matthews was no fool. He was a big fan of *Top Ten Dance Party*. His rationale was that if I could sing half as good as I could *talk*, with my popularity among the kids, they might even buy a record if I recorded one. He approached me with the idea and naturally, with all the Elvis sound-alikes springing up under every rock in the country, I thought, "Why not. It's Red's nickel!" So I rehearsed and rehearsed, then recorded two songs, one of which was another of Red's songs, "Thought It Was Moonlove." Naturally WHBQ played it, and I did a lip-sync performance of the song several times on *Dance Party*. Just as naturally, no other radio station in town would dare play the record because I was a competitor. Nonetheless, "Moonlove" sold enough copies to legitimately make the Memphis Top Ten sales charts. The record company even took me out on the road to several major cities to promote my record. But appearances on Baltimore's *Buddy Deane Show* and Washington's popular *Milt Grant Show* failed to create even an iota of interest, air play, and more importantly—*SALES*!

In short, my *second* try at record "stardom" was also a bust. But my six-city tour was fun for me because at the same time, I met several singers on tour promoting *their* latest record release: Frankie Avalon and "Dee Dee Dinah," and Sam Cooke with his trademark "You Send Me," among others. Frankie is a friend to this day, as was Sam, until his tragic and untimely death in the early Sixties.

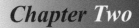

Chapter Two

ELVIS!
IN THE BEGINNING . . .

Beatle John Lennon said it best: "Nothing really affected me, until Elvis." And so it was for an entire generation. Since Elvis cut his first record in 1953, he recorded more than 500 different songs, sold nearly 300 million singles and albums, starred in 33 movies and changed more cultural habits than anyone before him.

Perhaps 1971, more than any other year was pivotal in the life of this Tupelo, Mississippi, man who had touched so many with his music since 1954. It was a year of uncommon events. The state highway which runs past Graceland Estate in Memphis was renamed "Elvis Presley Boulevard." When he appeared for a month at the Sahara in Lake

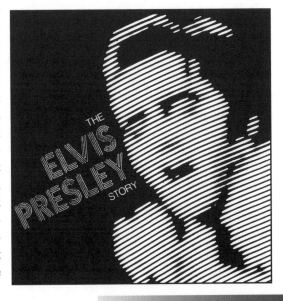

ILLUSTRATION ELVIS PRESLEY

Tahoe, so great was Elvis' appeal that every hotel and casino in town pitched in to meet Col. Parker's price. And for this engagement, like those in Las Vegas, the so-called "Memphis Mafia" was partially reformed.

RCA offered a four-record set of his million selling songs, including in the package a swatch of material from Elvis' personal wardrobe. President Nixon gave Elvis a federal narcotics badge for Elvis' badge collection, and the National Junior Chambers of Commerce named Elvis one of America's Outstanding Young Men of the Year. The date: January 16th. The place: The Municipal Auditorium in Memphis, the same huge concert hall where as a boy Elvis attended all-night gospel sings. At the ceremony, surrounded by his family and closest friends, Elvis walked briskly to the microphone and made these brief comments:

"I read comic books, and I was the hero of the comic book. I saw movies, and I was the hero in the movie. Every dream that I ever dreamed has come true a hundred times. And these gentlemen over here, are the type people who care...who are dedicated, and you realize that it is possible that they might be building the kingdom of heaven. It's not too far-fetched from reality. I'd like to say that I learned very early in life that without a song, a man ain't got a friend. Without a song, the road would never bend . . . without a song. So I keep singing a song. Good night."

Elvis Presley's Story

Not long after that memorable moment in Elvis' life, I was asked by Ron Jacobs and Tom Rounds of Watermark Productions to narrate an audiobiography entitled *The Elvis Presley Story*, which remains, in my view, the most definitive and complete story of his life from bright beginning to tragic end. I was requested because of my Southern upbringing and attendant accent. The producers were aware of my Memphis connection to Elvis, Sam and Dewey Phillips, and WHBQ Radio, where the very first entertainment chapter of Elvis' life really began. A little over a year before the night the first Elvis Presley record was played on WHBQ, I had mailed my audition tape from my home in Jackson, Tennessee, to station program director Gordon Lawhead in hopes of landing a job at the station I admired the most. Luckily in just a few weeks I received a reply from Mr. Lawhead suggesting I take the 85-mile drive to Memphis to meet and get acquainted. I was thrilled — but nervous! So this 19-year-old kid, two years removed from high school, asked his sister if she would go along with him. She consented.

Through the same front door my sister Gerry and I entered at WHBQ the 31st day of March 1953, would later walk the young singer who would singlehandedly change the course of popular music as we had known it. And fate dealt me the lucky hand to witness the beginning.

Elvis...The First Time!

Not long after my introductory meeting, I began as combination record librarian and host

This was Wink's very first publicity picture after joining WHBQ.

of WHBQ's popular morning drive show, *Clockwatchers*. I would be in place at the station just months prior to the "night of nights"— the night an Elvis Presley record would be played on Memphis radio for the first time.

Dewey Phillips was arguably the most popular deejay in Memphis and the Mid-South. His show was called *Red, Hot and Blue* — and the title was a perfect fit. He played the red hot hits. But not the so called " pop hits" you might hear on WHBQ during other hours of the day. The early Fifties was still a time of *vanilla* music. That is, hits by Eddie Fisher, Jo Stafford, Johnny Ray, Peggy Lee, Nat "King" Cole and Perry Como. Those were among the artists ruling the airwaves of popular music stations. But the winds of change were to beginning to blow. Dewey Phillips was a white jock who had gained enormous popularity among black *and* white teens by concentrating on "race" music, another term for music by Black performers. Another term for this black music was "rhythm and blues." (Thus the "blue" in *Red, Hot and Blue*.)

Phillips' ratings were more than triple his nearest competition between 9PM and midnight. He possessed an uncanny ability to pick the hits. Record company executives, from Chicago to New York to LA, knew that if Dewey jumped on a record and started playing it with any regularity, they had a hit!

So it wasn't unusual to see Sun Records founder Sam Phillips (no relation to Dewey) show up this night with an advance pressing (this was prior to cassettes or CDs) of a record by his new truck-driving singer, Elvis Presley. Sam had first met Elvis when the boy had walked into his Memphis Recording Service to make a birthday recording of "My Happiness" for his Mother. Sam had often said that, "If I can ever find a white man who can sing like a negro, I'll make a million dollars!" In Elvis he felt that he'd found that person. After over a year of rehearsing and searching for just the right songs, Sam Phillips felt "That's Alright Mama" and "Blue Moon of Kentucky" were the ticket.

Bear in mind that 99% of the music Phillips played was by black artists. So naturally when he followed a Little Richard, a Chuck Berry

or a Penguins record with an artist named Elvis Presley, everybody listening just assumed he was black too. And arguably, Elvis *sounded* black!

The Night the Music Changed

It was Thursday night, July 8, 1954. By happenstance I was at the station that night showing some friends the studio. And they were excited about meeting Dewey. Little did they know they were to get more than they bargained for. From the

Elvis seems to be giving great thought to Wink's question during the King's visit to WHBQ's *Top Ten Dance Party*.

first playing of the record the phone lines lit up. Phillips would play one side of the record, then flip it and play the other side. Over and over. The listeners couldn't get enough of this new sound, later to be termed "rockabilly." It was an exciting happening. No one there that night, least of all Dewey Phillips, had any way of knowing we were witnessing the birth of a musical icon, a legend in every sense of the word — perhaps the birth of rock n' roll.

It was only a relatively short time later that we realized the symbolism of that evening at WHBQ in the old Chisca Hotel on South Main Street. Soon there would be network appearances on The Dorsey Summer Show, then a multi-appearance booking on *The Ed Sullivan Show*. In short order, "Presley-mania" was here for the long haul. But on this night everyone began to ask questions. Who was this guy? Somebody said he was originally from Tupelo, Mississippi. George Klein, who worked for Dewey at the station, was a former classmate of Elvis' at Memphis Humes High School. George, who would later be considered one of Elvis' closest friends and one of the inner circle known as the "Memphis Mafia," was able to fill in many of the blanks.

As Shocked as Everybody

Naturally as the excitement mounted, Dewey wanted Elvis to come to the station. But where was he? A call was placed to his mother and daddy at their Lauderdale Courts apartment. They said their son had gone to a movie at the Suzores Theatre on Jackson Avenue (which wasn't that far from the Chisca). He had known Phillips would be playing his record that night, but he was too nervous about its reaction to listen. He was found sitting alone in that dark theatre and was coaxed into coming to WHBQ.

Elvis seemed just as shocked as everybody else at the commotion he was causing. Phillips, unbeknown to Elvis, began to ask his new-found star some of the questions everybody wanted to hear him answer. Nervously, Elvis was giving his first interview as a professional entertainer. He later confided that he had no idea that interview was on-the-air. Otherwise he'd never have been able to talk!

The next day Music Sales, Sun Records' distributor in Memphis, was deluged with calls for this new Elvis Presley recording. It's veteran manager, Bill Fitzgerald, told me he had never experienced such a reaction to a record. Joe Coughi, who owned one of the largest one-stop and retail-record outlets in the city, Home of The Blues, said he could easily have shipped

Elvis proudly shows off the diamond ring sugar heiress, Judy Spreckles, has just given him the week before this interview.

and sold over 10,000 records the next day, if he'd had them to sell. Problem was, nobody (least of all Sam Phillips) anticipated the kind of reaction this new singer generated overnight — beyond his wildest expectations.

The Word Spread

This first record would prove only a regional hit for Elvis. For although word was spreading about him far and wide, there were still many disbelievers. His first nationwide hit would come only after RCA record executive Steve Sholes negotiated the purchase of his contract from Sam Phillips and Sun Records. The price — $35,000. The biggest steal since the Louisiana Purchase.

With his first RCA release, "Heartbreak Hotel," any doubt about his ability to meet and surpass the expectations of even his harshest of critics was forever put to rest. The rest, as they say, is history.

Between his early tours, and all during his professional career, Elvis always used his beloved Memphis as homebase. He loved his roots. And he revered his mother.

She was in Memphis, so that's where he wanted to be—near her. I discovered that when at home, he, his mom and dad always watched a teen television show I hosted called *Top Ten Dance Party*. Similar to *American Bandstand,* the 5 to 6:30 P.M. Coca-Cola sponsored show was the Memphis clone of *Bandstand*, and I suppose I was Memphis' Dick Clark. I had a delightful co-host, Susan

Wink and *Top Ten Dance Party* co-hostess Susan Bancroft, convince Elvis to show his dancing prowess after interview.

Bancroft, who did most of the work while I received entirely too much credit.

The First Recorded Interview

It was during one of his visits home that I was able to persuade Dewey Phillips to approach Elvis, by now a *HUGE* star. Though I was an aquaintance of Elvis, I knew my best bet was to work through Dewey, for Elvis idolized Phillips and would be beholden to him always for "believing" from the start. There was an approaching Cynthia Milk Fund charity appearance Elvis was to make at Russwood Park, sponsored by TV columnist Bob Johnson of the *Memphis Press Scimitar*. I appealed to my friendship with Dewey (and his ego) to join Elvis on the show for a joint interview. He loved the idea, and convinced Elvis to do it. It would be Saturday, July 16.

Word soon spread about Elvis' and Phillips' impending guest shot on *Dance Party*. The station even hired a security guard to handle the excess crowd that day. Even many station employees suddenly found a reason to work, on a Saturday! My gal Friday, Martha Sherman, suggested that it might be a good idea to film the interview. There still were no videotape recorders at WHBQ-TV in 1956. Since it was not in the show's meager budget, I personally hired a local photographer to set up a camera in the studio and make a kinescope of what was, without question, one of the first recorded interviews with Elvis. Martha's idea was a good one, for that filmed interview later proved invaluable to me as Elvis' fame grew and grew worldwide.

Dance-Party Delirium

The show's director Stan Porter had the hardest job that day, just trying to retain some semblance of order due to the chaotic conditions. When Elvis strolled into the studio that day, it was sheer magic. The teen dancers were trying to be so cool, but it wasn't easy. We saved *the best* for the final half hour. Dewey had brought along a cheap guitar to use as a prop, also hoping we could talk Elvis into singing a song while there. But nothing doing. He had forewarned us all he planned to do was answer any questions I wanted to ask, and promote his upcoming charity show. That was it. But believe me, that was enough.

Phillips: There's your boy right there, Wink.

Wink: *Is this the fella you were going to bring in to see us today?*

Phillips: That's lover boy!

Elvis: Ahhhh!

Wink: *Elvis Presley! Dewey, thanks a lot for getting him here today. You were really one of the guys who helped to get this fella started, weren't you? Weren't you one of the first to play his records?*

Phillips: You ask Elvis, I don't know. What about it, Elvis?

Elvis: Nah-h! (laughs) I guess he was the first one in Memphis to play my record.

Phillips: I'll tell you what happened, Wink . . .

Elvis: It didn't cost me much.

Wink: *Didn't cost you much, huh?*

Phillips: He went out there. He recorded a record for Sam Phillips and one night Sam brought the record up to the radio station, and I listened to the record — and I said, "Man, one of them has got to go! That "Blue Moon" and "That's Alright." And I got Elvis' home phone number. I called and his mother answered the phone. I said, "Mrs. Presley, is Elvis home?" She said, "No, he's down there watching a western at the Suzore." And I called down to the theater and asked Presley to come up there (to the radio station). and he came up to the station and we cut loose with that record, "That's Alright"! You know what made that record?

Wink: *What?*

Phillips: "Dee Dee Dee Dee"! (Phillips "sings") How's it go, Elvis?

Elvis: I forgot.

Wink: *That's been a long time ago.*

Phillips: How about me singing a song here?

Elvis: "Yes it's me, and I'm in love again"!

Phillips: (Repeats) "Yes it's me and I'm in love again"!

Wink: That's the only one you know, isn't it?

Elvis: Naw. I know, uh . . . (Well, I better not give that one).

Wink and Elvis share a laugh after the "King" replies to Wink's question, "When you were in Humes High School, did you expect all this to happen?" Elvis: "I didn't expect to get outa Humes High School!"

Dewey Phillips, the first Memphis deejay to play Elvis' "That's Alright Mama" and "Blue Moon of Kentucky" in 1954, gives Wink and Elvis a lesson or two on how to 'pick and sing' during Elvis' visit to *Top Ten Dance Party* in 1956.

Wink: C'mon. One little chorus.

Phillips: You with me, Elvis?

Elvis: I'm with you.

Phillips: You got your knife with you? You got your pick?
              (Looks up) "Man, there's a flock of 'em flew over then"!

Elvis: Sing "Gee Dad, It's a Wurlitzer."

Phillips: "Gee Dad, It's a Wurlitzer"? Let's go cat, you ready?

Elvis: **You go ahead. I'll wind you up.**

Phillips: "The landlord rang my front door bell . . ."
Where's the mike at? I don't see a mike! That the mike?

Wink: *That's it. Go ahead.*

Phillips: You ready? I'll tell you what you do, Elvis. You hold the chord. I don't know how to hold it.

Elvis: **You're left handed. I can't . . .**

Phillips: Don't break it! Here it is. Let's go. What are we gonna sing?

Elvis: **"Money Honey"!**

Phillips: "Well the landlord rang my front door bell. I let it ring for a long, long spell. I went to the window . . .

Wink asks Elvis about his gyrations when he's singing: "Is this an unconscious movement that goes with the mood of the song?"

and I jumped straight up. I said what is it baby that's on your mind. She said, "Money Honey." Ho baby!

Wink: *Thanks a lot, Dewey.*

Phillips: Martindale, want you to meet one of the nicest guys in show business. Elvis Presley. He's a clean boy! *(Applause)*

He's one of the hottest guys that's ever hit show business.

Wink: *I realize that.*

Elvis: **You ain't kidding.**

Phillips: See ya' old buddy.

Wink: *Thanks a lot, Dewey*

Phillips: Anytime you want me, if you got the money I'll be back old buddy.

Wink: *Okay—(You cost too much)!*
            Elvis, it goes without saying that all of us here at Dance Party *appreciate very much you taking time out today to come by and say hello to all of our friends who watch* Dance Party. *And also the people who are here on the floor. And it's nice you were able to spend these past few days at home. How is it you've been home so many days in a row here?*

Elvis: **Well, it's the first time I've been off in months. I've been on the road. I've been on the West Coast and everything. I decided I needed a little rest.**

Wink: *A few days off, huh? You don't want to go too fast now.*

Elvis: **. . . And I'd like to tell you that, uh . . . I really enjoy being out here . . . all these people . . . .**

Wink: *Well, we're certainly glad to have you here. Elvis, we want to ask you a few questions and uh . . . .*

Elvis: **Shoot!**

Wink: *Here we go. Let's go back to the beginning first of all,*

*to your quick rise to fame. First of all, how old were
you when you first remember being attracted to music
and singing? And, well, how old were you? How'd you
get started? And when did you get that first guitar, and
where did you get it?*

Elvis: **Whew! Let's start with the first question again.**

Wink: *Okay. How old were you when you first . . .*

Elvis: **When I first started singing? Well, I never sung in
my life until I made my first record.**

Wink: *Uh huh. Where did you get the guitar?*

Elvis: **I got it in Mississippi. It cost twelve dollars I think.**

Wink: *Twelve dollar guitar, huh?*

Elvis: **It was a Gene Autry guitar. I got a Roy Rogers now.**

Wink: *What did you do with that first guitar? What happened to it?*

Elvis: **Well, I had some uncles that picked a guitar a little
bit, and I sat down and watched 'em all the time. I
just picked it up watching 'em. But, I mean, I never
thought I'd make anything doing it ya know.**

Wink: *Uh huh. Well now, when you were graduated from
Humes High School did you expect to pursue singing
and uh . . .*

Elvis: **I didn't expect to get out of Humes High School!**
(laughter).

Wink: *That takes care of that question. Very well answered.*

Elvis: **No. I'll tell you. I never even thought of singing as
a career. In fact, I was ashamed to sing in front of
any body except my mother and daddy. And all of**

a sudden one day I got a sudden urge to go into this recording studio; Mr. Sam Phillips Memphis Recording Service. And he told me he might call me sometime, ya know.

Wink: *And he called you.*

Elvis: So he called me. It was a year-and-a-half later. I was an old man.

Wink: *Elvis, regarding your hobbies. Would you consider cars or sports cars an interest?*

Elvis: I don't have any cars.

Wink: *I heard the opposite of that.*

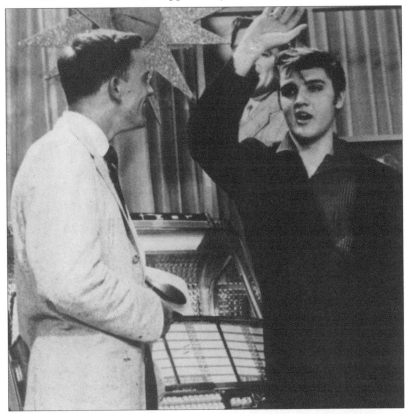

Elvis tells Wink about the night backstage in Kansas City when he "made a new door" in the wall!

Elvis: **My daddy's got Presley's Used Car Lot out on Audubon Drive.**
(laughter)

Wink: *How many cars do you have by the way?*

Elvis: **I've got four cars, and a Messerschmidt. And a motorcycle.**

Wink: *What kind of cars are included in the four cars?*

Elvis: **All Lincolns!**

Wink: *(He said that for the benefit of Dewey Phillips.)*

Elvis: **I'll tell you the reason I bought those cars. Maybe someday I'll go broke and I can sell some of 'em.**

Wink: *And have a little extra money on hand.*

Elvis: **Right.**

Wink: *You have experienced a phenomenal rise to popularity, Elvis, in the course of a few months time. How did you first feel when your records first started to be accepted by the people and bought by the public? Didn't you have sort of a sensation?*

Elvis: **Well, I'll tell ya Wink. It all happened so fast, and so I didn't even have time to think about it. And it just kept going and it's still doing that way. And I can't even think about it—in fact, I don't even like to wake up in the morning—I'm afraid I might wake up . . .**

Wink: *Afraid it might be all over, huh?*

Elvis: **Afraid I might be back driving that truck again.**

Wink: *That brings about this question. Some people have said they don't like the way you jump around — move*

— when you sing, Elvis. Now does this help you, or is it an unconscious motion which sorta goes with the mood of the song? Is that a hard question to answer?

Elvis: Well, I'll tell ya. I'm not — I'm not doing it on purpose. I mean, I'm aware of everything I do at all times. But it's just the way I feel. I mean, if I — I can just picture somebody singing a rock 'n' roll song standing still. Actually, I'd go nuts standing there, ya know?

Wink: *People everywhere say, well I know (and you've heard it too more than likely), all this type of thing is just a craze and a fad, and like other fads and personalities in the past, Presley and rock 'n' roll music will depart in due time. What is your feeling about this, along this line?*

Mae Axton, co-writer of Elvis' first million seller "Heartbreak Hotel," was a long-time friend of Wink and Sandy.

Elvis: Well, I uh — I'm inclined to agree with them. I mean, people change. Some time they like you. And then again, later on they don't. Rock 'n' roll is real hot right now and I like it. It's very good. It has a feeling, and people enjoy it. People enjoy dancing to it. And, uh — there are some very beautiful records made in rock 'n' roll style. Stuff like "The Magic Touch," "The Great Pretender." Stuff like that. I mean they just don't make any prettier songs

than that.

Wink: *Well now, speaking of records, "Heartbreak Hotel" sold over a million copies and, undoubtedly, that was a pretty thrilling experience to be presented by the RCA Victor people with a gold copy for you to keep for the rest of your life. Now, actually, didn't you like the other side better than "Heartbreak Hotel"?*

Elvis: **I liked "I Was the One," but I liked the royalty checks better on "Heartbreak Hotel."**

Wink: *Well, which record in your opinion, of all the ones you've recorded do you like the best?*

Elvis: **"I Was the One."**

Wink: *"I Was the One" huh?*

Elvis: **Yeah.**

Wink visits Elvis on the set of *G. I. Blues*, the King's first movie for MGM following Army duty.

Wink: *And that was on the other side of "Heartbreak Hotel" — and we could say that both helped to sell a million copies. Well how are things looking regarding your latest releases?*

Elvis: My latest record, "I Want You, I Need You, I Love You" has sold almost a million. It's only been out 15 days. Sold right close to eight hundred thousand.

Wink: *Pretty fast work isn't it people? (Applause). Elvis, you've made many personal appearances. You've played many one nighters and you've appeared on several big-time television shows. You've sung. Now, which do you get the biggest kick out of? Which do you enjoy the most? Do you like the live personal appearances, or television better?*

Elvis: I like live personal appearances better.

Wink: *Any particular reason?*

Elvis: I enjoy it. I mean, on television you're limited, ya know. You can only do so much, and so many rehearsals.

Wink: *You rehearse, you rehearse, and you rehearse some more don't you?*

Elvis: By doing only so much, I mean — you know, you can only do a couple of songs, and by the time you get warmed up—well, they're dragging you off.

Wink: *That's it. Well, in the cities and towns you've visited in the past several months you've met lots of people. You've signed lots of autographs and I understand you've lost several shirts in the process.*

Elvis: Well, uh — there's been some pretty wild stories. Like the one in Kansas City where my drummer was thrown in the orchestra pit. Uh—there wasn't even an orchestra pit there. Uh—what it was was a barn. Actually it was. It was more or less a great big barn we were playing in and, uh, and they overran the police (I think there were six policemen around the stage). And the people overran the police. And I was singing "You ain't nothin' but a ... hound"... and out I went! And there was a door, there was a door backstage that I ran through. (I mean I knocked a lock off). It was dark and I couldn't see where I was going. I just knew where the door was.

Wink: *You made a new door!*

Elvis: I mean—there's a lot of stories start, but ...
Wink: *Well now, that brings us around to something else, and we're getting around to the end pretty soon here. Some people (and we discussed this the other day) . . .*

Elvis: Aw, we got plenty of time ...
           And about this Judy Spreckles that I've been get ting a lot of — I've been getting a lot of publicity with Judy Spreckles. All that got started when Judy gave me a ring out in Las Vegas. She gave me this ring here (shows ring). And uh, that ring there.

Wink: *It is a pretty big ring, isn't it? Would you show it to us up close there?*

Elvis: Sure.

Wink: *Pretty big. Beautiful ring, too.*

Elvis: Uh — she gave me this ring because, uh, I saw it in the window and I just admired it. But Judy is a very good friend. Judy is older than I am, and she's engaged. She's going to get married next month. And she's a real good friend, nothing else. Some body started that we were wearing each other's rings. *(laughs)*

Wink: *That's the way it goes. How about the big show at Russwood Park scheduled for July Fourth? Bob Bob Johnson surely, I know, wants us to mention that, and we want to mention it. I believe the proceeds from this show go to the Cynthia Milk Fund, is that right, Elvis?*

Elvis: **Yes sir. That's right. And uh — I'd like to say that we're, uh, let's see — what would I like to say. I'd like to say that we have a diamond ring that we're going to have as a door prize. It's my initial ring, I've had it for some time and it has fourteen diamonds in it. And, uh, we're going to give it away at the door as a door prize.**

Wink: *And all the proceeds from this particular show — this is July Fourth [1956] at Russwood Park. Elvis is going to be there. He's going to sing and play. His band will be there. Many other stars will be there, too. We'll certainly want you to watch Bob Johnson's column in the* Memphis Press Scimitar. *Watch all the publicity on it, and get your tickets in advance.*

Elvis Presley, I want to thank you again, because we know you're a busy man.

Elvis: **Thank you, Wink.**

Wink: *And thanks a lot for coming by and seeing us at Dance Party, and saying hello to all your friends here in Memphis and the Mid-South. Anytime you're in town and want to come by we certainly will welcome you.*

Elvis: **Thank you very much, Wink, and I'll see you again.**

Wink: *Thanks a lot—Elvis Presley.*

(Applause)

The complete interview lasted almost fifteen minutes. It was sad when the show came to a close because we had all looked forward to it for weeks. Although I tried, I was never again successful at getting him to return. Several reasons for that, but at the top of the list was Elvis' manager Colonel Parker. The Colonel had not been happy when he learned of the "free" television interview his "boy" had granted, apparently without his knowledge.

During my four years as host of *Top Ten Dance Party*, my co-hostess changed from time to time. After Susie Bancroft left, the hostesses included Ina Poindexter, Donna Rae Jackson and Anita Wood. Like me, Anita was a former Jacksonian. Elvis became enamored with Anita when he saw her one Saturday on *Dance Party*. He started dating her and she was considered his steady for quite awhile. At one point there were even rumors of an impending marriage. History proves he eventually tied the knot, but not very tightly. And not to Anita.

The "Private Elvis" Connection

Although I never considered myself a close personal friend of Elvis Presley, we stayed in touch on occasion through the years. In 1959, when I was transferred by RKO General to their radio and television outlet in Los Angeles, KHJ, I began a new TV program similar to the Memphis show. To help kick off the first *Wink Martindale Dance Party*, I made a transatlantic call to Elvis in Germany. Unlike the in-person Memphis interview, the phoner was still something special. Elvis was in the Army. His personna was in short supply, so to his fans, Elvis' voice was better than no Elvis at all.

Wink: *Elvis, where are you stationed?*

Elvis: **I'm in Freiburg (Germany).**

Wink: *How is life in the service, Elvis? What do you do in your spare time?*

Elvis: **Well, if I don't have to work late, I usually have some people over here to the house — and we just wake all the neighbors up — and play music. It's nice over here, Wink. I mean—I've met a lot of nice people and I've seen a little of the country, not too much. I went to Paris, and a few places. But, uh . . . I'd like to come back over here someday as an entertainer.**

I'd like to come back and, uh, have a chance to travel around all over Europe, ya' know.

Wink: *Listen, we're hearing a lot of rumors in the states these days about a certain Elvis and a certain German girl. Any truth to those rumors, and how do the girls over there compare to American girls?*

Elvis: Well, I couldn't give you any comparison, Wink. The only thing I could tell you is that, uh, I find that the girls here are a lot like the ones in the states. The only thing is the language difference.

    I've been getting a lot of articles through the mail — that people have sent me about this little German girl. A movie actress, ya know—Vera [unintelligible], and uh, (chuckles) according to the — a lot of the articles in the magazines—uh, we're almost ready to get married! Actually, I haven't seen her since the first of the year. But it's funny, I get a lot of mail, ya know, people asking me about it. There's no chance of marriage, uh — over here, over there, or anywhere for a while, Wink, ya know. I will — I will get married some day. First of all I'm not ready for it. I've got a lot of things I would like to accomplish first, ya' know. Like the movie industry. I'd like to—I'd like to learn to act, ya know. That's what I've got my head set on right now.

Wink: *I've got to tell you that we receive nothing but glowing reports here of how you're conducting yourself in the service, Elvis. Anything you want to say to every body back here at home while we've got you on the phone?*

Elvis: Well—the only thing I can think of, Wink, is—the people who have stood by me during the time I've been in the Army, and everything. I owe everything to them and I can't thank them enough, really. Be cause, uh — I've tried to play it straight—in the army, ya know—it's the only way it could be. In other

words, I couldn't do any entertaining. Uh. I couldn't be, or do anything but just what the other boys do. That's the only way it could be, ya know. And — I'm drafted. And it's turned out the way it has, because I've made a lot of friends, uh, in the Army, among the men that I would have never met before, ya know.

And I'm glad of this. I would just like to say, I would just like to say that, uh, to all the people that have stood by me and written to me and so forth—it's really helped me get through it.

Wink: *Elvis, I want you to know that I speak for everyone here. We all miss you very much. And I also want you to know how much I appreciate, personally, you taking time from your busy schedule to talk to us, as we kick off our new* Dance Party *show. And we look forward to your return home.*

Elvis: **Okay—that's good. And, uh, best of luck to you and your new show, Wink. And, uh, I'll — uh — I'll see you when I get back.**

Wink: *Thanks again, Elvis.*

Elvis: **Okay—Good luck, boy—Bye bye!**

When he received his discharge and came home, his first picture at MGM was *G.I. Blues.* I remember my producer, Al Burton, and I visiting Elvis on the set. We had a picture made together. He looked sensational following his stint for Uncle Sam. In the final years of his life my memory traveled back to that day at MGM, a day still bright and full of promise.

In a touch of irony, Sandy, my wife of twenty-five years, met Elvis in April of 1960, during the filming of *G.I. Blues,* eleven years before our paths would cross by chance in Palm Springs. Sandy Ferra met Elvis Presley at her father's nightclub, The Crossbow. She grew to love him very much. So much that by her own admission, the day he died, a part of her died. Sandy's memories are bittersweet:

More Vulnerable Than He Knew

"Those of us who were lucky enough to have had their lives touched by Elvis are truly blessed," Sandy remembered. "To have experienced the excitement of his presence in a room was electrifying, and so was the joy of his infectious laugh, his magnetic smile, and the fun of his devilish, little-boy pranks. He was capable of great sensitivity, friendship and love. He was more vulnerable than he knew, which I feel is one of the reasons he is no longer with us.

"I am extremely lucky!" she said. "I am happily married to *another* Tennesseean—Wink Martindale—who makes me feel as secure and complete as Elvis ever did. I remember once telling Elvis he was responsible for me having fallen in love with a man from Tennessee."

The last time Sandy and I saw Elvis alive was backstage at the Las Vegas Hilton following one of his performances in 1976. Just the three of us were chatting very quietly by the bar in his dressing room. It was somewhat eerie, but a moment frozen in time for us. His body and his handsome chiseled face were showing the ravages of time. Though there were many people in the room, including Ginger Alden, his then current fiancee, he insisted on chatting with Sandy and me. We had just guested that day on a CBS Television show hosted by the late Bert Convy, *Tattletales*. Elvis had seen the show and commented how much he enjoyed it—and how well we seemed to know each other.

It was then that Sandy tearfully told him how much we loved him, and thanked him for teaching her just how nice and mannerly Southern boys could be. Then we all enjoyed a hearty laugh when Sandy recalled that her mother, Mary Lou, used to come along on their dates. He *had* to be mannerly! No other choice.

Incidentally, Sandy has always been a terrific dancer. So good, that she was cast as a dancer in several Elvis movies, including *Viva Las Vegas, The Trouble With Girls,* and *Girls, Girls, Girls.*

Somehow we knew as we turned to leave that night, that this was our final farewell to our friend. But he will always be very special to both of us. We still miss him, and we will always cherish our memories of this very special man.

HE GAVE US ALL HE HAD!

Elvis! In the Beginning . . .

That Was Elvis to Me
August 16, 1977

Few dates are as indelibly printed in our memory as that one. Pearl Harbor, that infamous day in Dallas, perhaps two or three more. Odds are you can still pinpoint just where you were, even what you were doing at the moment you learned that the man who reshaped the music of a generation was gone.

This might be considered an open letter, not only to all his fans, but more importantly to those who attempted to tarnish the memory of Elvis Presley, some even making a mockery of his passing.

Were the accusations and claims in the dozens of books truthful and accurate? Did the doctors ever really level with us about the cause of his death?

I answer those questions with two of my own. Why ask? For there are no answers that can bring back to us this person we loved so much.

What is it about human nature that makes many of us more interested in a person's shortcomings than successes? Nobody will ever convince me that this man was anything but a good, kind, generous human being. That was Elvis to me.

Talented? Beyond words! God-fearing! Yes, for all of his 42 years. His humble beginnings in that little Tupelo shack and the Christian upbringing by a devoted Mama and Daddy lighted the path he would follow for the rest of his life. Stray from that path? Of course! No question about it. For, like you and me, he was only human. And humans make mistakes.

The absolute truth is, we made him a god, but he was only a man. We called him the king of rock and roll, but his response to that was always the same: "There is only one King, Jesus Christ."

Elvis loved his country. He served it proudly and with honor at the height of his career, asking no special treatment and with no complaints. His love for his fellow man, his loyalty, his generosity are legend, befitting a legend. He found great joy in giving. For him material things were few as a child. As a man, he had it all. And, my God, he loved to share.

The most precious gift he gave many of us was his friendship. That was the Elvis I knew.

Those of us who played and bought his records, those of you who attended his concerts and movies by the millions helped buy him a Memphis mansion, gold cadillacs, and clothes embroidered in silver. To watch an Elvis performance, in person, was something more than just memorable. To have done so, you know what I mean.

How many times were you there? How many times did you witness, in wonder, the sea of popping flashbulbs illuminating a darkened hall? The frenzied excitement that carried a tingle to your toes. That undeniable chill down your back. All this so much a part of an Elvis Presley concert since the mid-Fifties.

The swelling sound of "2001" let us know that waiting in the wings stood the man whose first name alone had won more recognition than any other full name in the world.

Then finally — that so familiar stride on stage, in that so familiar jump suit was truly an unforgettable moment. We laughed with him when he sang about that dog. We cried real tears when he left the stage in the summer of his last year, the words of "Can't Help Falling in Love" still ringing in our ears.

It's a sad irony, but true, that on the day Elvis died a steady rain began to fall on a parched Las Vegas. The same Las Vegas that Elvis had conquered so many years before. Near the end, friends and fans alike wanted with all our hearts to see him healthy and happy again, because he had brought us so much happiness.

Elvis once said, "I watch my audience. I listen, and I know we're all getting something out of our system. Nobody knows what it is. But the important thing is we're getting rid of it. And nobody's getting hurt."

THAT WAS ELVIS TO ME.

Between the sarcasm of sightings and untruthful but seemingly never ending revelations about his life on this earth, I conclude my letter of remembrances with these thoughts:

Those of you who still feel a great emptiness and void in your hearts, always remember his good gifts to you.

Elvis said shortly before he died, "I'm here to make people happy. That's my mission in life. I was chosen by God to do it. My happiest moments have always been on stage. I'll never stop until the day I die."

He kept his word.

In the aftermath of Elvis' death, and the subsequent publication of several cruel and inaccurate books, I felt the need to express my personal feelings about the man as I had known him. "That Was Elvis to Me" was my attempt to set the record straight relative to the good side of Elvis Presley. I first read this on my radio show in 1978, and still share it with my audiences, usually on the anniversaries of his birth and/or his death.

Elvis ended one of his final concerts with the words, "I hope I haven't bored you." I think it's safe to say Elvis Presley was a lot of things, but boring was *not* one of them.

"That Was Elvis to Me" and Wink's
interviews with Elvis are available on
Century Hill Recordings.

"Winking at Life" is also available
on audiocassettes.

To order either or both
click on
e-mail: wmartindale@earthlink.net
www.winkmartindale.com

Chapter Three

IT WAS ALL IN THE CARDS

A Career Hit

My graduation from Memphis State University in June, 1957, was a red letter day in my life for many reasons. First and foremost, after just two quarters at Lambuth College in the fall of '51, I had determined that I knew everything I needed to know in order to further my radio and television career. I had a job already, I was earning $50.00 a week, buying a car, and was totally "independent." My view was only "up." Why spend any more time studying geometry, English literature or biology? Fortunately, two people I was very close to, and whose opinions I valued greatly, interceded. Those two people were Madelyn's dad, Bill Leech, and WHBQ Station Manager John Cleghorn. In their own words and ways, they let me know that a young

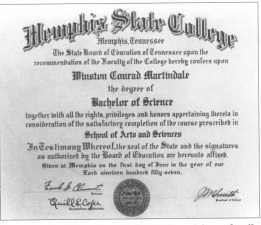

Wink worked in radio and TV while raising a family and attending Memphis State University, where he received his B.S. degree in 1957.

man of twenty, who seemed to already have the world by the tail, stood a far greater chance of conquering the world with a well rounded liberal arts education. Though my young mind still questioned their years of experience and good judgment, my heart was overjoyed with happiness and pride that warm day in June as I was handed my Bachelor of Science degree, with a major in Speech and Drama and a minor in Journalism.

All my family had driven over from Jackson to join in this most festive of accasions. I know my mother and dad were particularly proud, as were Bill and Erin Leech. But no one was prouder than Mr. Cleghorn. I remember looking out at the hundreds and hundreds of families gathered in the athletic fieldhouse, and zeroing in on the three smiling faces of a mother and her two daughters . . . Madelyn and two-year-old Lisa, and one-year-old Lyn! Perhaps they had given up more than I . . . to make this day a reality. After the ceremonies, we had arranged to have our immediate families and friends join us at Holiday Inn for dinner. Six years had elapsed between receiving my high school diploma and a college degree. But the wait was worth it. I have discovered over the years in ways that have sometimes been obvious . . . and at times less obvious, furthering my education was one of the smartest decisions I ever made. Countless times in the future, I would be asked the question of a young admirer with his eyes on a radio/TV career, "Mr. Martindale, what can I do to get started in your business?" Without the decision to go back to school, how could I have possibly answered in the way I always did, "Get as much education as you possibly can. You won't regret it!"

It almost seemed we were marking time between my graduation from college and our move to California. Naturally there were many good times and much fun for all of

The Martindale Christmas card, 1962. (Top to bottom) Wink, Jr., Laura Leigh, Madelyn Lizbeth, and Lisa Dawn.

(Left to right) Lyn and Lisa Martindale join their Dad in celebrating his graduation from Memphis State.

us during those final years in Memphis. But for me, I felt there was little more for me to accomplish in Memphis . . . that if I really wanted to test the waters elsewhere, the time was nearing for me to do so. That was my state of mind as I walked into Bill Grumble's office on a day in January, 1959. He would tell me later that he wasn't really shocked at my decision. He too felt I had much to offer elsewhere. I had been at WHBQ Radio and Television for seven years, almost an *eternity* of consistent employment in our business! With the transfer to KHJ Radio and Television in Los Angeles set to occur in March, Bill Grumbles set about to make a really big deal of my departure. With his brilliant promotional mind working overtime, he and Program Director Mark Forrester laid plans for a huge "going away" party at the Memphis Fairgrounds, to take place following my final Saturday *Dance Party*. It would be open to the kids from every school who had been featured on the show during my years as host.

WHBQ News Director Gene ("Five hundred words in five minutes") Roper acted as emcee for the night. And some night it was! The venue was packed to the rafters with humanity, but not a single incident was reported all evening. It's interesting to note the changes in teen behavior in the years since that decade. Very honestly, it was a time when drug use, as we know it today, was almost totally non-existent. The music of this night was the music of the day. Rock and roll had long since taken over. The sounds of Lloyd Price's "Stagger Lee" and The Coaster's "Charlie

Wink and Madelyn's Martindale "Four" began in Memphis with Lisa, then Lyn—California would produce Laura and Wink, Jr.

Brown" filled the dance floor, along with Richie Valen's love song for his "Donna," and "Smoke Gets in Your Eyes" by The Platters. In addition to the love expressed in those lyrics, I, too, felt a great deal of love in that room. It was as if these kids were saying "thanks" for being a small part of their life. I felt like a million dollars! It was one of those events during one's lifetime to cherish forever. And I shall!

Looking for a Home

When Madelyn and I bought our first home on Chickasaw Road, we immediately began looking for a Methodist church home. We found it at Mullins Methodist Church on Walnut Grove Road, a gorgeous new church with traditional architecture

Dot Records founder Randy Wood presents Pat Boone with one of his many gold records.

the likes of which we both had grown up with in Jackson. The Reverend Jimmy Elder was one of those rare men of God who delivered a sermon as though he was talking directly to you. He literally brought the *Bible* to life. Madelyn and I hit it off with Jimmy, his wife Billie, and their family from our very first Sunday at Mullins. We had dinner in their home, and they in ours. It grew into a warm and friendly relationship. As it happened, the Elders were regular viewers of *Dance Party*. They loved keeping abreast of the currently popular music and dance crazes. I could look for Jimmy Elder to drop by WHBQ at least once a week just to have coffee and chat. That's the kind of relationship we had.

"How would you like to have Randy Wood as a guest on your *Dance Party*?" That was the question Jimmy posed one morning in the Chisca Hotel coffee shop. I was floored. "I'd love to have Mr. Wood on the show!" I knew the name well. Little did I know how *well* I would get to know Mr. Wood. As a prelude to founding the independent Dot Record label in the early Fifties, and with it the careers of Pat Boone, The Hilltoppers, Billy Vaughn and many others, Randy Wood was in the wholesale/retail record business in his hometown, Gallatin, Tennessee. But long before the Blockbuster method of merchandising records, Randy devised his own creative and innovative method of selling records to the masses.

The Popularity of Black Artists

Randy's Record Shop would purchase blocks of air time each night on clear channel, 50,000 Watt WLAC in Nashville. By buying post-midnight hours, the time was purchased at a big discount. Then by buying records from the manufacturers in quantity, Randy could put premium packages together for a premium price. For example, Ten Top Hits of the Day for the

In 1958, on the movie set of *Let's Rock* in the Bronx, New York. Wink's role in this low-budget flick was small, but he was in his first movie.

price of EIGHT, and perhaps two "future hits" thrown in as a bonus. Every package had a special name and number to avoid confusion when

Randy Wood founded Dot Records in this small mail order record store in Gallatin, Tennessee.

ordering by mail. And "The Voice" of Randy's Record Shop was longtime WLAC announcer Gene Nobles. Gene had the pitches down pat. He could literally sell ice to the eskimos, he was that kind of salesman. And like Dewey Phillips later at WHBQ, Randy recognized early on the power and popularity of black artists. Rhythm and blues records made up probably 75% of all his package sales. By the very nature of the mail order business he was engaged in, Randy was among the first industry figures to notice that Caucasian teenagers were buying "race," or rhythm and blues music, ten or twenty to one over the long established white performers.

With its powerful signal, WLAC, during the early morning hours, reached practically every state in the union, every nook and cranny of the United States. As a youngster growing up and listening to the radio in the mid-Forties and early Fifties, I can attest to the popularity of Gene Nobles' *Randy's Record Shop* nightly on WLAC. Fact is, I ordered many of those record packages myself. As a result of Randy Wood's enormous success in the retail end of the business, his own record label just seemed the proper extension of his entrepreneurial abilities. He also had an uncanny ability to pick hit records even before they were exposed on the radio. This would prove an enormous asset in future years through the selection of songs for his artists to record, and the commercial sound to be recorded. The magic began for real in 1952, bigtime!

A Stream of Hits

The first Dot release was a hit! Not a smash, but a big enough hit to get the fledgling label off and running. The Hilltoppers were four undergraduates at Western Kentucky University. The athletic teams used the name "Hilltoppers" for the hilly Kentucky countryside on which the college campus was located. The group had auditioned for Randy using a song written by one of the singers, Billy Vaughn (who later became the multimillionaire instrumental artist/music director for Dot). "Trying" was the song's title, recorded with no more than a piano as background. With Jimmy Sacca singing lead, the group turned out hit after hit, titles that ran the gamut, from an original song, "I'd Rather Die Young (Than Grow Old Without You)," to a re-make of Gershwin's "Love Walked In." With Randy Wood picking the songs and producing the record sessions, The Hilltoppers could do no wrong.

A stream of hits began to flow from this "little engine that could" known as Dot Records in Gallatin, Tennessee. "The Crazy Otto Rag," by ragtime pianist Johnny Maddox, Pat Boone's first hit, a pop cover of Fat's Domino's "Ain't That A Shame," followed in fast succession by "Don't Forbid Me," "Friendly Persuasion," "April Love," and the multi-million selling standard, "Love Letters in the Sand." Pat was a prime example of Randy Wood's innate ability to place the right voice with just the right song. In 1955 Randy selected a piece of music for Billy Vaughn to record, a piece that had been originally copywritten in 1903. "Melody of Love" was one of that year's biggest hits. (I would not be the first disc jockey on Dot to sell a million records with "Deck of Cards," 1959). New York deejay Jim Lowe brought Randy a nov-

in COLOR

Hear
Jackson's
WINK
MARTINDALE
Sing The Hit Tune
"LOOK AT ME"
In The Lively Set

JOANIE
SOMMERS
sings
BOBBY
DARIN'S
LATEST
HIT
TUNES

WINK

Wink had Bobby Darin to thank for his singing role in *The Lively Set.*

elty song he'd written in 1956 titled "The Green Door." Nobody ever did figure out what was behind that green door, but well over a million members of the record buying public laid down a dollar to *try* to figure it out. And so it went. Hit after hit. Year after year. The little label that had been spawned from Randy's Record Shop in Gallatin, Tennessee, was now the most powerful independent in the business, rivaling long time powerhouses RCA, Columbia, Decca, and Capitol.

Randy's company had outgrown its little origination point by the late fifties. In order to continue to compete with the big boys, he felt compelled to move to the West coast. And even more success came with him. So much, that when Paramount made Randy "an offer he couldn't refuse," Dot became a Paramount subsidiary with Randy retained as President to continue running the company as he had in the past.

The Silver Screen

Reverend Jimmy Elder, our pastor at Mullins Methodist Church, had been Randy and Lois Wood's pastor in Gallatin. They were very close friends. Needless to say, though I knew Randy by reputation and had played most of his Dot Records through the years, I didn't know him personally. When Jimmy asked, "How would you like to have Randy Wood as a guest on *Dance Party?*" I fell all over myself accepting! Randy and Lois were to be in Memphis visiting the Elders the following weekend, and after the Saturday show Madelyn and I were invited to dinner at the parsonage. I was excited for a couple of reasons. First and foremost, I admired and revered the man as a person of high morals and ideals. To me he personified the American dream.

Secondly, I looked forward to interviewing him about the incredible story that was Dot Records. As with the Elvis interview a couple of years before, I really did my homework, carefully preparing each question to be asked, playing little edited snippets of past Dot hits, and getting him to comment on each: "Tell me how you first met Pat Boone." What makes a hit record? The song, the singer, or a combination of each?" My questions literally cascaded from my lips. I was truly in awe of this man and his accomplishments. AND, since the release of my record, "Thought It Was Moonlove" happened to coincide with Randy's visit that day, perhaps it wouldn't be a bad move to sing it on the show. I thought, *maybe, just maybe . . .* Well, I did sing it that day, and at dinner that evening, sure enough he asked, "How would you like to be on Dot?"

Trying to be so cool so as to not totally embarrass myself, I told Mr. Wood that I really didn't consider myself a singer. I related to him the story of "Red" Matthews asking me to make a record for his local O. J. label. It turned out that Randy knew "Red," and said he would arrange to buy my contract from O. J. And as far as singing was concerned, he felt I had a pleasant enough voice. But what would I think of spending a little time in New York working with Carlo Menotti, Pat Boone's voice coach?

Type Casting

Needless to say I was almost speechless. But in time, all of that happened just as Randy suggested. In fact, the sequence of events was interesting. During 1958 I received a call from a producer in New York asking me to appear in a low-budget feature film titled *Let's Rock*, starring Julius LaRosa and Phyliss Newman, and featuring several record acts such as Paul Anka, Roy Hamilton and Danny and the Juniors. It was to be shot in the old Gold Medal Studios in the Bronx. I was to play, what else? Host of a teenage *Dance Party*! Type casting or what? But again, it was a hot thing to be asked to be in a movie, regardless of the budget. (I think my fee was a thousand dollars plus first-class air transportation, hotel and per diem.) Plus it would be only my second trip to New York. (Madelyn and I had been given a trip to the big city by her Mom and Dad upon my graduation from Memphis

State the preceding year.)

The Memphis papers played up the fact that I was to be in a movie! Plus I was to sing a song as well. "All Love Broke Loose" was recorded while I was in New York, and I sang it in the movie as the kids danced around me on my "show." It was a mediocre song at best, and a lousy Elvis imitation at its worst! In any event, it subsequently was released (or escaped) on Dot Records. I can't even be sure my *family* bought it—not to mention my friends and fans of *Dance Party*.

Forgettable Moments

To this day I don't know what was most embarrassing. My bad imitation of Elvis Presley, or the premiere of *Let's Rock* at the Malco Theatre in Memphis. When the movie finally came out, someone, somewhere, concocted the idea that this premiere should be handled as a really big deal. You know. Local deejay goes to New York to "star" in a movie! I think WHBQ-TV was behind the promotion for obvious reasons. But I was "there" during the filming. I knew how bad this picture was. Yet I did nothing to contain the publicity and promotion surrounding it. I had only myself to blame when on the night of the initial showing, my friends, family and co-workers walked out of the screening not knowing what to say to me. What had they expected? *Casablanca*? *Gone With The Wind*?

It was not a great moment to relish. I have since done many cameos for movies as well as television, but none equal (let me rephrase that); none as LOUSY as *Let's Rock*. To add insult to injury, even now I will see that movie listed in TV Guide from time to time. Hopefully always at three or four in the morning. And how did "All Love Broke Loose" rate among the three records I had made up to then? To

45 RPM single records during the fifties and sixties were most often packaged in a "sleeve" featuring a picture of the artist. This is the original sleeve for Wink's "Deck of Cards," showing a *song* on the flip side, "Now You Know How It Feels."

be honest, lower than "The Bug-A-Bop"! And that is a generous assessment.

Bobby Darin

Let's Rock suffered a miserable but quick death at the box office. I did enjoy a photo my friend Bob Neal sent me from Hollywood, showing the picture's title on the marquee of a theatre on Hollywood Boulevard. Sadly the picture failed to show any patrons *lined up* to get in! The only other motion picture worthy of mentioning in which I had a role came my way in 1963, thanks to singer Bobby Darin. *The Lively Set*, starring Pamela Tiffin, James

Ed Sullivan, taken from the 1959 kinescope, introducing Wink on *The Toast of the Town*, a title later changed to *The Ed Sullivan Show*.

Darren, Doug McClure and Bobby, was another of those low-budget, innocuous scripts designed to take advantage of some of the day's hot young names.

Bobby, then with Capitol Records, was also assigned the job of writing the songs and scoring the music for the picture. There was a part which called for a nightclub emcee to make a brief appearance on stage and sing a ballad titled "Look At Me," while Pamela and Doug chatted over a drink. Playing the part of the emcee was a piece of cake. But having to record the song on a soundstage at Universal Studios was some kind of challenge.

As you are aware, songs in movies are pre-recorded, then the actor/ singer will lip-sync the song during shooting as if singing it live. I was never at ease standing before a mike to sing. Talk yes. Sing no! Circumstances kept placing me in the uncomfortable position of attempting to do something that was foreign to me, outside my shower. To be honest, I'm sure the reason I got this quickie role was because I was the morning man on LA's most popular Top 40 station, plus I was host of the daily *Wink Martindale Dance Party*. I had only met Bobby Darin briefly in a visit to the Atlantic Records offices during Madelyn's and my college graduation trip in 1958. (Incidentally, that was the day that

Atlantic Records executives Ahmet Ertegun, Jerry Wexler, and Bobby, asked my opinion of Bobby's first soon-to-be-released Atlantic record. I can honestly say it didn't take a rocket scientist to determine that "Splish Splash" would be a smash as it came through the speakers.)

Outside My Shower

That instance, and one other occasion when Madelyn and I had been invited to spend a delightful Sunday afternoon at Bobby's and his then wife, actress Sandra Dee's house,

Wink as he nervously recites the narration, "Deck of Cards," before a national television audience on *Toast of the Town*, the number one variety show on TV, and consistently in 1959's Top Ten.

were the only times I ever had the occasion to be around him for any period of time. But for whatever reason, he personally called me one day to meet him at the Capitol Tower to talk about the picture he was co-starring in and writing the music for *The Lively Set*. There was this one part that I would be "perfect" for, complete with a song to sing! Here we go again! But I could hardly say no. After all, I was in Tinseltown, U.S.A. and I still had vague visions of somehow using my radio and television work as a springboard to movies.

The day I had to show up at Universal Pictures to record "Look At Me," I was mortified. Though I had worked endless hours with a piano track Bobby had given me to learn the song (I did not read music), the vision of walking onto that soundstage and seeing all those musicians was almost more than my heart would take. I remember so well feeling weak, as if I was going to faint. Many of these musicians were the same as those accustomed to recording soundtracks on this same stage with the likes of Henry Mancini. What would they think when they heard a playback of my voice singing with *their* music? We did take after endless take trying to get it right. I was sweating profusely and becoming more uncomfortable by the minute. Finally someone mercilessly uttered those magic words from the control room, "I think

KFWB *Fabulous Forty Survey*

• 98 •   FOR THE WEEK ENDING OCTOBER 21, 1959   **• 98 •**

		LAST WEEK
1. MACK THE KNIFE	BOBBY DARIN—ATCO	1
2. MISTER BLUE	The Fleetwoods—Dolton	2
3. DON'T YOU KNOW	Della Reese—RCA Victor	4
4. YOU WERE MINE	The Fireflys—Ribbon	6
5. PUT YOUR HEAD ON MY SHOULDER	Paul Anka—ABC/Para	3
6. PRIMROSE LANE	Jerry Wallace—Challenge	7
7. DECK OF CARDS	Wink Martindale—Dot	8

Los Angeles' number one radio station, KFWB, showing one of their competing deejays, Wink Martindale, with the number 7 hit during the week of October 31, 1959 — the same week the nation's number 1 hit was Bobby Darin's "Mack The Knife."

we've got it!" He never asked, "Got what?" But I know I *got* out of there as quickly as my feet would take me. Randy Wood at Dot Records, who had granted me permission to record this song for the sountrack album, never released a single of the song on his label. That spoke volumes to me of his opinion of this effort. In retrospect, neither the picture nor the soundtrack broke any records. Nor did the picture further enhance the careers of any of its stars. It just sort of disappeared into the atmosphere.

A career hit

"Can you hold for a moment, Mr. Martindale? Mr. Wood would like to speak to you." With those words, Fran Kirk (Randy Wood's executive assistant) connected me with the president and founder of Dot Records. "Wink, as you know I've been looking for just the right song for you to record . . . and now I think I have something that might just give you a million seller! When can you come by the office? I want you to hear this." I blurted out as fast as my Tennessee tongue would allow me to

Former Dot Records Vice President of Sales Chris Hamilton called Wink one morning in 1959 to tell him "Deck of Cards" was a smash in Boston!

say, "Right now!" As a deejay at KHJ Radio in Hollywood, just a block away from the Dot offices, I knew I could be there in five minutes. And judging from the excitement in his voice and the six months I had been anticipating this call, I wanted no grass to grow under my feet!

I felt I had wings on my shoes as I walked the short distance to the famous corner of Sunset and Vine where Dot Records offices were located. My mind took me back to the day in January earlier in the year (1959) when I had interviewed Randy on my teen *Top Ten Dance Party* in Memphis, and during dinner he asked me if I would like to record for Dot, unquestionably the most successful and prestigious independent record label in the business. The same

Wink received a gold copy of this record in 1960 from Dot Records president Randy Wood, denoting sales in excess of a million copies.

label that just a few short years ago had launched the career of Pat Boone! I said, "Mr. Wood, I hardly know what to say . . . except . . . of course! I am honored that you even asked me"! That was six months ago. In those six months, my request for a transfer from RKO's Memphis station to their Los Angeles station had been approved, and now I was hosting a morning radio show as well as a Saturday evening *Dance Party* on television.

As Fran showed me into the fanciest office I'd ever seen, the plush carpeting seemed to swallow up my loafers. The walls were decked with gold records, and I couldn't help but dream that I might be included among those names some day. Randy proceded to tell me about a narrative country recording by T. Texas Tyler he remembered selling by the thousands around 1948 when he owned Randy's Record Shop, a mail-order record business in his hometown of Gallatin, Tennessee. He felt if we made a pop version of the same narrative with a choral background, chances are "Deck of Cards" could be the hit we were looking for!

My Heart Sank

He placed an old, scratchy 78RPM record on his hi-fi turntable and it began to play. "During the North African campaign a bunch of soldier boys had been on a long hike. . . ." As the droll, country voice of a hillbilly singer I'd never heard of continued his story, my heart sank! I tried to keep a straight face, but it wasn't easy. The hot records then were "Kansas City" by Wilbert Harrison; Elvis' "A Fool Such As I," and "The Battle of New Orleans" by Johnny Horton. How would a religious "talking record," by somebody most of the country had never heard of, be received? But this was the same Randy Wood that had successfully selected hit song after hit song for Pat Boone and the rest of the Dot roster of talent. His record of picking hits, and hit material, was a matter of record.

As he took the needle off the record, Randy asked, "Whatta you think? Isn't that

THE DECK OF CARDS
By T. TEXAS TYLER

Recorded by WINK MARTINDALE on Dot Records

Sheet music sales were once depended on to generate almost as much income for a song's publisher as a hit record. Because of the narrative nature of Wink's "Deck of Cards," sheet music sales were unusually high.

great?" What was I to say? In a Tennessee second I replied, "Randy . . . *I LOVE IT!*" He picked up the phone, asked arrangers Billy Vaughn and Milt Rogers to come to his office. After a couple of weeks of rehearsals, we recorded the memorable narrative that has literally followed me my entire career.

"Toast of the Town"

"Now here is a handsome young man from Memphis, Tennessee who has one of the big record hits of the day. I'm sure you've heard it on radio. It's called 'A Deck of Cards.' So let's have a big welcome for . . . Wink Martindale!"

As each word of that typically halting introduction formed on the lips of Ed Sullivan that Fall evening in September of 1959, my mind flashed back to all those Sunday nights I, too, had sat watching, as this icon of entertainment had similarly introduced in his own inimitable and often grammatically incorrect manner, other acts, ranging from circus clowns to the entire Russian ballet; from a stage full of jugglers to a single current Broadway star; from Senor Wences to Elvis Presley; to the Beatles screaming televised introduction to America; *and now me!*

As I stood there counting the moments until the camera's little red light cued my opening line, I truly felt that I was going through an out-of-body experience. Was this a miracle? Was this really happening to me? Am I about to recite some narrative lines to music before millions and millions of TV viewers all over the country? Me? Little "Winkie" Martindale from Jackson, Tennessee who used to dream of being a radio announcer from the time he was knee high to a duck!

Before being placed by the stage manager in my designated position on stage, in front of a series of hanging oversized playing cards, I had said a quiet prayer backstage asking God to please help me through this most demanding, though opportune, moment that I had experienced in my young career. I could almost hear my teeth chattering in rhythm to the knocking of my knees as I stood looking out at the packed audience in this relatively small theatre within a stone's throw of Times Square. The same theatre that would see its marquee change in later years from THE ED SULLIVAN THEATRE to the DAVID LETTERMAN THEATRE.

But tonight, this storied stage was mine, all mine. At least for about three and a half minutes. Thanks to a lucky series of events that almost seemed providential, here I was on *The Toast Of The Town*, as *The Sullivan Show* was called prior to taking his name exclusively the following year. Naturally word of my exciting opportunity had spread far and wide among my friends, family and fans. The unspoken realization that the odds of a non-singer enjoying the fruits of a Top Ten hit record were a million to one.

But the odds of that non-singer performing that narration on CBS Television's number one variety show were more like hitting the lottery. A "talking" record? Years before rap? At a time when the year's biggest hits were Bobby Darin's "Mack the Knife" and Lloyd Price's "Stagger Lee"! Yet that was the case. And here I was. About to tell the tale of a soldier who on a Sunday morning during the World War II battle for Casino, Italy, took a deck of cards to worship service to use in place of a *Bible* — and for doing so was arrested by the Provost Marshall.

Just Another Wild Card

Obviously this wartime story with religious overtones had caught the public's fancy at just the right time, for whatever reason. Years earlier, the story had enjoyed a modicum of success. Recordings by its author, country singer turned minister, T. Texas Tyler, actor Phil Harris and cowboy star Tex Ritter, each had sold a number of records. But no version had enjoyed the popularity with the record buying public to the extent mine did. It had been recorded on a hot July afternoon during the summer of '59. But not until a Boston deejay played the record one day, was there any reaction to it whatsoever. I remember thinking that my "Deck of Cards" was going to be just another wild card among the hundreds and hundreds of records received each week by radio stations.

But then came the phone call from Christine Hamilton, Dot Records vice-president of sales. A call as vivid in my memory as if it were yesterday. I had just ended my daily morning radio show on KHJ in Hollywood. It was nine o'clock. I picked up the phone and Chris said, "Are you sitting down?" I said, "I

wasn't, but I am now — why?" She practically screamed into the phone, "We just got an order out of Boston for 10,000 copies of 'Deck of Cards!'" My reaction to that initial order was one that Chris and I had so many laughs about during the following months. I asked, "Is that good"? **"IS THAT GOOD,"** she yelled! "If we got a first-time or-der for 10,000 on every

Ed Sullivan welcomes the transplanted Tennes-seean to his show thanks to "Deck of Cards."

record we produced and shipped to our distributors we'd put out 10,000 records a month!"

Gold Record!

From that first listener reaction in Boston just weeks after the record's release, radio stations couldn't seem to play the record enough. Station managers, program directors, record librarians, and deejays themselves reported listener response the likes of which they hadn't experienced in years. With every airing the station switchboards would light up like a veritable Christmas tree. My morning sales calls from Chris Hamilton at Dot became as regular as a clock! Another 25,000 order from Boston . . . 50,000 from New York . . . Dallas, 20,000 . . . Los Angeles, 35,000! It was like a dream. But one from which I didn't have to awaken!

Before the rollercoaster ride was over my introduction to the world of *Billboard* and *Cashbox* Magazines found "Deck of Cards" peaking at number four on their sales charts, reflecting final sales of well over a million copies. The recording enjoyed not only domestic popularity but became a giant hit in many other parts of the English speaking world, most notably the United Kingdom where it has hit the charts twice since its first introduction in 1959. Randy Wood presented me with a framed gold copy of my record denoting sales of over a million. It still hangs proudly high above any and all memorabilia collected during my career.

The rehearsal for my "Andy Warhol moment of fame" on national television had certainly not been a thing of beauty. Mickey Addy, Vice-President of Dot Records East Coast operations and a close personal friend of Ed Sullivan, had been assured a week before the Sunday show that cue cards would be available to me. For in addition to having a lousy ability to memorize, my greatest nightmare was that I would forget the words to this lengthy narrative smack dab in the middle of my performance.

Sure enough, when Mickey and I arrived at the theatre for rehearsals with the Ray Bloch Orchestra, no cue cards! Suddenly to add to my obvious nervousness I was forced to endure the embarrassment of the entire theatre rehearsal audience, crew, musicians, EVERYBODY, aware that the kid with the hit record didn't even know the *words*! To make matters worse, since rehearsal time is carefully planned for each act on the show, the question suddenly arose as to whether my cue cards could be written in time for me to rehearse with the orchestra. If not then I would have to be bumped from this week's show, with the possibility that I might not be rebooked due to prior scheduling. Chester A. Riley's oft used expression from "The Life of Riley" began to ring in my ears: "What a revoltin' development this is!"

Fortunately, thanks to Mickey's close association with Ed Sullivan, and more importantly with Ed's son-in-law and the show's producer Marlo Lewis, somehow the cue cards were written. I made it through both the dress rehearsal and live show without a hitch, and, if I may say so, the audience seemed to love "Deck of Cards" whether they had heard it prior to that night or not. In fact, as a direct result of the Sullivan appearance, sales of the record more than tripled the following week. It should be noted that in the Fifties and Sixties, prior to MTV, VH-1, The Nashville Network and all the other cable outlets showing music videos, the primary means of exposing a recording artist and his or her single or album was through appearances on the major network variety shows, of which there were several. But leading the pack was always *The Ed Sullivan Show*.

Deck of Cards

During the North African campaign a group of soldier boys had been on a long hike. They arrived in a little town called Casino. The next morning being Sunday, several of the boys went to church. A sergeant commanded the boys in church and after the chaplin had read the prayer, the text was taken up next. Those of the boys who had a Prayer book took them out, but this one boy had only a deck of cards — and so he spread them out.

The sergeant saw the cards and said, "Soldier, put away those cards!" After the service was over the soldier was taken prisoner and brought before the provost marshal. The marshal said, "Sergeant, why have you brought this man here?" "For playing cards in church, Sir."

"And what have you to say for yourself son?" "Much, Sir," replied the soldier. The marshal said, "I hope so. For if not, I shall punish you more than any man was ever punished." The soldier said, "Sir, I have been on the march for six days, and I had neither Bible nor Prayer book; but I hope to satisfy you sir with the purity of my intentions." And with that, the boy started his story.

"You see sir, when I look at the Ace, it reminds me there is but one God, and the deuce reminds me the Bible is divided into two parts, the Old and the New Testaments. When I see the trey, I think of the Father, the Son and the Holy Ghost. and when I see the four, I think of the four evangelists who preached the Gospel. There were Matthew, Mark, Luke, and John. And when I see the five, it reminds me of the five wise virgins who trimmed their lamps. There were ten of them. Five were wise and were saved; five were foolish, and were shut out. When I see the six, it reminds me that in six days God made this great Heaven and Earth. When I see the seven, it reminds me that on the seventh day God rested from his great work. And when I see the eight, I think of the eight righteous persons God saved when he destroyed this Earth. There was Noah, his wife, their three sons, and their wives. And when I see the nine, I think of the lepers our Savior cleansed and nine of the ten didn't even thank him. When I see the ten, I think of the Ten Commandments God handed down to Moses on a table of stone. And when I see the King, it reminds me there is but one King of

Heaven, God Almighty. When I see the Queen, I think of the blessed Virgin Mary, who is Queen of Heaven. And the Jack, or knave, is the devil. When I count the number of spots on a deck of cards, I find three hundred sixty-five, the number of days in a year. There are fifty-two cards, the number of weeks in a year. There are four suits, the number of weeks in a month. There are twelve picture cards, the number of months in a year. There are thirteen tricks, the number of weeks in a quarter.

So you see sir, my pack of cards serves me as a Bible, an almanac, and a Prayer book."

And friends, this story is true. I know, for I was that soldier.

Deck of Cards - T. Texas Tyler
© 1964 - Fort Knox Music Inc., Trio Music Company, Inc. and Songs of Polygram International, Inc.
Copyright renewed
Used by permission   All rights reserved.

To underline the importance and prestige of a spot on the Sullivan show, everywhere I went in New York the next day I was constantly confronted by viewers who had seen my performance. Naturally since I was in New York City, the number one market for record sales at that time, it was only natural that I be taken around to the various radio stations that had been playing my record to meet the jocks and to personally thank them. I recall standing in the record library of WINS Radio, at the time the Number One rated music station in New York. Suddenly in walks Tony Bennett, an idol of mine since I first played his "Because of You" as a teenage announcer (even before we were called deejays) on Radio Station WDXI in Jackson. Therefore, you might imagine my amazement as he walked up to me, said he recognized me from last night's Sullivan show, and proceeded to tell me how much he loved my record! Not only was I floored. I could hardly utter the words, "Thank you Mr. Bennett. I am such a fan of yours I hardly know what to say. Thank you very much."

I could tell he sensed my humble embarrassment, and I never forgot his words of kindness to me each and every time I played his countless hits in later years. In fact, years later when we were both attending a charitable event for Danny Thomas' St. Jude Children's Research Hospital he still recalled, as I certainly did, that morning at WINS Radio and his words of praise and encouragement.

Never Again Duplicated

It's still a constant source of amazement to me that to this day I have people ask me if I'm the same Wink Martindale who made that record, "Deck of Cards." Little did I know that day in July in 1959 when I walked into United Studios on Sunset Boulevard in Hollywood, that I would be creating a small piece of pop music history, one that will still be played and talked about long after I'm gone. As they say, it was in the cards.

Even though I was fortunate enough in future years to appear on network television many, many times as host of my own game shows, the thrill of appearing on the one and only *Ed Sullivan Show* would never be duplicated. Remember the feeling of that first kiss? Or when you bought your first car? Your first house? Feelings, experiences never to be captured again. Fortunately those moments with Mr. Sullivan *were* captured on kinescope (or film) and I was given a copy for my library, which I cherish dearly. Not simply to have a piece of memorabilia to gather dust on a shelf. But you see, when I finished my number that night long ago, I believe Ed took note of the audience applause and motioned for me to come over to where he was standing stage left, a gesture not accorded every guest on his show.

Because I was relieved that I had completed my narration and partly because I was thrilled he was calling me over, I made my way across the stage smiling from ear to ear, the smile that would later become my game show hosting trademark. Ed asked, "Are you married? I'm sure there are many young ladies out there who would like to know." Delighted at the thought anyone would care for such vital statistics, I answered "Yes sir, I'm married and the father of three lovely daughters." He said, "Well I know they are all very proud of you tonight."

As he once again called my name and mentioned Memphis, I walked into the wings as if I had wings on my feet. A night never again duplicated in my show business career.

From Wink's Photo Album

From Wink's Photo Album

Wink's Gold Record from Dot Records in 1960, denoting sales in excess of a million copies.

Do you recognize Andre Agassi with all that hair?

Naomi Suarez has been Wink and Sandy's housekeeper for fifteen of their twenty-five years of marriage.

Sandy joined Wink in celebrating his 45th high school reunion in 1997. Can you spot those two?

Jim Hook and Brian McManus took care of Wink's wardrobe and makeup for most of his game shows.

Paula Haynes listens as Wink recites "To a Sleeping Beauty" during his *Cerebral Palsy Telethon* in Jackson, Tennessee.

Wink and longtime friend Bill Smith hosted the *Wink and Bill Show* on Talkradio KABC.

Wink hosts a 1999 music video for the popular rock group Everclear.

Wink and Sandy with her dad Tony, and veteran Dodger Manager Tommy Lasorda.

All three of these gentlemen were hosting Merv Griffin produced shows simultaneously in 1985; Wink (*Headline Chasers*) Martindale, Alex (*Jeopardy*) Trebek, and Pat (*Wheel of Fortune*) Sajak.

Wink pictured here with game show legend Bill Cullen.

The grandkids (almost) grown! Circa Christmas 1999. (Back row, L to R) Erin Cuff, Matthew Klodt, Blake Lucas, and Hannah Klodt. (Front, L to R) Emilee Lucas, Tara Cuff, and Stephen Lucas.

Wink and Sandy's favorite home away from home—complete with typical Maui sunsets like this, snapped from their balcony.

Bobby Hatfield and Bill Medley, The Righteous Brothers, got their start at Sandy's Dad's Hollywood night club.

Promotional picture for Wink's first NBC
show *What's This Song?* (and he can't
play a note!)

The Martindale's Christmas card for 1995 featured "Rocky Elvis" (far right) singing "Jingle Bells"!

One of Wink and Sandy's Christmas cards, starring Santa and their Chihuahuas.

Sandy's first bubble bath in her Malibu digs called for a special toast.

Wink and Sandy's Serra Retreat at Malibu was just that—a treat!

Wink and Sandy
pose prior to
attending a charity
dance in Memphis.

Daddy Wink
surrounded by
pretty ladies at
Laura's wedding—
Emilee and Lisa
Lucas, Sandy
and Lyn Klodt.

Wink and Sandy with her mom Mary Lou and dad Tony Ferra.

Sandy's bridesmaids were Wink's daughters Laura, Lyn and Lisa. Her sister Christie was her Maid of Honor.

Wink's grooms-
men—Bill Smith,
Tom Kratochvil, Ed
Lojeski and Best
Man Wink, Jr.

The Martindales
celebrating their
10th Anniversary by
renewing their vows at
their Malibu home.

Sandy and Wink celebrate with newlyweds Wayne and Kathleen Newton in Las Vegas.

The day Lisa Martindale became Lisa Lucas.

The "Mad Martindales" pose during a Jackson, Tennessee reunion, summer of '97 (and not all were there for the picture).

The gang meets at Lawry's for prime rib, for Daddy Wink's birthday dinner in 1997.

Daughter Laura and Kevin Cuff's future surfing champs Tara and Erin.

From Wink's Photo Album

Lisa and Jim Lucas'
daughter Emilee,
Wink's first grand-
child to graduate
from high school
(1999)

Wink's daughter Lyn
and granddaughter
Hannah Klodt

Son-in-law Ed, Lyn,
Hannah and
Matthew Klodt.

The "young" Lucas grand-
children—Stephen, Blake
and Emilee.

Handsome Leonardo Gilmore,
son of Sandy's sister Christy
and husband Gene.

Wink visits *Live with Regis and Kathie Lee* to promote his show *Debt*.

Wink's "Big Numbers Game," the popular *High Rollers*.

The long-running game show most associated with Wink.

HOORAY FOR HOLLYWOOD
The Career Continues . . .

I had witnessed the lights and skylines of Chicago and New York as my plane had descended on those cities on past occasions. But even these two giants among cities could not prepare me for that crystal clear night in March 1959, when I laid my eyes on the miles and miles of lights making up the megalopolis we call Los Angeles, California. As our American Airlines jet grew closer to touchdown at Los Angeles International Airport, I turned to Mark Forrester, who had accompanied me on my first flight from Memphis to LA, and wondered aloud, "Do you think I've made a mistake?" I was sort of King Of The Hill in Memphis. Making a good living for my family and me. Nice house. Two-car garage! And here I was entering this unknown world, at my own request. Would I live to rue the day I uprooted my family in the name of fame and more success?

"Don't worry! Everything's going to be fine," were Mark's consoling words. He said, "People are people wherever you go. Only the faces change. All you have to do is be yourself, just as you were in Memphis." Whether he really believed that, or was simply trying to make me feel good, I never knew. But it was music to my ears! I was the transplanted country boy. No doubt. Truly frightened. Excited! But frightened.

During the cab ride from the airport to the Beverly Wilshire Hotel in Beverly Hills, I can still remember staring at palm tree after palm tree lining the streets. Though I had first been exposed to real palm trees in Florida when Madelyn and I had honeymooned in Ft. Lauderdale years before, it didn't seem the same. This was CALIFORNIA! Sunshine! Orange, lemon and grapefruit trees in front yards! Hollywood! Movies! And yes, palm trees! As Mark and I checked in at this famous Four Star Hotel, I wanted to pinch myself to see if this was really happening. As I turned the key and opened the door to my room, there was no longer any question. After hurriedly unpacking, I called Mark and asked if we might go downstairs and take a Beverly Hills walk. It was around nine o'clock, still early in LA. But a bedtime eleven P.M. back home! After phoning home to assure Madelyn and the girls we'd arrived okay, I met Mark in the lobby. We ended up at Marshall Edson's "Ye Little Club," a popular small jazz club in Beverly Hills. It was here that I was introduced to a song that would become a favorite of mine from that night forward. Featured singer Marilyn Lovell sang "I Wish You Love," and I recall thinking it was one of the prettiest songs I'd ever heard. I later learned it had been introduced on Capitol by Keely Smith. Guess I had been too busy playing "Stagger Lee"!

As we headed back to the Beverly Wilshire (now The Beverly Regent Hotel), I mentioned to Mark that I would never forget tonight's feeling of flying into Los Angeles and viewing those miles and miles and millions and millions of lights. And I never have, after dozens and dozens of night flights.

At Home in La La Land

Happily, within months, my fright of the big city and resulting homesickness gave way to self assurance and a feeling of belonging. As the saying goes, "I never looked back." My first two weeks in Los Angeles I was lodged at the Beverly Wilshire, thanks to my new bosses. Not a shabby beginning! But the permanent arrangement would place the four-and-a-half

Daughter number three, Laura Leigh, was born in 1959, the year Dad went west. Here is Laura with hubby Kevin on their wedding day.

Martindales in a small, rented Spanish home in San Marino. (Did I say four-and-a-half Martindales?) Indeed! Madelyn was pregnant with our *third* daughter as we headed Westward. Laura Leigh would be born at Huntington Memorial Hospital in Pasadena, July 29, 1959. I felt like the second coming of Pat Boone! All girls, no boys. Wasn't this carrying the Dot Records story just a bit too far? Incidentally, my first week in LA, I received a call from Randy Wood inviting me to join him and his family for church on Sunday. I was delighted, as it made me a lot less homesick to be with some fellow Tennesseeans. Plus, I had much for which I could give thanks! The Woods came by

Wink's new radio home in Hollywood; KHJ Radio and Television—1959.

the Beverly Wilshire, picked me up, and we attended services at the First Methodist Church of Hollywood. Then they were kind enough to invite me to have lunch with them. It was a perfect ending to my first week in what's jokingly known as "La La Land."

Two weeks after I had arrived, I was officially "On-The-Air"! As in Memphis, I was the morning man. But unlike WHBQ in Memphis, I did a *split* shift. That is, I did the 6-9AM show, took a two-hour break, then hosted the 11-2PM show. Unusual to say the least. But KHJ was not your run-of-the-mill radio station. For years it had been the West Coast anchor for the Mutual-Don Lee Network in radio's drama-filled halcyon days. Then along came a new medium called television, and network radio became the perverbial white elephant. The owners, RKO General, were faced with streamlining, not only KHJ, but their entire chain of broadcast stations. And who did they select to lead this monumental task? None other than my long time mentor, Bill Grumbles, and his very able assistant Mark Forrester. They both had steered WHBQ into ratings success and profitability back in Memphis with a solid Top Forty music format. So why not duplicate that success with the rest of the stations? This turn of events was a great plus for me, for it gave me the chance to learn the ropes in the second largest radio market in the country without as much pressure as I ordinarily would have been under.

However time would soon prove that to knock the Los Angeles radio market on its ear would be a formidable task. Already the city's number one station since 1958, KFWB was a ratings powerhouse! At times it quadrupled the audience of its nearest competitor. And to make the competitive factor even tougher for KHJ, management didn't condone playing certain hits because they were too "rock," or they were an "embarrassment" to the image of the station. Thus we became known as the "chicken rock" radio station. The format, as conceived by Bill and Mark, was doomed to failure from the start.

It never had a chance to succeed, to get off the ground. I was the only deejay on the staff who had any Top Forty experience. The other guys, Larry Carroll, Henry Travis, Paul Compton, George Crowell and Larry

THE REVIEWS ARE IN

AND THEY'RE TERRIFIC!

WINK MARTINDALE'S
DANCING PARTY
(Sat., 6:30-7:30 p.m., KHJ-TV)
Years ago Zeke Manners staged dancing parties in the cramped quarters of what passed for a studio. Al Jarvis came along later with a ditto of the leather pushing adolescents. But it really never caught on big until Dick Clark gave it the big personality push. Comes now a chap from Memphis named Wink Martindale, who is well equipped to duplicate his success, at least, on the local level.

Such a format as this must rise or fall on the man who is the ringmaster. In Martindale it is halfway home. He's a bright, refreshing youngster who doesn't try to be a comic and keeps his place when the others are on view. There's nothing new in dance parties, per se, but "Wink" has laced in a few features to give it pace and variety Faves of the record spinners in the juvenile stakes are trotted out to lip-sync their biggest sellers and a game is played to immobilize the dancing feet. A variation of musical chairs, with a cowbell as the device, had three losers make a pizza pie. It was the show's fun spot.

Read this "rave" from Variety!

Among the recording artists were Eddie and Betty Cole, Jan and Dean and Dave "Baby" Cortez, the latter a swinging hipster on the electric organ, who may have nnger-synced. His beat was hotter than the others and he came off with the neftiest applause. The big money for the hoofers came when Martindale resurrected a filmed interview he did with Elvis Presley long enough ago to ask the question, "I see you're going to make a picture." What cared the shufflers from San Berdu when it was done. Here was their idol to swoon and sigh to.

That not all rock 'n' rollers are in the delinquent class was amply evidenced by three of the dancers, who told of their efforts to help the underprivileged with fund drives and a boys' ranch to help straighten out the wayward. A nice touch of respectability. Al Burton produced and Bob Searles directed competently. *Helm.*

This Variety *reviewer looked favorably on Wink's new KHJ-TV* Dance Party.

Chatterton were terrific network announcers with marvelous pipes. But they just weren't cut out for this format change that had been thrust upon them from the outside. As hard as they tried to acclimate themselves to it, it just wasn't working. And one of the main reasons — they all loved jazz, but hated rock and roll!

Magic Moments

Though it never became a morale problem, I was viewed as "Grumbles' boy"—the *intruder* from Memphis. So during my first months in California at KHJ, I hardly felt at ease in my new surroundings. But I was lucky from the start. No sooner had I begun my radio show, than KHJ-TV's General Manager Norm Boggs (with a bit of a boost from Grumbles) set aside five 'til six-thirty every Saturday for *The Wink Martindale Dance Party*, and renewing my familiar association with Coca-Cola. Enter another one of the influential and driving forces in my career, Al Burton, a creative talent in every sense of the word. Al was brought on board to produce the show, and I didn't know in the beginning just *how* valuable he was. Though a young man, Al had been producing youth-oriented shows for years. He made it his business to keep his finger on the pulse of what and how the kids were thinking, almost *before* they thought it. We struck up a friendship with that show in 1959 that has endured through the years. Later, in the Seventies, Al would be the creative force behind most of the Norman Lear television hits, of which there were many, including *Maude* and *Fernwood 2-Night*. Then he cre-

Teen idols Jan and Dean were Wink's guests on his first KHJ *Dance Party*.

ated the enormously successful and long-running hit *Charles In Charge* starring Scott Baio, which only *added* to Al's growing wealth and reputation. With Al Burton at my side, once again God — and fate — smiled upon me.

As we began to lay out the format and plans for *Dance Party*, Al and I wisely decided to retain much of the format that had worked so well in Memphis, and sure enough, the decision proved to be a good one. It was decided that to live up to the advance press and publicity the show was receiving, it would be wise to use my 1956 Elvis interview as the centerpiece of the show. This would help to bring more attention to the show, as well as give the new LA name of Wink Martindale some immediate credibility. We surrounded the Elvis kinescope with some in-person, hot names on the charts that summer, including Jan and Dean and Dave "Baby" Cortez, whose instrumental of "The Happy Organ" was riding high. The show was staged in one of the former network radio studios that had been converted to television use, complete with comfortable theatre seats for the audience of approximately two hundred. I couldn't help but make the comparison to our small, cramped studio at WHBQ in Memphis. For our show, the facility was perfect. The first show came off without a hitch. And everybody was even more thrilled when, on Monday, the reviews in both trade papers, *Hollywood Reporter* and *Variety*, were very compli-

mentary. The show became an immediate hit, and continued as a weekly fixture on Saturdays until the following summer, when it was taken on location and broadcast live daily, outdoors from Pacific Ocean Park in Santa Monica. This would be in addition to the Saturday show.

Dollars and Sense

Business manager Bob Stilwell with Wink and Sandy at Wink's birthday party.

On the subject of good, sound business decisions, how about one I made on a day in August 1959? As you will later learn, my bad decisions far outnumber my good ones. But this one must be considered one of the latter. Stan Borhman was an announcer for KNXT (now KCBS) in Los Angeles. It so happened that since both KHJ and KNXT were housed in the same large building at Fountain and Vine in Hollywood, we became speaking aquaintances in the hallways. Stan, armed with the knowledge of my record's growing popularity and climb up the sales charts, recognized that I would eventually be coming into some appreciable royalties. Never one to

Wink and Sandy seen here with Charlie and Ginny Ryder, and Jim Considine, Wink's longtime business managers.

mince words, Stan walked up to me one day and said, "What are you going to do with all that money? You're going to put it away I hope?" Frankly, I hadn't really given it that much thought, but I probably should. "Why do you ask?" He said, "Do you know what a business manager does?" I said, "Not really!" Then he proceded to give me a quickie primer on the world of business management. Stan began his explanation. "A business manager takes your income and writes all your checks; sees that your bills are paid in a timely manner; handles your bank deposits and withdrawals; seeks out and makes investments in stocks, bonds, real estate etc.; and for this he receives a fee."

"I have a business manager named Charlie Ryder. He and his wife have a small office up on Hollywood Boulevard in the Security Bank Building. When I go in for my weekly meeting, why don't you go with me? You can meet Charlie and Ginnie Ryder. Without high-pressuring you they can give you a more complete idea of what they do. Who knows, it may be just what you need." I took Stan up on his offer of an introduction. That was 1959. To this day I am still a client of Ryder-Stilwell, Incorporated. It was one of the smartest moves I ever made. Never a rocket scientist with a buck, I *needed* a guiding financial hand. Madelyn and I made that decision together, and we never regretted it. Not only were they our financial advisors, they became two of our nearest and dearest friends. Several years ago, Charlie and Ginnie retired to Laguna Niguel, California. Shortly after we helped the Ryders celebrate their fortieth wedding anniversary, Charlie, suffering from acute emphysema, lost his battle with this consuming disease. For years he had smoked three packs of cigarettes a day. He died in 1995. But he loved reminiscing about the good days, studying pictures from past parties and good times — the fun we all had, while at the same time sealing our financial futures.

Earlier I described in detail the story of my appearance on the Ed

Friend and fellow Memphian Johnny Cash "mix it up" during Wink's POP *Dance Party*—1961

Sullivan Show. 1959 was some kind of year for me. In January, I had requested, and received, a transfer to KHJ in Los Angeles. In a few short months I had my own morning radio show, my own 90-minute television show, a million selling hit record, and an appearance on the number one variety show in the country. I could easily have thought, "Wow, this is easy! I come out here, go on radio and TV, make a record and everybody wants to buy it!" Even if I entertained such thoughts, they soon dissipated. I learned in due time that what had happened to

Then, as now, a hit single called for an album, including material similar to that featured on the 45. Wink's "Deck of Cards" LP spotlighted other narratives, such as Joyce Kilmer's famous poem "Trees," and the Ken Nordine/Billy Vaughn classic, "The Shifting, Whispering Sands."

me was far from the ordinary. Following custom, Randy selected a dozen add*itional* narratives to be included in my first album, naturally titled "Deck of Cards." As a result of the single's success, the album sold moderately well. But though I would record at least a dozen more records and four additional albums for Dot, I was never able to come *close* to duplicating the phenomenal success of that initial country narrative. There was a six-month period in 1962 when I said goodbye to radio completely, and at Randy's request accepted the position of National Promotion Director and Assistant in the Artists and Repertoire Department at Dot Records. Between 1959 and early 1962, I had moved from KHJ Radio to KRLA, a fast rising competitor to KFWB. I could see early on that KHJ had far too many hangups to ever become a ratings factor in the marketplace. KRLA made me an offer I couldn't refuse, and with their studios in the Huntington Sheraton Hotel in Pasadena, the station was a 15-minute early morning drive from the house we had just purchased in Pasadena.

Cooke on the Cusp

As morning man at KRLA, unfortunately I never really felt "at home." Like KHJ, the station was always just on the cusp of overhauling KFWB. But the station's owner, Don Cooke (brother of then Washington Redskins owner Jack Kent Cooke) was never willing to cut loose with the necessary funds to properly promote the station. In the second largest radio market in America (now the largest), a competitive edge could easily swing on the funds management was willing to spend to merchandise its product! KRLA had come knocking on my door at KHJ because they could clearly see an advantage to having someone on their air who was hosting a daily *Dance Party* television show, wooing the same audience they were looking for and playing essentially the same music. It was like "free" bonus advertising.

After about a year and a half at Radio 1110, KRLA, I decided to hang it up — my mike, that is. My passion for radio wasn't what it once had been, and I also wasn't particularly thrilled with the direction of music at that moment in time. There seemed to be a sameness. A stagnancy of sorts. Perhaps I thought, in my own mind, as an A&R man at Dot Records I could change all that. If indeed that is what I thought, I was in for a rude awakening. However, during those final months at KRLA, there was one awakening that occurred, one that would prove blissful at the time but somewhat heartbreaking down the road.

The birth of our fourth and final child, Winston C. (Wink) Martindale, Jr. came on August 15, 1961. The place, once again the historical Huntington Memorial Hospital in Pasadena, where Laura had been born two years earlier. Naturally, I was thrilled to have a son, after experiencing the birth of three gorgeous girls. We truly felt that now our family was complete.

California Dreamin'

After having lived in a small but cozy Spanish rental home at 755 La Mirada in *upscale* San Marino our first couple of years in California, we settled into our new digs in the Hastings Ranch area of Pasadena. Our real estate broker came across an excellent buy at 3840 Greenhill Road. It was certainly not an imposing house from the street, but it had everything we needed for a family of six — 3500 square feet of living space (including three bedrooms), and most importantly, a 20' x 40' Olympic-size swimming pool! Needless to say this proved a big hit for the kids and grownups alike. It would be the first of three houses (and pools) our family would share while we all were together.

Though we loved the house, there was a period when we had second thoughts about its purchase. It seems the seller's husband had committed suicide in the house just months before. However, after a few dives into the pool in the heat of summer, we were able to put that unfortunate incident out of our minds!

Friends

The Martindale family was blessed with good, true and lasting friendships from the moment we first settled in the San Gabriel Valley. For example, following our first Sunday morning worship service at the beautiful San Marino Community Church, the pastor introduced us to Dr. and Mrs. Henry D. ("Red") Austin. The Austins, like us, were transplanted Tennesseeans with two girls and a boy the same ages as ours. So we hit it off immediately. In fact, they invited us to their house that day to swim and have dinner. Funny how the most unlikely things will impress you. I recall the Austin's front and backyard had the lushest stand of dichondra (a native California grass/groundcover) I had seen! It was like a thick, forest-green carpet. Once again I was so impressed! Obviously it didn't take much to impress this Tennessee boy. From that day forward, Dr. Austin, a graduate of the University of Tennessee School of Medicine at Memphis, became our family dentist, and the Austin family became closest of friends.

At virtually the same time we met the Austins at San Marino Community Church, we met another family that would prove to be close friends. Bill and Shirley Cole were the parents of three lovely daughters, again the same ages as Lisa, Lyn, and Laura. They owned a lovely home in San Marino, which would be the site of many wonderful birthday, social and holiday gatherings in future years. In fact, from our first Christmas as friends, we began a tradition of exchanging gifts and hosting holiday dinners. And in an unlikely twist of fate, Bill Cole, a

Lyn holds her new baby brother, Wink, Jr. while Mom keeps a close eye and Laura looks skeptical.

professional soloist with the Jack Halloran Singers, sang background on my recording of "Deck of Cards." We had barely met at the time, but together as friends we had the pleasure of enjoying the record's climb up the charts. Small world indeed.

In mentioning close friends during this wonderful growth period for our children, I would be remiss not to mention Barbara and Gordon Hyde. Just like the Austins and the Coles, the Hydes were the parents of three girls — that's right, the same ages as our gals! Gordon was a stockbroker with E. F. Hutton, and Barb was vice-president of raising those three girls of theirs! And she did a good job of it. As with the two other families I've mentioned, we enjoyed some great times together. There seems to be a bonding that occurs when similar age parents are faced with raising teams of kids with similar ages. Much like going through grade school and high school together. Yet so sad when the time comes to go separate ways. It's all a part of breaking away, and we all experience it.

Merry Christmas!

The perfect ending to a perfect year was made possible when Bill Grumbles came up with the idea of a *Top Ten Dance Party* homecoming! He would fly my family and me back to Memphis during the Christmas holidays, and while there, I would host the Saturday show one more time. Thanks to the hit record, I had received a lot of publicity both in the national and local press. Grumbles seized upon this promotional opportunity in a big way. The TV date was set, and the promotion started weeks in advance. Thanks to my LA radio and television exposure I was able to get former Mouseketeer Annette Funicello (who had recently enjoyed a big hit with "Tall Paul") and another red-hot teen-singing heart throb of the day, Bobby Rydell, to make the trip with me.

The day of the much ballyhooed *Dance Party* was really quite special to me. I couldn't have asked for more. The dancers on the show seemed genuinely happy to be a part of my return home. But I didn't get the same feeling from my replacement host! Ron Meroney was the young deejay selected to fill my shoes when I left for California, and I got the feeling that day he would have been delighted had I *stayed* in California! But the show came off in a big way. Annette, her mom, Bobby and his manager, Madelyn and several more from the station were all feted at dinner that night. The perfect conclusion to a superb homecoming idea. Next day, Annette and Bobby flew back to California, while Madelyn, the girls and I drove over to Jackson, spent the remaining holidays with our families, then we, too, flew home to California, wondering if the New Year could rival the outgoing year in terms of career advancement and old-fashioned excitement.

Wink and Sandy share a backstage picture with Kathleen and Wayne Newton.

The architects of *"Dance Party"* at P.O.P., Al Burton, "The Winker," and Arnold Shapiro.

A MOST WONDERFUL SUMMER

1960

W hen I allow my mind a tender, nostalgic moment, I think of 1960! Remember the brilliant and descriptive movie slogan, "In everyone's life, there is a Summer of '42." I might paraphrase that slogan to work for me, personally, in remembering the summer of '60. I had experienced a dream of a year in 1959. So much had happened in a relatively brief period of time. My transfer from Memphis to California. My experience of recording a million-selling record and performing it on national television. The successful debuts of my radio and television shows. The birth of our third daughter, Laura. And finally my Memphis homecoming at Christmas time.

Luckily, in many ways, 1960 mirrored the *prior* year. While a young and vibrant John F. Kennedy was waging the political battle of his life with Vice-President Richard M. Nixon, my *Dance Party* from Pacific Ocean Park was dancing its way into the hearts of young people, creating excellent ratings for KHJ afternoons between four and five o'clock, and Saturday nights, 6:30 'til 7:30.

Pacific Ocean Park was an amusement park bounded by the blue Pacific on the west and Santa Monica to the east. Having been in a run-down state for several years prior to being pur-

Wink and one of his regular dancer/cheerleaders taking a tour and enjoying the fun of a day at Pacific Ocean Park in Santa Monica.

chased in 1958 by CBS, the park had lost its lustre in terms of popularity. The surrounding neighborhood had deteriorated greatly, causing attendance to drop dramatically. CBS instituted a renovation and cleanup of the facility, along with a promotion campaign that proved quite successful.

Popular Pricing Policy

But with CBS' subsequent sale of POP to a private investment group led by entrepreneur Jack Moorheart, the park was given a million-dollar facelift, along with a brilliant pricing policy that turned this former white elephant into an overnight financial winner. The idea was to make the letters **P.O.P.** (Pacific Ocean Park), translate to **Pay One Price.** That is, a visitor to the park need only pay the low admission price of $1.55 to be allowed to stay as long as he wanted, and use all the rides and facilities of the park that day. Such a deal! Imagine that today!

The Wink Martindale Dance Party, along with an aggressive and expensive media advertising campaign, brought young people and their parents to the park in record numbers. The fact that the Santa Monica Freeway had not yet been constructed and the main traffic arteries, Olympic, Pico and Wilshire Boulevards, provided the only real access to the park from other areas of Los Angeles was another tribute to the park and what it had to offer in the eyes of the public. One of the features of Disneyland that always appealed to me was its cleanliness. Almost as soon as a piece of paper hit the ground, there was an attendant to pick it up! That cleanliness factor was in place at POP as well. The park was a real pleasure to visit. It was a family paradise, in terms of cost and entertainment. For me, personally, once again I was in the right place at the right time to continue making a name for myself with the young people of Southern California.

Pacific Ocean Park! The perfect place to spend a hot summer day close to the beach! Imagine the screams of frightened kids on the roller coaster with the aroma of fresh peanuts, popcorn, hotdogs and cotton candy. Then listen for *more* screams of delight and excitement as I would introduce the number one teen idol of that summer to a predominantly female audience of over a 1,000 *standing* souls gathered in the Sea Circus Arena and several hundred more hanging over the surrounding fences: "And now here he is. The young man you've all been waiting in the hot, summer sun to see *in person!* He grew up in Philadelphia, the same city that gave us Bobby Rydell [screams], James Darren [screams], Chubby Checker [screams], Fabian [louder screams], and Dick Clark's American Bandstand [screams]! Welcome, Francis Thomas Avallone. We know him as *FRANKIE AVALON!*"

Sea of Screaming Humanity

As his recording of "Venus" began to reverberate through the giant speakers, the song could hardly be heard through the din of continuous screams. The moment was reminiscent of the Saturday Elvis walked into the *Dance Party* studio in Memphis. Sheer magic! As Frankie tried making his way down the isles through a sea of humanity while attempting to lip sync his biggest number one hit from a year earlier, I turned to my producer, Al Burton, and asked in all seriousness, "Do you think he's going to be all right out there?" Al, always the confident one, replied, "No problem! Look at that. Can you imagine watching this at home on television?" Al, ever the producer, was seeing this as it was on TV. I was concerned for Frankie's safety! And would he make it to the stage for our interview? That was my main concern. I liked to get to the bottom of where singers found their hit songs. That was of great interest to me. Naturally, as Al had predicted, Frankie *did* weather the storm of gals.

Frankie told me, "A guy named Ed Marshall brought me that song. He came to my house one day and asked if I would listen to something. He sat down at the piano and started playing 'Venus.' I asked him to play it twice, I loved the song. I called my manager Bob Marcucci, he came over, listened to the song and totally agreed it could be a hit. Three days later we recorded it in New York. Took nine takes before I felt I nailed it." I asked him if he was as excited about the song *after* recording it as before? Frankie almost seemed insulted. "Are you kidding?" He said, "I

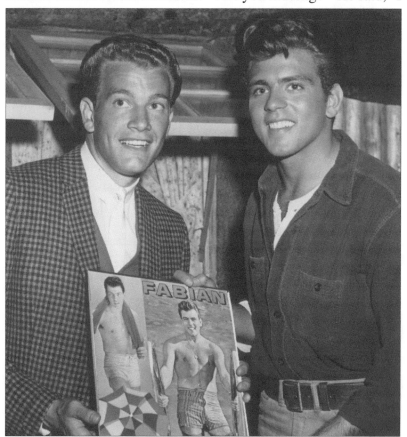

Teen heartthrob Fabian shows off his second Chancellor album to all his fans during previous night's *Wink Martindale POP Dance Party*.

waited till 4 A.M. to get a dub of it, and when I got back to Philly I stayed up all next day playing it over and over." A week later it was released, and four weeks after it hit Billboard's Hot 100 at number 99, it was the number one song in America.

Frankie's *first* hit had been nothing like "Venus." Since we had planned to use it as his encore, he reminded me that "the day I walked into the studio, they were rehearsing the song, and it sounded very staccato to me.

One of Wink's many fans during his Pacific Ocean Park *Dance Party*.

So I started singing along with it *holding my nose*! Everybody laughingly said let's make a couple of takes like that. And that's how the dumb, nasal sounding 'Dede Dinah' came about. Went as high as number seven!" When the engineer let that one go, I thought the bleachers were going to collapse. The kids were jumping up and down, stomping their feet so hard it sounded as if a train was passing through the park!

Frankie, Fabian . . . Fabulous!

Another similar day was when Frankie's friend and label-mate on Chancellor Records, Fabian, stopped by! He was another good looking hunk with five pounds of hair that Bob Marcucci had created, in the image of Frankie Avalon. The big difference however, was Frankie could really *sing*. It was another case of utter pandemonium when I introduced Fabian singing his big hit, "Tiger," and later "Turn Me Loose." Again, one handsome face in a sea of females! I remember asking him one of the dumbest questions I could ever ask a teen idol. "When you were out there among all those screaming admirers, was it fun?" Fabian answered rhetorically, "What do you think?" I took that to mean it sure beat working for a living!

In addition to producer Al Burton and dozens of recording superstars, the *POP Dance Party* introduced me to several lifelong friends, without whom the show would never have been as successful as it was. Larry Sloane was "the man in charge." He ran the park and was instrumental in seeing to it that our show became a fixture that first summer. Larry, Al, Producers Bart Ross and Frank Danzig all recognized how important television exposure was in reaching the

Young and lovely Joanie Sommers visits Wink at POP to sing her hit "Johnny Get Angry."

teen demographic needed to put Pacific Ocean Park over the top. It was their vision that prevailed over early cost concerns of the owners. Incidentally, years later Larry Sloane would realize enormous success as a partner in the Price-Stern-Sloane publishing empire.

Arnold Shapiro, Emmy and Academy Award winning producer of the *Scared Straight* documentary and executive producer of the long-running series *Rescue 911* for CBS, was the glue that held the POP *Dance Party* together. He worked harder behind the scenes than any of us did in front of the camera. Arnold had

Actor/singer Tab Hunter came to POP on "Oldies But Goodies" Night to sing his million-selling "Young Love."

known Al, his mentor for several years, and worked for Al on two or three local shows. So it was only fitting that Arnold be invited to join our team when the KHJ *POP Dance Party* began the prior year. Arnold had the innate ability to get the job done, whatever that called for, while at the same time keeping his cool no matter what. Obviously that has served him well in later years. And I must say Arnold thoroughly enjoyed working alongside the lovely ladies of *Dance Party*! He used to say, "That goes with the territory." Linda Mintz was another of the unsung heroes who was totally devoted to ensuring a top-flight show day in and day out. There were many other important persons behind the scenes. Suffice it to say, as in any creative endeavor,

Wink Martindale *POP Dance Party* regular dancer/cheerleader Linda Walsh gets a little hug as Fabian's official "greeter." Fabe later sang both "Tiger" and "Turn Me Loose" on the popular teen show the previous night.

without each doing his or her task, the successful end result would have been impossible to achieve.

Off the Charts

Johnny Mathis was one of those stars who would always make his way to POP when Columbia released a new single. His career had skyrocketed with the release of "Wonderful Wonderful" and "It's Not For Me To Say" in 1957.

His manager in those days was Helen Noga, who had discovered Johnny singing in a small San Francisco club and had brought Johnny's talents to the attention of Columbia executive George Avakian. The rest, as they say, is history. Johnny, Helen, her daughter Beverly, and Johnny's national promotion director since 1957, George Russell, befriended me early on. As Johnny be-

"Chances Are" you'll recognize a youthful Johnny Mathis as he visits Wink at POP to sing "Misty."

came the superstar that he remains today, they would never refuse our call to make an appearance on the POP *Dance Party*. His first appearance was on our Saturday night show, and he sang to every-one's delight the song that had introduced him to the world just three years hence, the song that remained on the sales charts for 39 consecutive weeks, "Wonderful Wonderful." I couldn't

Wink, "Laugh In" announcer Gary Owens, Sandy Martindale, Johnny Mathis and Johnny's long-time promotions director George Russell at Johnny's house for dinner in 1976.

resist asking Johnny if he could recall the day A&R genius Mitch Miller played him the song. Johnny said, "Mitch came into his office and laid a big stack of acetate demos on his desk for me to listen to. I chose 'Wonderful Wonderful,' 'When Sunny Gets Blue,' and 'It's Not For Me To Say.' If you notice, the instrumentation on these recordings is very light. I was new to the label, and there was almost no budget set aside for my recording sessions in those days." Johnny laughed and said, "That's changed a little bit now!"

"Misty" by the Sea

Actually Johnny was on the show to promote his new single, Errol Garner's great classic, "Misty," which Columbia almost didn't release because they preferred a Broadway show tune in favor of "Misty." Johnny mentioned, "I used to listen to Errol Garner play "Misty" when I first met him in San Francisco. I vowed to record the song if I ever had the opportunity." As the familiar opening piano notes filled the Sea Circus Arena this clear and balmy Saturday night, the audience let Johnny Mathis know just how much they appreciated his talent By then Johnny had grown in stature to the point where our live audience for him was about half young adult men and women and half teens. Regardless, he was always greeted with the kind of love and adulation he still receives to this day. Few stars can lay claim to the degree of longevity, widespread popularity and album sales Johnny Mathis continues to enjoy today.

When Columbia Records issued the four CD set in 1993, "The Music Of Johnny Mathis–A Personal Collection," I devoted a great deal of one of my five-hour radio shows to the introduction of this Mathis compilation. I was so impressed with this body of work, that I sent Johnny the following note: *What a pleasure it was to tell Southern California about this marvelous CD package. CONGRATULATIONS! This collection of singing majesty should be required listening for everyone, young and old alike! It's hard to believe that I have known Johnny Mathis since 1960. The days of Pacific Ocean Park. Sandy and I count you as the kind of friend few people enjoy having. Our love and best wishes for continued health, happiness and success. And thanks for your many kindnesses over the years.*

Unlike Dick Clark's *American Bandstand* on the ABC Network, which could make a new record a hit almost overnight, the POP *Dance Party* was strictly a local show, seen only in the Los Angeles area, albeit a *very large* area. So an Avalon, or a Fabian, or a Mathis, or a Pat Boone, or a Connie Francis, or a Duane Eddy, was doing a bigger favor for *me* than I was for *them*. Although that went unsaid, I'm sure it was a recognized fact among artists and their promotion people.

He Could Make the World Disappear

Thus it was even more appreciated, for example, when Sam Cooke's manager, Jess Rand, called *our* office asking if we would like Sam to be on the show while he was in town! Would we ever! Late in 1957, while I was still a jock in Memphis and just out of Memphis State University, Sam's "You Send Me" had literally exploded on the pop music scene and in no time at all had shot to number one. It was recognized as a phenomenal debut by a handsome but young unknown. But in African-American areas of this country, the name of Sam Cooke was already one of gospel music's most charismatic stars—and his crossover into rock 'n' roll heralded the beginning of a new era.

With stunning good looks, devastating charm and a smile women said "could make the rest of the world disappear," Sam Cooke mesmerized young girls and their grandmothers too! "You

Send Me" had sold over two million copies, and in so doing he broke the supposed taboo of gospel singers doing secular music. As author Dan Wolff points out in his recent book, *You Send Me— The Life & Times of Sam Cooke*, "The supposedly uncrossable border between Saturday night and Sunday morning was mostly talk." Sam's first appearance on our new show was just what the doctor ordered. For some reason there didn't seem to be an over supply of African-American performers hitting the charts the summer of '60 and Sam Cooke was the major exception. We welcomed him with open arms. And so did our audience.

Arnold Shapiro and Linda Mintz map out the day's *Wink Martindale Dance Party* at P.O.P.

When the spotlight outlined Sam's image singing "Only Sixteen," his second big hit, the kids literally came unglued. It was as if he was singing "their" love theme. We had secretly taken him *under* the bleachers to the far end of the stands, and didn't reveal to the audience his whereabouts until the song had begun. It was so effective we began using that method of introducing an act on a regular basis, bringing artists into view from the most unexpected places. Since Sam agreed to lip sync three songs this night, it left very little time for talk, other than the basic "thank you" for being there. We decided to hold his signature song 'til last since we felt it would have an unbelievable effect on the audience.

But as I was attempting to introduce his current hit, "Chain

Gang," I had second thoughts about our decision. Everybody went wild at the familiar pick and shovel sounds introducing this latest Sam Cooke smash. Here was a man who recorded or wrote 29 Top 40 singles—more than Little Richard, Buddy Holly and Jerry Lee Lewis combined. In 1986, he was one of the first 10 inductees into the Rock 'n' Roll Hall of Fame. So was it any wonder these kids, regardless of color, creed or nationality, were reacting in this way?

Former Mouseketeer Annette Funicello was a POP *Dance Party* favorite singing "Tall Paul."

Obviously not. By the time Sam had completed his third song on that show, "You Send Me," we all knew we had just witnessed perhaps the most exciting show of the summer. On Monday I could hardly wait to call Jess Rand with words of appreciation. And a question. When can we get Sam back? Well, luckily we did. Several times.

Percy Faith "Captured" that Summer

Without question, 1960 was the most memorable of all my years as a deejay on radio and television. And the number one *recording* of that year, oddly enough, was not "Venus," "Chain Gang," "El Paso," "Stuck On You," "Everybody's Somebody's Fool," "I'm Sorry," or "Cathy's Clown," all smash hits by Frankie Avalon, Sam Cooke, Marty Robbins, Elvis Presley, Connie Francis, Brenda Lee and The Everly Brothers, respectively. *Billboard Magazine's* biggest single hit of the year was an *instrumental,* from Max Steiner's score for a 1959 film starring Dorothy Malone, Richard Egan, Sandra Dee, Troy Donahue and Arthur Kennedy, "A Summer Place." Percy Faith had enjoyed success in 1953 with another popular film theme, "The Song from Moulin Rouge," the best-selling single of that year. Then he duplicated that feat with "Theme from a Summer Place" eight years later. Though not an immediate hit, it enjoyed a run of nine weeks at the top of the charts, and was truly the "love theme" of the year!

Percy had joined Columbia Records as musical director of the pop division, recording over 45 albums in that company's catalogue. His arrangements of "Because of You," "Cold, Cold Heart," and "Rags to Riches" helped Tony Bennett win three gold records. And Percy's own composition, "My Heart Cries For You" won a gold record while launching the singing career of Guy Mitchell. He also helped develop such stars as Rosemary Clooney, Jerry Vale, Johnny Mathis and many others on the Columbia label. His very first film-scoring effort, "Love Me or Leave Me" in 1955, brought him an Academy Award nomination.

Obviously long accustomed to winning awards, a 51-year-old Percy Faith was nonetheless overjoyed with the success of "Theme from a Summer Place," and our *Dance Party* audience was delighted to meet the face behind the name they were hearing so frequently on radio. Could he still get excited about winning another gold record? "It's always a thrill for those of us in the instrumental field to get gold records, because it was never easy," he told me. "It's monstrously tough now to get one, you know, with the competition we have from vocalists, vocal groups, and rock groups. To get a gold record for an instrumental is quite an achievement."

In the early seventies, I would have the pleasure of a more in-depth look into the career of this man, who as a young Canadian student was forced to abandon pursuit of a concert pianist's career to become a world famous popular music composer, conductor, and arranger. While preparing to leave on a tour of Japan with his orchestra, February 9, 1976, Percy Faith died at the age of 67, a victim of cancer. The musical legacy he left with us is timeless. His recordings of "Song from Moulin Rouge" and the number one latin hit "Delicado" were among the first records I remember playing as a young radio announcer in Jackson, Tennessee. The impression his music made on me in those days was enormous. I shall cherish always the opportunity I had to share a microphone with Percy Faith.

1960. President Eisenhower was winding down his presidency and the largest nuclear-powered submarine in the world was circumnavigating the globe on a submerged voyage of 41,519 miles in 84 days. We said hello to *Can-Can,* the top money-making motion picture. We said goodbye to *The Romance of Helen Trent* (after 27 years on radio); Oscar

Wink and Dot Records star Pat Boone during a between songs interview on *Dance Party* from the Sea Circus Arena at Pacific Ocean Park.

Hammerstein II, Emily Post, and Lawrence Tibbett. John Fitzgerald Kennedy of Massachusetts nosed out by a small popular majority his Republican opponent, Vice-President Richard Milhous Nixon, in part thanks to four nationally televised debates—a new political technique! On a much lesser scale of importance, I was making an indelible print on my memory, my second year as a transplanted Tennesseean. And it all happened at Pacific Ocean Park. When the park finally gave way to the wrecking ball in favor of high rise condominiums in the mid-Seventies, a dear friend from KMPC was aware of how much POP had meant to me. On the first day demolition began, Jane Hassler drove

"The Terrific Twosome," Dance Party producers Arnold Shapiro and Al Burton, went on to great television success.

to Santa Monica and picked from the rubble a decorative circular metal piece that was part of the park's entrance way, had it painted and fitted with a glass top, and gave it to me as a small cocktail table, which I still have to this day. Who knows, perhaps "in everyone's life, there is a summer of '60."

It's obvious from this candid moment at P.O.P. that Wink and Arnold took their jobs quite seriously!

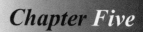
A LIFE OF FUN AND GAMES

Better than Work!

"In the department store of life, I'm in the toy department." That's game show host Bob Eubank's stock answer to why he's been hosting since 1966. But *The Price Is Right* host Bob Barker's "excuse" for not pursuing another line of work is so good he should bottle it and sell it to the rest of us. Says Bob, who pulls down several million dollars a year for hosting *Price* since 1972, "I give refrigerators away for a living. I don't sing. I don't dance. I don't tell jokes. I don't act, and it's too late for me to learn now, *because I'm a star!"*

The question I am asked most often (aside from "Is Wink your real name?"): How did you get into game shows? The truth is so simplistic, I have thought at times about making up some incredible story that shocks and entertains! I had been playing rock 'n roll deejay since Bill Haley and the Comets exploded on the scene with "Rock Around the Clock," from *Blackboard Jungle* in 1955. I had experienced the Elvis phenomenon from the ground up, first hand. And as morning man at Los Angeles' KFWB, I saw the British invade our shores and our airwaves, and still lived to tell about it! The Beatles "I Want To Hold Your Hand" debuted at number 45 on Billboard's chart, jumped to number 3 the following week while "She Loves You" debuted at number 69. Next week "I Want To Hold Your Hand" hit number 1.

Off the Charts

"She Loves You" had advanced in short order to 21; and enter "Please Please Me" at number 68! The 14th of March, 1963, those three records held the top three positions on the popularity chart . . . (by this time we needed a scorecard to keep up). Then on March 28th "Twist and Shout" had joined them in the top four, and a week later along came "Can't Buy Me Love," moving from number 27 to the top of the chart. That gave the Beatles an unprecedented stranglehold on *THE TOP FIVE!* A week later the Beatles hits held 14 spots out of 100, another all-time record.

THE TOP FIVE
Week of April 4, 1964

1	Can't Buy Me Love
	Beatles

2	Twist and Shout
	Beatles

3	She Loves You
	Beatles

4	I Want to Hold Your Hand
	Beatles

5	Please Please Me
	Beatles

It was during this period that I became truly disenchanted with playing records on the radio and began thinking about alternatives I might pursue. Although I had majored in Speech and Drama at Memphis State, I never seriously considered acting as a vocation due mainly to my difficulty at memorization, which dated back to high school. By process of elimination, I settled on the possibility of hosting game shows. Early on I had admired the ad lib abilities and personable styles of people like Arthur Godfrey, Art Linkletter, Bill Cullen, Garry Moore and during the early Sixties I became absolutely addicted to Allen Ludden's marvelous hosting of *Password.* So my agent Noel Rubaloff began sending me on auditions for game show hosting.

How It All Began

I won my first job as host of a local game show on Los Angeles station KTLA, Channel Five. "ZOOM" was produced by Ralph Andrews and Bill Yagemann (Andrews-Yagemann Productions). The format called for two competing contestants to answer questions to win the right to see a high-powered camera lens "zoom" closer and closer to an object until one of the two recognized that object. The show ran for 13 weeks, but did not create enough viewer interest, i.e. *ratings*, and slowly descended to game show heaven. While my next local show eventu-

Wink getting wrapped up in his work on NBC's *What's This Song?*

ally hit pay dirt with a slot in the daytime lineup at NBC, it didn't happen overnight.

What's the Name of That Song? had enjoyed considerable popularity as a local Los Angeles radio game on the Mutual Network. Host Dud Williamson would challenge studio audiences to identify songs and then sing their lyrics. Cash prizes of $5 to $50 went to contestants and to those sending in questions from home. It was this show that led producer Harry Salter to broaden the pool of players through the use of the telephone, and the result was one of radio's all-time game show hits, *Stop the Music.* Its debut in 1948 made host Bert Parks a household name.

Early in 1963, Stu Phelps partnered with Jack Reeves and Jesse Martin and obtained the rights to long-dormant *What's the Name of That Song?* They made a 13-week development deal with KTLA and

Actress Ruta Lee, Wink, and (then) *Tonight Show* bandleader Skitch Henderson try their skill at *singing* lyrics to popular songs on NBC's daily *What's This Song?*

NBC, then began fishing around for a host who could *sing!* My shower singing talents were just enough to win me the job, and I was ecstatic! The plan was for Phelps-Reeves-Martin to produce a nightly strip for Channel 5 (13 weeks/65 shows), and depending on the show's popularity, NBC would have the right of first refusal to bring the format to their daytime schedule.

The show didn't set the woods on fire, but the audience response was just good enough to put it over the top. So October 26, 1964, this guy from Jackson, Tennessee, who dreamed of being a radio announcer as a kid, realized yet another extension of that dream with his first network game show. With a shorter, TV Guide-friendly title, *What's This Song?* replaced Merv Griffin's *Word for Word.* It required two teams, each composed of a celebrity guest and a studio contestant, to identify songs. If a team guessed correctly they earned 20 points and an opportunity to earn 20 more points by *singing* the first two lines of the chorus, verbatim. If the opposing team felt the lyrics were incorrect they could challenge. If correct in their challenge, they could win points by singing the *correct* lyrics. First team to hit 100 points won the game.

Elvis Presley's friend and former high school classmate George Klein, welcomes Wink to WHBQ-TV Talent Party to promote his latest Dot LP "My True Love" (1963).

Exposed!

This show not only gave me valuable network experience and exposure, but working with such diverse celebrities as Lorne Greene (*Bonanza*), Andy Devine, Phyllis Diller, Michael Landon, Walter Brennan, Betty White, Angie Dickinson, Ryan O'Neal and many, many others, gave me the self-assurance that would come in handy on future celebrity driven shows. Any chances of winning a daytime Emmy would have been offset by the occasional need for me to break into song! Outside of the fact that I was often off-key and out of meter with the music, I was *adequate!* If it was my singing that drove us off the air, I was spared that fact. But I wasn't spared the news that the show's final airing would be September 24, 1965, a month short of a one-year run.

My first network outing on *What's This Song?* left me anything but disenchanted with the process. As the saying goes, "What goes up must come down"—so the first of many subsequent game show cancellations I would experience, though disappointing, was taken in stride, though I distinctly recall, in my quiet moments, asking myself if there was anything I might have done differently to alter the fate of the show. One of my most common failings is that of being too hard on myself in such situations. Even today, I must constantly remind myself that more than 400 game shows have been produced for network and syndicated television since 1946. That first show, *Cash and Carry*, was hosted by Dennis James. Since then, not one weekday has passed without a game show being broadcast on television!

The host "plays" the horn, while Deborah Walley and Gene Pitney play *What's This Song?* on NBC.

Half a Loaf

Everybody's Talking was another short-lived show on ABC daytime in 1967 that proved somewhat of a disappointment to me. Local TV personality Lloyd Thaxton and I were the two finalists as host, with Lloyd getting the final nod for the job. However, ABC and producer Jerome Schnur asked if I would agree to be the on-camera announcer. I reasoned that "half a loaf" was better than . . . etc. . . . so I accepted their offer. On this show three celebrities competed for cash and merchandise for *home viewers* by attempting to guess the person, place, or thing being described by pre-filmed man-on-the-street interviews, edited into a series of short clips. My job consisted of introducing Lloyd at the top of the show, as well as the contestants during play of the game. Again, not my most exciting job, but I continued getting my size-twelve foot in the door of the tightly-held world of game shows. In fact, in a touch of irony, Jack Barry (who had been prevented from producing game shows in this country resulting from his involvement in the 1959 rigging scandal), was actually the creator of *Everybody's Talking,* though prohibited from a hands-on role in its production. Jack and partner Dan Enright would later select me to host the long-running syndicated success, *Tic-Tac-Dough.* And who knows? Perhaps my acceptance of that secondary role on *Everybody's Talking* impressed Jack in some way when time came to select a host for the show most people still associate most closely with my name.

Dream Job

A most unlikely break came my way during the 10-month run of *Everybody's Talking.* Chuck Barris, who was riding high as the new game show maven thanks to the success of *The Dating Game,* then *The Newlywed Game,* was producing yet a third daytime show for ABC titled *Dream Girl '67.* Four contestants were judged by a panel of celebrity bachelors on the basis of poise, personality, and fashion consciousness. Each daily winner returned to compete on the Friday show

Dream Girl '67 **for Chuck Barris on ABC was tough duty for Wink, but somebody had to do it!**

to become "Dream Girl of the Week." All weekly winners returned at the end of the year to compete for the title "Dream Girl of '67." Six months into the show, Chuck was forced to replace Dick Stewart as host, and I got the call.

This was a delightful assignment for a lot of reasons, not the least of which was the opportunity to gaze upon a lovely group of young ladies each show. It also gave me another chance to hone the art of interacting with a panel of celebrity judges each day. I had discovered early on that working with celebs required a somewhat different skill than those used in dealing with everyday game players. As a "people person," I al-

Wink Martindale, with comics as "defense attorneys" to three worthy Moms on *How's Your Mother-in-Law?* Seen Monday thru Friday on ABC.

ways felt right at home with "pedestrian" contestants — but celebrities, by the very nature of their often egotistical personalities, could sometimes prove difficult. Thus a separate dynamic usually came into play.

As host of *Dream Girl*, I never did really feel at ease in the job, as pleasant as it was. Why? Would you feel at ease when the very *title* of the show would put you in the unemployment line after saying goodbye to 1967? I mean, nobody was contemplating a *Dream Girl '68*! Fortunately, an unusual circumstance threw me into yet another Chuck Barris creation in the middle of the year. I had taken over *Dream Girl* in June, and in September I handed over hosting duties to Paul Peterson (of *The Donna Reed Show*), so I might be free to host ABC's *How's Your Mother-In-Law?*—the show that has remained my stock answer to the question, "Of the 19 shows you've hosted during your career, which was the worst?" The premise? Well, as weak and as uninviting as it was, a trio of guest celebrity comedians served as "defense attorneys" in defending a mother-in-law against the accusations of her son-in-law. A bachelor jury then voted on which mother-in-law was the best of the group! The show lasted the minimum 13 weeks before being cancelled, but I've jokingly said it came and went so fast, it seemed more

Wink and three contestants prepare to play the new NBC game "Words and Music" for cash and prizes!

like 13 minutes! Most amazing about this experience was that the pilot show was sensational. Advance audience testing was through the roof. Chuck Barris was on a roll. He had the Midas touch, and he could seemingly do no wrong—until *How's Your Mother-In-Law?* Chuck assigned art director George Smith to design a set emblematic of Mom, country, and apple-pie, so we ended up with a loud but patriotic red, white and blue background, podium, and seating areas. To this day, if you looked up the word "gauche" in the dictionary, chances are you might see a picture of that set.

"Hello 1970!"

In saying goodbye to my first five years as a host, I entered the decade of the Seventies firmly entrenched in a business that was now knee-deep in game shows. As popular as talk shows would become during the Nineties, that's the way it was with games as we said hello to the Seventies. In fact, in addition to getting back into the radio wars again with a daily adult-contemporary show on KGIL in the San Fernando Valley, I would host not one, but two shows at the same time: *Words and Music* on NBC, and *Can You Top This?* in first-run syndication. The former was a badly conceived musical quiz that debuted on the network September 28, 1970. Though musical in nature, that's where the similarity stopped in comparison to *What's This Song?* With this show, three contestants competed using a game board of 16 squares. Each square contained a clue that was associated with a word to be sung by one of our five singers. The first player to correctly guess the word after it was sung won cash and the opportunity to select the next clue. The player with the highest cash score at the end of the show won and returned to play the next day. If the player could continue to win for three straight days he/she won a new car! As simple as that explan-

Morey Amsterdam, wide-eyed producer of "Can You Top This?" with Danny Thomas, Henny Youngman, and Milton Berle.

ation might sound, the show never really got on track. The original producer, Army Grant, was replaced by New York game-show "doctor" Howard Felsher. But his "patient" never really recovered. The game rules seemed to change from minute to minute, so as a host it was extremely difficult to reach a comfort zone. *Words and Music* was laid to rest with its final airing February 12, 1971.

A Life of Fun and Games

The Laugh Meter

Two actors approach each other on the street. *"You working?"* says one. *"I'm doing a one-man show,"* says the other. The first guy says, *"Is there a part in it for me?"*

Can You Top This? had been a smash hit on radio in the forties. The premise was so simple. Listeners sent in their jokes, the jokes were told by emcee Peter Donald, and the studio audience's reaction was registered on a "laugh meter." Then three panelists would follow with a joke of their own in the same category and try to top the home joke on the laugh meter. Nothing more. Nothing less. A good example of a simple concept designed to make people laugh, to feel good. A television version of the radio show attempted to capitalize on the show's popularity in 1950 but failed to translate to TV. Comedian Morey Amsterdam, always a fan of the show, secured the rights in 1970 and produced 65 shows for first-run syndication. The home viewer joke tellers were Richard Dawson (later to host *Family Feud*), and actor/comic Dick Gautier. Morey was able to get his comedian friends to guest on the show, people like Red Buttons, Milton Berle, Soupy Sales, Danny Thomas, Nipsey Russell, Jack Carter, Dick Van Dyke, Rose Marie, Mickey Rooney, Steve Allen, George Gobel, Arte Johnson, and many others. What a pleasure it was to have the opportunity to share a stage with these giants of our industry! Here is an example of a typical home viewer story. Then we'll see if Morey can top it!

Top This!

WINK: *This story was submitted by Joseph Lahane of Brooklyn, New York. The category is CLOTHES.*

DICK: *This bus driver had his mind set for years on this special suit. He saved and saved till he had what he needed, $200! He goes to the tailor, has it made, puts it on, and is walking down the street proud as punch, when he sees a friend. The friend says, "Hey, you got a new suit, nice, very nice. But it's got a little kink right there on the lapel." So the bus driver runs back to his tailor and says, "Hey, $200 dollars ain't hay. What about this kink on the lapel?" The tailor says, "No problem. Just grab it like this and hold it. It'll look fine." Now he's struttin' down the street again, and runs into another friend, who compliments the suit but says, "The buttons — shouldn't they be adjusted? They don't lay right!" So it's back to the tailor. "Look, these buttons don't seem to be quite right, can you fix 'em?" The tailor brushes that off by saying "Nah — just take your hand, grab the buttons and hold 'em like that. Gonna' look fine." The bus driver leaves, heads up the* *street and runs into another old friend. "New suit? Good lookin'! But the pants — see how they drag? They're way too long." So back to the tailor. "These pants are too long. What can you do about it?" The tailor says, "No problem, just reach down, pick 'em up and hold 'em like this." Now the bus driver's walking down the street and two doctors pass by. One doctor says, "Look at that poor man. Isn't that awful?" The other doctor says, "Terrible! But look how good his suit fits!"*

WINK: Good job Dick. You got a 60 for that story on CLOTHES. Now, here's a Dapper Dan, if I ever saw one. Morey Amsterdam!

MOREY: The biggest kick for me is when I go shopping with my wife. But this one day I didn't go shopping with my wife and she came

Host Wink Martindale, home viewer joke teller Dick Gautier and fellow comedians watch Morey Amsterdam relate another hilarious story on "Can You Top This?"

home with a mini-skirt. Now I have seen mini-skirts, but this looked like something a silk worm knocked off during his lunch hour. I think she kept it on by suction! Darndest thing you ever saw. She says, "How do you like it?" Well I never fight with my wife. I said, "Sweetheart, it's beautiful! I love it." She said, "What'll I wear with it?" I said, "Jockey shorts, what else?"

The Marriage Game—Loser/Winner

This show was a good combination of fun, silliness and old fashioned entertainment. But like its predecessor, it didn't find its audience and lasted just one season.

Between *Can You Top This?* in 1970 and my first taste of genuine game show success (the four-plus years of *Gambit* beginning in 1972), I would experience the end of my 18-year marriage to my wife Madelyn, tempering any elation with the bittersweet taste of divorce. It is very difficult to put my finger on just when our marriage began to falter. I had always heard from others that balancing family life with a career in any phase of show business wasn't without problems. I used to think I was doing it quite well, but in fact it's not an easy task. I think I compromised so much in trying to take advantage of every potential break that came my way, trying to have it all. Somewhere along the line something had to get neglected, and too often it was my family rather than my career! I was blessed with lots of energy, but you can't do *everything* well. I made some big mistakes along the way causing some irreparable damage to my marriage. In all candor, I cast no stones. I

A Martindale family Christmas card in their Pasadena home, 1961. From left to right: little Wink, Jr., Lyn, Madelyn, Lisa, Wink, and young Laura Leigh.

Daddy Wink with his line-up of future Olympic swimming stars in 1961. From left to right: Lisa, Lyn, Laura and Wink, Jr.

Wink's family of kids, sons-in-law and grandchildren. Left to right, front row: Steven and Blake Lucas, Matthew Klodt. Second row: Laura and Erin Cuff, Emilee and Lisa Lucas, Hannah and Lyn Klodt. Third row: Kevin Cuff, Wink, Jr., Jim Lucas, and Ed Klodt.

take the full blame for whatever went wrong. I was married to a good and wonderful wife and mother. She was the glue that tried very hard to hold our marriage together.

In hindsight, always 20-20, I have come to realize that I never really got close to any of our four children. For that I shall always feel a deep sense of sorrow. I missed so much of their young lives. For that I shall always feel a deep sense of guilt. As the years passed it seemed I was taking most business and recreational trips without Madelyn. That is not a healthy habit in holding a marriage together. Perhaps that is the reason a cardinal rule in setting the course for my 25-year marriage to Sandy, and a rule I would suggest for any couple getting married; Whenever possible, include your wife on your trips. Interestingly, I find that many of the mistakes I made in my first marriage help me in the role of husband to Sandy.

Wink's first legitimate hit! Contestants answer trivia questions to win cards, and the game, *Gambit*, Monday thru Friday on CBS.

Where Were You Then?

There are certain moments in our life frozen in time. I remember as a boy of 8 standing in front of our house in Jackson, Tennessee, the morning of December 7, 1941. I might have been too young to know the real meaning of the bombs dropped on Pearl Harbor, but I knew only too well that my Mother's tears meant something quite sad had happened. I remember my own tears four years later when I heard that President Roosevelt, the only president I had known, had succumbed to the ravages of polio and WWII. The deaths of President Kennedy, singer Elvis Presley, the beginning of the Gulf War, and President

Truman's firing of Gen. Douglas McArthur, all bring vivid pictures to my mind of where I was and what I was doing at the time I heard the news.

On a less serious but more personal note, I recall in a similarly vivid way the telephone call from my agent Mike Phelps informing me that *Gambit* had been picked up by CBS for a September 4th start! Then as now I had gone through the audition process in the offices of Heatter-Quigley Productions on Sunset Boulevard in Beverly Hills.

Left: Wink, Bob Barker and Jack Barry saw their shows, "Gambit," "The Price is Right" and "The Joker's Wild" all debut the same day on CBS: Monday, September 4.

Three classic game shows debuted Monday, September 4, 1972. In addition to *Gambit,* the audience said hello to Bob Barker, hosting *The Price Is Right,* and Jack Barry with *The Joker's Wild.*

From the day it hit the air, *Gambit* spelled winner, and it taught me a basic tenant of any truly successful game show: KISS! "Keep It Simple Stupid!" Like playing *Old Maids* as a kid, *everybody* knows how to play 21, i.e. Blackjack.

The long-running hit *Wheel of Fortune* called for a practical way to play the age-old kids game of "hangman." With *Gambit* (meaning a "calculated move"), veteran producers Merrill Heatter and Bob Quigley created a set of

Gambit **host Wink Martindale with his co-hostess and dealer Elaine Stewart, holding the best of all hands, 21! This popular blackjack game was seen every day on CBS.**

brilliantly simple rules for playing blackjack on television. Two husband and wife couples competed against each other in answering questions, with a correct answer giving them the option to keep or give away an oversize playing card from a regulation deck. The object was to score exactly, or get as close as possible to 21, without going over before your opponent did.

Long-time announcer on *Gambit* and many other game shows, Kenny Williams awards another "brand new car!"

A best two of three games determined the winning couple. Elaine Stewart, former actress (*The Bad and the Beautiful*) and Merrill Heatter's wife, was the dealer of the cards.

All Good Things End

"I don't know what you're doing right, but keep on doing it!" That's what Bud Grant, CBS Vice-President of Daytime Programs said to me on the set one day, after *Gambit* had been soundly beating its competition on NBC and ABC for over two years. But all good shows must come to an end. Ours eventually met its Waterloo when a new show debuted on NBC January 6, 1975. I remember saying to my producer Bob Noah one day, "I've seen our new competition on NBC, and frankly I don't think we have anything to worry about!" Bob's response proved prophetic. "I don't know about that. I have a

Veteran game show producer Dan Enright striking a typical pose on the set of *Tic-Tac-Dough.*

rule. Don't ever sell a new show short. Chances are, it will come back to bite you in the butt!" Sure enough, from its premiere January 6, 1975, *Wheel of Fortune* took off like a slowly rising rocket. The show slowly but surely ate away at our ratings. *Gambit* fell from a near 40 share of audience (homes watching television) to a 26 (which in *today's* daytime marketplace would denote a bonafide hit) the day we aired our final show, December 10, 1976, roughly four years and two months after premiering. What a lousy Christmas gift! But our little Silky Terrier, born in 1975, we had named Gambit, and until his death in 1989 Sandy and I felt our love affair with the TV show was very much alive.

Sidebar (to coin a phrase): A season or so later, *Wheel* actually had received its notice of cancellation from NBC due to falling ratings, but received a last-minute reprieve and continued on the network for several very successful years. The syndicated version of the show was

The real producer/owner of the CBS hit game *Gambit.* That's the little silkie's name, belonging to the show's host, Wink Martindale and his wife Sandy.

launched in September, 1983, and remains the number one show in syndication.

The Three "Stages"

He shook my hand firmly and said, "Wink, I enjoyed your work on *Gambit.* I must say, you really look good." Though I only knew the man by reputation, I shot back, "But you know the three stages of man — youth, middle age, and *you really look good*! That was my introduction to game show producer Dan Enright, who along with partner Jack Barry, did more for my hosting career than anybody else when they cast me as host of *Tic-Tac-Dough.*

Dan, always ready with a good joke and a laugh, loved my retort, and from that day forward in 1978 we were fast friends. Dan was a difficult person to get to know, but in the six weeks of rehearsals leading up to the CBS pilot, I came to know him as a kind and loving person and a close personal friend until the day he died. He methodically taught me *more* about the approach to hosting a question/answer game show than even I recognized at the time. The right and wrong way to read a question, how to dramatize that question, when to raise your voice and when to speak quietly — little nuances I never dreamed existed.

I would meet Dan, line producer Ron Greenberg, director Richard Kline and several contestants each morning in their Century City offices, Saturdays included. We rehearsed, and rehearsed, and rehearsed for the upcoming pilot. The purpose was to make me feel so at home with the game that I knew it like I knew my name. So that, if all the cue cards were thrown away, I could wing it without difficulty. I had never

Wink and Sandy vacation in Hawaii with *Tic-Tac-Dough* fans and friends, Homer and Joyce Formby.

before experienced such a woodshedding process, but it really paid off when the little red light went on.

The entry of *Tic-Tac-Dough* into the CBS morning lineup July 3, 1978, was heralded as a show that "couldn't miss." It had enjoyed daytime and primetime success in the late fifties on NBC. But the show was a paradox. Less than two months after its premiere, it was canceled off the network. It simply failed to attract an audience. Now it was panic time for all those television stations that had already bought the syndicated version of the show to begin airing in September! Here was a show that had failed miserably on CBS, and now it was headed for access time periods five nights a week worth millions of dollars in commercial spot sales to the stations that had gambled on its success. To say there were furrowed brows and considerable hand-wrenching by station managers all over the country would be an understatement.

Nielsen Smash!

But lo and behold! From the very first Nielsen rating books reflecting the all-important November sweeps (which sets the price stations get for their commercials), *Tic-Tac-Dough* was a SMASH! At the NATPE (National Association of Television and Program Executive) Convention, I was treated like a king by Dick Colbert, the show's distributor, station managers and program directors, even advertising executives. Overnight I had gone from the outhouse to the penthouse. It was another lesson in show biz for me, still

Lt. Thom McKee in one of his 48 straight championship appearances with Wink on *Tic-Tac-Dough*.

wet behind the ears in terms of how to handle such a turn of fortunes. But I took it in stride, counted my blessings and felt fortunate that I had been in the right place at the right time.

A Matter of Pride

"Are you going to be proud to tell your grand-children that you were a game show host?" That

Live! With Regis and Kathie Lee **executive producer Art Moore, star Kathie Lee Gifford and Wink get together and wonder where Regis is!**

was the very first question asked of me as I hit the road in September 1978, visiting several major cities in a media blitz to assure those eventual winning ratings. The question was posed by a major television critic with the Philadelphia Inquirer. As I sat across from this young lady in the beautiful oak-paneled conference room at Philly's number-one station, WPVI, I had no doubt she was out to nail me!

The station's promotion and publicity director Art Moore (now Program Director at WABC in New York and Executive Producer of *Live! With Regis and Kathie Lee*) had pre-warned me of her negative opinion of game shows. But I was determined more than ever to win her over. Her resulting story was quite complimentary and any resemblance to the lady who opened with such a leading question and the lady who wrote the story the following week was strictly coincidental! Ironically, for the eight-year run of the show, WPVI (the *number one* ABC affiliate in the country) reflected the highest *Tic-Tac-Dough* ratings of all stations carrying the show, year in and year out. For this reason I was invited to participate in WPVI's annual Variety Club Telethon, drawing some of the biggest TV stars in the business and hosted by Monty Hall.

By its second season, *Tic-Tac-Dough* was being programmed successfully back-to-back on many stations with Barry & Enright's *The Joker's Wild,* hosted by Jack Barry. The shows were the talk of the industry, the first games to break the "checkerboard barrier," the stations inclination to program a different show in the same time period each night of the week.

After 57 straight matches, all-time "Tic-Tac-Dough" champ Thom McKee finally lost to Eric Kraepelien, who went on to win $66,000.

They Could Feel the Tension

"What leading actress appeared in both *The Wind and the Lion* and *Starting Over*?" The studio audience and the viewers at home could *feel* the tension, just as they had during the prior 47 shows. Record-setting *Tic-Tac-Dough* champion Naval Lt. Thom McKee stood quietly, thinking about his answer. A close-up of his wife Jenny, in the same seat that had proven lucky through all those questions and 20 defeated contestants, clearly showed the strain of 48 straight championship days on the show. As the seconds ticked off, this voracious reader of encyclopedias, almanacs and National Geographic Magazines, could not come up with the correct answer, Candice Bergen. After 57 straight matches, Tom had been defeated in this classic X and O game by computer analyst Erik Kraepelien. But, between the first and 57th match, this handsome 24-year-old Lieutenant stationed in San Diego, had enjoyed a nine-week winning streak of 88 games. Ratings on the show went through the roof as Thom and the show became the favorite subject each morning around the office water cooler.

Quintessential Contestant

When Thom and Jenny McKee first began to make the weekly drive from San Diego Naval Station to CBS Television City for tapings of *Tic-Tac-Dough,* they would drive up on Saturday for the five shows to be taped that evening, then drive back to San Diego,

Decathlon champs Rafer Johnson and Bob Seagren flank host Wink Martindale on *Tic-Tac-Dough's* celebrity tournament for charity.

then make the drive on Sunday for another five shows. One Saturday night they decided to take a room at the Farmer's Daughter Motel on Fairfax Street across from CBS. By now Thom had amassed winnings in excess of $25,000. But when they arrived at the desk to register, they discovered they had no cash and no credit cards on

Naval Lt. Thom McKee, whose total winnings, $312,700 in cash and prizes set an all-time *Tic-Tac-Dough* record, flashes that million-dollar smile as he beats the infamous "Dragon."

them. It was quite late and as hard as Thom tried, he couldn't convince the desk clerk that he was good for the $45 dollar room, that he was the winning contestant on *Tic-Tac-Dough* and had won lots of money. After some time, the employee either got tired of Thom's pleading or believed that he and Jenny were indeed more than just a young couple looking for a place to bed down for the night. He took Thom's word and the next day was happy to receive the 45 bucks and a couple of tickets to the taping as well.

"If we had conducted a nationwide search for the quintessential contestant, we could not have found anyone more ideal than Thom McKee," said Dan Enright on many occasions. "He was young. He was handsome. He wore the uniform of our country. In fact, he was a graduate of the U.S.Naval Academy, and Jenny was the daughter of a Navy man! He possessed an insatiable appetite for knowledge. He had an almost photographic memory. His wife was as pretty as he was handsome, and she just happened to be *pregnant*! Now was that an All-American couple or what?"

As host, I was in awe. I had never seen anything quite like it. I looked forward to each show wondering if *this* would be the one? The fighter pilot's total winnings came to $312,700 in cash and prizes, including eight Buick automobiles, 3 sailboats and 16 vacation trips. He shipped one car to his brother, a missionary in Africa, sold the remaining seven and purchased a shiny new Mercedes Benz with the personalized license plates, *Tic-Tac*. Thom's winnings made him, to that time, the all-time single top champ on a game-show series. This record would be erased in 1999 with the phenominal success of ABC's *Who Wants to Be a Millionaire?* Runner-up Teddy Nadler, back in the fifties, won over $250,000 on the *$64,000 Question* and its companion show. Thom's lucky streak had made him an overnight celebrity, but I sensed that he was growing somewhat weary of his new found wealth and status. Thom later admitted that, "I wasn't unhappy at all when I lost. Two months of competition had taken their toll. And I lost to a very smart individual who did very well himself." (Erik Kraepelien won $66,000).

Jenny McKee joins husband Thom on the set of "Tic-Tac-Dough" as the Naval fighter pilot continues his record-breaking winning ways.

To this day I have viewers ask me about Thom McKee. Where he is and do I ever hear from him? The first few years after his appearances on the show, Sandy and I would talk to Thom and Jenny from time to time. In fact, Thom made one return appearance on *Tic-Tac-Dough* as part of a Tournament of Champions, but was defeated early on.

When he retired from the Navy and moved to Atlanta, we lost track of the McKees. But their impression on my viewers and me in the spring of 1980, will never be forgotten.

A TV Guide cover and story in 1984 features six
popular game show hosts, all with shows airing
at the same time. Front row: Jack Barry (*The
Joker's Wild*), Bill Cullen (*Hot Potato*), and Wink
(*Tic-Tac-Dough*). Back row: Pat Sajak (*Wheel
of Fortune*), Monty Hall (*Let's Make a Deal*),
and Bob Barker (*The Price is Right*).

MORE FUN AND GAMES . . .

"I've learned one thing," says game show veteran Bob Barker of *The Price Is Right.* "Real people are much more exciting than a bunch of fake dramatic characters in a script." And I heartily agree. Most contestants, "real people," are down-to-earth, honest people who just want to add a few bucks to their bank accounts. Or they are simply looking for their fifteen minutes of fame. Monty Hall, creator and host of *Let's Make A Deal,* feels that "people love to be winners . . . and they embarrassed themselves to the point of making total jackasses of themselves to take home money or gifts." Adds Monty, "Some guests had terrible tempers. No one wanted to go home empty-handed and I can understand that. Game shows have had their greatest success in America, where there has always been a strong sense of competition and fair play."

By the way, in 1980, right in the middle of *Tic-Tac-Dough's* third season, producers Merrill Heatter and Bob Quigley sold NBC on the idea of bringing *Gambit* back to daytime, but this time set in what seemed to be the ideal location. *Las Vegas Gambit* premiered October 27 and taped at the Tropicana Hotel amid much hoopla, flashing lights and glamour! We had two card girls during the show's 13- month run, first Beverly Malden then Lee Menning handed out those lucky 21s (most of the time). Our schedule kept us hopping between L.A. and Las Vegas, taping 10 *Tic-Tac-Dough* shows one weekend then 10 *Las Vegas Gambit* shows the next weekend. But it was really a kick to play

Wink found an exciting and new setting for one of his long-time favorite shows when NBC revived the "21" game as *Las Vegas Gambit*.

the big room at the Tropicana, where our show was staged. The audiences were absolutely teriffic, and were standing around the block on tape days waiting to get in. What show could possibly be better suited for Vegas than our classic blackjack game? It was fun while it lasted! I read a most complimentary quote by Merrill Heatter, printed in Jefferson Graham's excellent game-show book, *Come On Down*. Merrill said, "Wink gives you kind of a *Music Man* approach. There's a performance. He's having a great time. He'll break up when something's funny, and he'll put his arms around you when it's appropriate. That's just his style!"

Watching Lives Change

Sometimes a person will still ask me what I eventually want to do. I'm *doing* what I want to do. I love working with contestants, interacting with the audience—and to a degree, watching lives change. Winning a lot of cash can

Wink has a laugh between matches on a *Tic-Tac-Dough* celebrity tournament featuring two former Miss Americas—Cheryl Prewitt and Debbie Moffat.

cause that to happen. In 1964, I—temporarily—gave up radio, teen-age dance parties and a score of other opportunities to host and eventually produce game shows, and I'm thoroughly happy with my decision. The late game show guru Mark Goodson once described the perfect emcee like this: "You are in a car with 12 gears on top of a mountain, and I want you to steer backwards down the mountain looking through the rear mirror, and while you are doing that, I want you to be witty. Not a lot of candidates."

How much money have I given away on game shows? Producer Dan Enright once told me that in the seven years I hosted *Tic-Tac-Dough*, we gave away over 7 million dollars in cash and prizes. My favorite of the 21 shows I have hosted? I count *two* as favorites— *Gambit* and predictably, *Tic-Tac-Dough*. The latter perhaps because it gave me the longest period of employment, keeping me out of those *long, long* unemployment lines! Incidentally, some of my fondest moments on *Tic-Tac* occurred during special tournaments we would hold, designed to bolster ratings during the all-important sweeps periods, held four times per year.

These octogenarians are having a ball with Wink all this week on Tic-Tac-Dough's annual "Over 80" tournament.

Celebrity players would be paid a fee for their appearance, but their winnings would be designated to their favorite charities. One season we featured a tournament pitting former Miss Americas against former stars from the world of sports. Among the Miss Americas were Elizabeth Ward (whom I had help select the prior year as a judge in Atlantic City), Cheryl Prewitt, Debbie Moffat (whom I also helped judge as the winner two years prior at the Miss America contest), and Nancy Fleming, wife of game show host Jim Lange. The sports personalities included decathlon champs Bob Seagren and Rafer Johnson, former St. Louis Cardinal base stealer Lou Brock, former pro and U.C.L.A. basketball great Bill Walton, and former pro football Hall of Fame linebacker Dick Butkus. These tourneys were usually entertaining as well as interesting. The stars would dive right in with their very best efforts for charity, but occasionally an unusual, even embarrassing answer would be forthcoming. Like the response one of the Miss

Left: Wink welcomes former sports greats (left to right) Bob Seagren, Lou Brock, Bill Walton and Dick Butkus to his celebrity tournament on *Tic-Tac-Dough.*

Right: Wink congratulates Dr. Reba Kelley and Bobbi Tremain as finalists in the *Tic-Tac-Dough* " $100,000 Over-80 Tournament."

Americas gave in answer to the question, "What popular, long-running broadway show, later made into a successful movie, starred Carol Channing? Was it *Hello Dolly*, *Hello Tilly*, or *Hello Lucy*? Her unpredictable response was, believe it or not, *"Hello Tilly!"* (Her charity came up short that week).

Elder Excitement

One of the most anticipated events each season came to be the "$100,000 Over-80 Tournament." As the title implies, all the participants were over 80-years young. With such a big cash prize at stake, these octogenarians went at this game in a big way. An 82-year-old general practitioner from San Diego, Dr. Spangler, was a tourney contestant several years running, an excellent player with a marvelous trivia recall. Once backstage, minutes before the taping began, Dr. Spangler noticed me nervously smoking a cigarette (a sometimes habit I have long since given up). He proceeded to give me hell down the river! "Why would a nice young man like you harm your body by puffing on one of those filthy things? *And* one who depends on his voice so much as well!" Needless to say I never let him see me do that dastardly deed again. Several weeks after each tournament, I could expect a letter from Dr. Spangler, an avid runner, reminding me of the hazards of smoking! He lived into his mid-nineties.

One of our elderly players gave us a good laugh with his answer to this question. It was one of my all-time favorite responses. "The category is U.S. cities. The question: What major city in Pennsylvania produces over 9 billion candy bars per year?" Without giving the question a second thought he confidently answered, "*NESTLE!*" It

Mrs. McNeely and Dr. Spangler are two "Over-80" contestants in the *Tic-Tac-Dough* tourney with host Wink Martindale. Mrs. McNeely gave Wink one of the biggest laughs he's ever experienced on any show!

took awhile for the audience to settle down to the point where we could continue. (Privately, I thought about sending him a box of Hershey bars for giving us such a good laugh). Dr. Reba Kelley, 96 years young, told me she was an expert at raising roses, her favorite flower. I made the mistake of comparing myself to a rose and asking her how she would insure that I would open up into an award-winning rose. Without hesitation, and minus her dentures, she said, "The first thing I would do is check your *stem*! If you want a nice, full blossom at the top, you must have a good, strong stem." That woke me up and cleared my sinuses!

But my favorite Over-80s contestant was an 86-year-old African-American, a Mrs. McNeely. She provided me with a clip that was so funny I have used it over and over when guesting on various talk shows. An absolutely priceless moment, it happened when, during the interview with her just prior to the start of the game, I asked her if at her advanced age she ever had a desire to go out on a date? She answered,

Wink enjoying a fun moment with deejay icon "Wolfman" Jack.

"Honey, I have *four* boyfriends. I get up with *WILL POWER*, I go for a walk with *ARTHUR-ITIS*, I come home with *CHARLIE HORSE*, and I go to bed with *BEN GAY!*" It was one of those rare moments that a host dreams of. I laughed till I cried, and the audience joined me. Her family in the audience seemed stunned, but they laughed louder than anybody.

Flying High

Someone once coined the phrase "the higher they fly, the harder they fall!" *Tic-Tac-Dough* had flown uncommonly high during its first six years, but in season seven we all detected a noticeable slide in the ratings. Sometimes it happens quickly to a show, other times at an imperceptably slow pace. Without even realizing it, I began to search my mind for ideas from which I might *create* a show for myself. I had no assurance producers would be waiting in line to offer me a new show. With that in mind, I was standing in the kitchen one early morning in April of 1984 sipping coffee and reading the *Los Angeles Times*. Glancing at a headline, it occurred to me that if I hadn't *seen* that headline,

Wink's own creation based on everyday headlines was originally titled *The Front Page*. Merv Griffin re-titled the show *Headline Chasers,* and it aired in first-run syndication during the 1985 season.

but given a series of clues relative to the story content, could I mentally conceive the proper headline? I happened to have one of those newspaper headline books. I got it out and proceeded to rip out pages right and left to test the concept, which was quite simple. (Remember my KISS rule? — Keep It Simple Stupid.) The idea was to ask contestants questions about the news and have them try to fill in the missing letters of the headline, i.e. "Truman Fires MacArthur" became "- - - man Fires Mac - - - - - -." In testing some news and sports headlines with my wife Sandy, then with various friends, we had so much fun I got serious about trying to structure the idea into a viable game show."

Meet Merv Griffin

After a few weeks of woodshedding various ideas and titling the show *The Front Page*, I prepared a leather-bound presentation book, and decided to run it by my friend Michael King. We had become acquainted when brothers Michael and Roger sold *Tic-Tac-Dough* to stations for Colbert Syndication Sales. They had later formed their own company KingWorld, procured the rights to the NBC daytimer *Wheel of Fortune*, and in short order turned it into the hottest number one show in first-run syndication. It still occupies this lofty position, bringing almost 400-million dollars a year to KingWorld's bottom line. Sandy and I met Michael for drinks in the lounge of the Westwood Marquis Hotel and showed him my 15-page presentation. He was impressed, but because of KingWorld's exclusive game show distribution agreement with Merv Griffin, Merv would have the final say about the possibility of the concept becoming a reality.

At Michael's suggestion, I invested $20,000 into a 12-minute professional video presentation, expanding the game to include two additional components — "Cover Stories"— famous news personalities silhouetted on magazine covers which players would have to identify, and "Front-Page Headliners"— offering *voices* of past and present newsmakers.

The meeting with Merv was set in his Hollywood offices on Vine Street. At the appointed hour, 3PM, Michael, Merv, Bob Murphy and Murray Schwartz (Merv's top executives), and I convened in Murray's office to watch the demo tape. Knowing full well the importance of this meeting personally and professionally, and being aware that Merv had never before bought an idea from outside his own company, I nervously described the genesis of the show, its concept, and hit the tape!

Literally two minutes into the presentation, Merv got up, moved

Bumper Stumpers was a show idea that came to Wink after seeing an Avis ad in the *United Airlines* magazine displaying the license plates of all 50 states. The result was a three-year run on the USA Network, hosted by Canadian Al Dubois.

to the arm of my chair and said to me, "Wink, this isn't just another game show — *this* is a very important game show!" Needless to say, I was elated, but floored. The best of all worlds had just happened. Merv not only *liked* it, he *loved* it. As promised, I picked up the phone and called the Hollywood Brown Derby across the street where Sandy, Nona and Ed Lojeski were waiting for the verdict. They came over, we all had a celebratory glass of wine, and made plans on how to proceed with *The Front Page.*

Good News, Bad News

In summary, Merv retitled the show *Headline Chasers.* We produced a pilot, took it to NATPE where it was well received and sold to stations covering over 80% of the country, making the show a go for Fall 1985. But just weeks into the new season, it was obvious *Chasers* would not find its audience. The show was either too difficult for the audience to find compelling and interesting, or it just failed to meet my long held "KISS" Rule: "Keep It Simple Stupid."

I will never forget while I was on a promotional trip to Miami, the program director of the station carrying Headline Chasers said to me, "Can't you dumb it down a little?" I knew then my show was doomed to only one season.

Two additional concepts that I have been proud of in the creator role are *2nd Honeymoon* and *Bumper Stumpers.* The former was an idea of Sandy's, where children of all ages competed to win their mom and dad a second honeymoon by trying to match hypothetical situations posed by the host, Canadian Wayne Cox. The game was played in three rounds and the family that ended up with the highest point score at the end of the three rounds was the winner for the day. *2nd Honeymoon* premiered September 2, 1987 on cable's Christian Broadcasting Network, but as the only game show on the network, it never found an adequate following.

License To Steal was a game based on personalized or vanity license plates. During the show's development process, pro-

Santa Claus is pictured here with Wink and Sandy Martindale's five Chihuahuas; Bumper, Stumper, Rocky, Winkie and Maui. As you might have guessed, the first two (brother and sister) were named for Wink's show *Bumper Stumpers.*

ducer Mark Maxwell Smith came up with the ideal title, "Bumper Stumpers." Sandy and I were on a flight to Hawaii. An Avis ad featuring colorful license plates from all 50 states featured in the *United Airlines* magazine caught my attention and started me wondering if there wasn't a way to incorporate the plates of all the states in a game show format.

Who among us has not tried to read the meaning of a vanity plate on the car in front of us? About a year later I presented the idea to Dan Enright. He saw promise in the concept, and together we developed the format that eventually made its way from Canada's Global Network to the U.S.A. cable network on June 29, 1987, where it enjoyed a three-year run, hosted by Al Dubois. The object of *Bumper Stumpers* was to solve the Super Stumper, a personalized license plate whose seven letters or numbers are revealed one at a time. To earn the right to have another blank filled in, both teams compete against each other to solve a "jump-in." The "jump-ins" are two license plates and a question that pertains to one of those two plates. The team guessing which plate gets a chance to spell out its meaning. Sandy and I named our two Chihuahuas Bumper (the male) and Stumper (the female). They have been joined by three of Miss Stumper's off-spring — Rocky Elvis, Winkie Tennessee, and Maui Martini!

Haven't we all done it at one time or another? Come across a new product on the market, something simple and practical, and thought, "Now why didn't I think of that?" For example, there's the guy next door, who's designed a revolutionary new egg beater — or electric socks — or an automatic goldfish feeder — that he dreams will soon be on retail shelves around the world!

Why Didn't I Think of That? was a weekly series in first-run syndication who's purpose was to celebrate good ol' American ingenuity by inviting our country's best home inventors to demonstrate their original (and outrageous) creations. The show put everyday people with extraordinary ideas into the spotlight. From a fool-proof flyswatter called the "Fly-A-Later," to a motorized spaghetti fork that makes pasta twisting a breeze, to an "Ecology Hat" that keeps smokers happy in a non-smoking world, *Why Didn't I Think of That?* was an idea that Memphis friend (and inventor) Ron Hoffman brought to me. I put it on hold for a coupla years. Then Ron, my partner Bill Hillier and I produced 52 shows in association with Samuel Goldwyn Television for the 1992-93 seasons. Host Wil Shriner introduced the inventors, who in turn demonstrated their ideas for a studio audience. We took selected inventions *outside* the studio and gave them a try with members of the unsuspecting public, who gave their opinions about the product. At the end of the show, the studio audience voted on their favorite idea, and the winning inventor received cash and prizes. In the show's final segment, an inventor who had developed a successful product explained to the audience how it grew from an idea to a reality. Like Arthur Fry, a 3M product researcher and church choir member, who came up with a winning idea in 1980 after bits of paper marking his place in the hymnal kept falling out. We know his invention as POST-IT NOTE PADS! I'll say it one more time, *"Why Didn't I Think of That?"*!

Hot Pursuit

When four young Canadian businessmen decided to attempt to sell a toy company on mass producing a parlor game they enjoyed playing with their friends, little did they know their game would eventually afford each the opportunity for early retirement in Barbados with a bank account for each in excess of 300 million dollars! *Trivial Pursuit* has fast become a part of our American culture. So it was with pride that Martindale-Hillier Entertainment was successful in acquiring the rights to create and produce a television version of this popular board game from Hasbro/Parker Brothers for The Family Channel. The straight-forward, easy to understand rules and questions immediately made it one of the most fun and entertaining game

Wink and another contestant enjoying his "15 minutes of fame" on *Trivial Pursuit.*

shows on cable television during 1993-94.

Game play: Three *Trivial Pursuit* contestants face-off in three rapid-fire rounds. For each correct answer, a wedge is illuminated on the game boards, and the first player with all 12 wedges wins and moves on to the bonus round.

Trivial Pursuit, the television show, was created to be the anchor of The Family Channel's daily game block. We called it TV's "hot pursuit" for trivia facts.

Interactivity

In addition to the classic game, we were asked by The Family Channel to round out the hour with television's first LIVE, REAL-TIME, play-at-home game show, *Trivial Pursuit—The Interactive Game.* Using touchtone telephones, viewers across America were given the opportunity to call in and compete for great prizes! Also, throughout the games on FAM, viewers were invited to call in and play our Trivial Pursuit Playbreak. Winners of the PlayBreaks during the three-hour game block then competed in a LIVE, INTERAC-TIVE national Trivial Pursuit Playoff every day.

To help kick off The Family Channel's entry into the

game show field mid-day, they asked us to create additional real-time interactive games with individual Playbreaks.

In *Boggle—The Interactive Game*, studio contestants and at-home viewers played by finding five words in a grid that resembled the telephone keypad. Each number and symbol on the keypad corresponded to a different letter. A clue was given for each word hidden in a grid. The player with the most correct answers in the shortest amount of time won. For example, if the clue was "home sweet home to a bee," the player would spell out the answer "hive" by pressing the appropriate numbers.

In *Shuffle—The Interactive Game*, studio contestants and at-home viewers played by selecting the correct order, chronologically, for a list of shuffled answers and pressing the corresponding numbers on their telephone keypad. For example, if the list was "1-aspirin," "2-false teeth," and "3-eye glasses," and the question was, "Which item came in use first?" the contestant would have 10 seconds to punch in number 2, "false teeth," the correct answer. After the top answer was revealed,

Boggle—The Interactive Game gave home viewers the opportunity to play at home, real time, on their touch-tone telephones to win cash and prizes.

the contestant would have five seconds to determine that number 3, "eye glasses," came into use next. Each game consisted of three lists and the contestant with the highest score, combining the most correct answers in the shortest amount of time was the winner.

In both shows, four studio players competed against one another to answer quickly—and accurately—each question. At the end of the first round, the three players with the highest scores moved on to the next round. One player was eliminated during the second round, leaving the final two contestants to compete in the last round for the grand prize. The viewers at home could take part through the interactive Playbreaks.

With these original shows, combined with classic hits such as *Let's Make A Deal* and *Name That Tune*, among others, The Family Channel made a giant stride toward capturing some the worldwide audience of over 58-million game players.

Wink in Debt . . .

"This show will do for you what MTV did for Tony Bennett!" Those words from the mouth of Disney producer Michael Davies caught my attention in a Tennessee minute! This particular afternoon in 1995, Michael had summoned me to his office to describe a new game in development by the Disney syndication and production arm, Buena Vista.

"The show is called *Debt*. It's truly a game show for the Nineties," Michael told me. And that it was. The show was one of the most exciting I had seen in a long time. On *Debt* players were matched by how much they owed on their student loans, mortgage and credit cards. Each correct answer to a pop-culture question whittled away the contestants' debt. For years I had given away cars, toasters, refrigerator/freezers and numerous other prizes on shows. But Michael pointed out to me that, "Today people already have those. Now they have to pay for them." Made sense to me! Paying off debt means more to most people than receiving cash or prizes. It's a sense of relief, like a burden lifted off a person's back. *Debt* seemed right for its time.

Michael Davies had picked a winner! Just four months after its 1996 debut, this show that gave its contestants a shot at winning their way out of real-life financial jeopardy became the Lifetime cable network's biggest hit series. There was a retro-hipness look to the show that appealed to young and old alike. In fact, the show was crafted to

look like a classic Fifties or Sixties game show. Add that to the fact that each show opened with me silhouetted in a *Saturday Night Fever* pose, carrying through that theme with tongue-in-cheek demeanor with categories to match. You felt a charm about the show that, personally, I had never experienced as a host or producer.

Wink strikes the familiar pose from *Saturday Night Fever* **that opened every** *Debt* **show on Lifetime.**

The *Debt* **security guard holds an attaché case full of cash as the show's winner decides whether to stop or continue to play.**

For example, try these categories on for size:

Larry King Geography

These are questions about U.S. capital cities. Each answer has to contain the city, state, and end with "Hello," just like Larry King says it on his talk show.

1. $100   Larry picks up the phone to talk to Ted in Georgia's capitol. I'm the city and state he gruffly announces.
                     Answer: **ATLANTA, GEORGIA . . . HELLO!**

2. $200   Scooter from Oregon's capital is dying to get on. I'm the city and state Larry snarls as picks up the phone.
                     Answer: **SALEM, OREGON . . . HELLO!**

THINGS THAT SOUND DIRTY BUT AREN'T

1. $200   I'm the most famous dice game in Las Vegas.
                     Answer: **CRAPS**

2. $100   I'm the breed of dog that's a cross between a poodle and a cocker spaniel.
                     Answer: **COCKAPOO**

3. $300   Nestled in the Andes between Bolivia and Peru, I'm the world's largest lake that big ships can still navigate.
                     Answer: **LAKE TITICACA**

Unique Concept

Debt had been designed to appeal to the largest and most dynamic segment of today's population: Baby Boomers (ages 30 - 49) and Baby Busters (ages 18 - 29). Together this group was nearly 130 million strong and made up nearly 50 percent of the total population. Plus, from the start, the show scored high in Lifetime's target demographic of women 18 - 49. These numbers made *Debt* a good alternative to talk and a prime show for first-run syndication, where the financial return to Disney would be the greatest.

In all the years I have been involved in game shows, I had never experienced the kind of press, publicity and promotion *Debt* received during its premiere season, 1996. This included a feature on the *NBC Nightly News* and a banner story in the financial section, Sunday edition, of the *New York Times*. Suddenly here was a game show, during

Award-winning song writer and producer David Foster with wife Linda (far right), and longtime Elvis friend Jerry Schilling enjoy an evening out with Wink and Sandy.

a period when the genre was overwhelmed by talk shows on television, that was the talk of the town, and on a cable network no less!

What was my take on why *Debt* took off like a rocket? It had all the elements of a successful game, most important of which might have been that all important moment when a player could either win everything, or lose it all—a moment where that person had to make a big financial decision. The game incorporated a compelling play-a-long factor. It was a classic elimination game, i.e. each round different than the one before. Plus the questions on *Debt* involved subjects we all knew about. These were things we might read about in the morning paper or see on the evening news. But most important of all, three players bringing their *REAL LIFE DEBT* to the show and competing to WIPE IT OUT!

"There has never been a game show quite like this," said Judy Girard, at the time senior vice president of programming and production, at the network's annual upfront presentation to advertisers where the program was unveiled. "We think the fun approach and the uniqueness of *Debt* will make it a popular choice with our viewers."

. . . and Out of Debt

I am asked to this day whatever happened to *Debt*. Why did it go off the air after only two seasons on Lifetime Cable? I have no definitive answer, but I do have several thoughts on the subject. First and foremost, while *Debt* was turning the genre on its ear in that premiere season, Disney could have made the show available to broadcast stations in first-run syndication. With its outstanding ratings and incredible amount of publicity, it had everything going for it. Although Lifetime had made a two-year deal for the show, that cable network is also owned by Disney. So had the hierachy so willed, two years on Lifetime could have become one.

Also the writing in year one was far superior to that of year two. A new Disney game show was waiting in the wings to premiere on Comedy Central, *Win Ben Stein's Money,* which incorporated a similar Q & A format to *Debt.* Good new writers for the type material needed for both these shows were few and far between, so it seemed the more qualified writers began writing for Ben Stein.

Looks as though Wink has found the perfect "contestant" on the set of *Tic-Tac-Dough,* circa 1979.

As host of *Debt,* I recognized early on in year two the difference in question and category quality. But in my view, with a great number of our staff attempting to produce our show while involved in pre-production of a second show on the adjoining stage, we had little chance to survive.

Indeed, after a hard-fought but futile daytime attempt to test *Debt* as a viable first-run syndication entry for Fall 1998 (using reruns seen several times already on Lifetime), the show, to no one's

During rehearsal of *Tic-Tac-Dough,* Wink is caught in a somewhat "thoughtful" moment!

surprise, was given the official pink slip by Disney. While it's true that every show eventually gets cancelled, I felt in the case of *Debt* it went down swinging prematurely. Here was a show with a definite *edge,* incorporating pop culture while paying off people's debts. Everybody could relate. Everybody could play. Personally speaking, saying goodbye to *Debt* was almost as difficult as saying hello to debt. For those who enjoyed the concept, I have a feeling this show will return someday to a better fate.

Good Pay, Good Hours, Good Service!

From my first network game show 'til now, as you read this, I can assure you I still enjoy my work. I love *hosting* shows for it's always fun to be recognized wherever I go. Getting good tables in restaurants is always nice. The pay is beyond my wildest dreams when I entered the business as a boy. The hours ain't bad either! But to have the opportunity to be involved in the development and the actual production of a show is indescribable. Having hosted many shows for several different producers was an excellent training ground, since you are exposed to all the elements it takes to make a good concept come together. It is somewhat similar to my years as a deejay being so helpful to me as a game show host, because radio work calls for constant ad libbing, teaching you the art of handling almost any situation on the spur of the moment.

These are the "golden dice" a winning contestant was given to roll during the bonus game of *High Rollers*.

And speaking of High Rollers . . .

So You Want to Own a Restaurant?

At sometime during my life I must have been extremely hungry with no place to turn for a square meal. Otherwise, why would I have harbored the insane idea of someday owning my own restaurant?

Whatever the reason, in 1982 my youngest brother David, by now a successful builder in Jackson, decided to join me in realizing another dream of mine. A dream that turned into a nightmare, that of building a family-style restaurant in our hometown. We would call it, what else, WINK MARTINDALE'S, in an attempt to take advantage of my new found notoriety thanks to the very successful run of *Tic-Tac-Dough*.

"Wink Martindale's" would prove to be Wink's most expensive "meal."

Since neither of us really knew anything about the business (our first mistake), we determined to overcome that by building our bistro by the book. The plan was to build a Victorian-type structure on a prime piece of property, hire our chef right out of the Culinary Institute in Hyde Park, New York, and with him carefully plan each item on the menu to conform to our original concept of family dining, which we felt would be perfect for Jackson, Tennessee, and fill a need that was lacking there.

This we did — to a point. We hired local architect Grady Barnes, the plans were drawn, the financial plan completed, and chef Bob Nichols (Keating Award winner from the Culinary Institute) was in place. All was in readiness to make Wink and David restaurateurs extraordinaire. But wait! Just before ground-breaking took place, during a trip to Memphis, I was told of a restaurant for sale in a "hot spot" of that city, Overton Square, and if we acted quickly perhaps we could buy it at the right price. It was just enough to whet my appetite to speed up our entry into this "can't miss" business of serving people their favorite meals.

Guess what! David and I did, indeed, "act quickly." As it turned out, too quickly for our own good! We dropped our well-conceived plans to open Wink Martindale's fam-

Hudson & Saleeby mug for the camera with country star Tanya Tucker.

ily restaurant in our home town, and purchased the former Mississippi River Company Restaurant in that Memphis hot spot. Had we done our homework, we would have known that the large and experienced ownership of Dobbs House Restaurants, the sellers, had closed their doors here after discovering Overton Square had already enjoyed its peak period as Memphis' place to go for action and discriminating dining.

Grand Opening

In our effort to do it right, our opening was as grand and special as we could make it. We hired one of the cities most reputable public relations firms, invited the city fathers, important business and political leaders, friends and family. Then opened our doors to a completely redecorated and if I may say, lovely Southern, pink tablecloth restaurant featuring continental and Southern cuisine that rivaled the other restaurants on the Square. But, as well as things began for us, as the months passed both David and I began to realize what a mistake it is to enter a domain about which you know very little.

Hudson & Saleeby

However, from start to finish, our gorgeous lounge was truly one of Memphis' most popular and talked about hot spots for late night entertainment. We had brought to the city a duo from Las Vegas — Hudson & Saleeby. We signed Chris and Doug to a multi-year contract and made our lounge their lounge, with custom signage that featured their names in lights on stage. They were an immediate hit! Had the restaurant side kept pace with the lounge, Wink Martindale's at Overton Square might still be humming today. You never knew who you might see there. It wasn't uncommon for celebrity performers to be found on stage with Hudson & Saleeby.

"The Killer" and Wink clown around on stage at the restaurant.

In spite of David putting his own construction and building business on hold in Jackson to oversee our food business 85 miles away, and despite Sandy and me taking over 50 flights from Los Angeles to Memphis during our first year of operation just to be there for some serious glad-handing with the customers, we constantly had to infuse more and more money into the operation just to keep the doors open. Our lounge business couldn't overcome the "other side." Sandy used to laughingly say, "Each night we gave a party for hundreds of people we didn't even know!"

The glamour of owning your own restaurant contrasts with the fact that running one is tough, considering all the hard work and constant problems. But, at the same time, the business can be very gratifying if, after making the place very comfortable and inviting, someone has really enjoyed their meal.

A Life of Fun and Games

The wake up call for me to stick with radio and television came on several different occasions. With every trip from L.A., Sandy and I used the same routine. After landing at the Memphis airport, we would rent a car and drive to Overton Square. It seemed odd that we would continually discover that another lounge employee would be driving a brand new automobile. That was disconcerting only because it was usually a better car than we were driving! But the straw that broke the proverbial camel's back came the night we discovered a key employee and lady friend on the floor of our main dining room at 3 a.m. sniffing lines of co-caine. Thus, about half-a-million dollars later my brother and I left the restaurant business to those who could spend twenty-five hours a day at it. We quietly stepped back into our respective careers, happy only with the fact that, at that stage in our lives, we could afford to take such a loss without it becoming a financial disaster.

Mary Vickery, Wink's second manager, flashes her patented smile with David Martindale.

One of the more pleasant sidelights of our brief sojourn into the world of food and fun was the many new friends we made. Suffice it to say there were hundreds and hundreds of regular customers who enjoyed our place, its food and atmosphere. One of my biggest laughs came one night as we were about to close the lounge. I happened to look towards the lobby and saw what seemingly was one of our large corn plants moving out the front door, complete with brass planter. Upon closer examination, I discovered a somewhat drunk bar patron with plant and planter in hand. Naturally I asked the obvious, "Where do you think you're going with that?" To which he replied, as best he

Doug Saleeby, Barry Manilow and Chris Hudson visit at Wink's during Barry's concert visit to Memphis.

could, "My wife asked me to bring home a souvenir from Wink's, and I thought she'd like this!"

Another joy during our many stays in Memphis during that period was the friendship of people like one of the top executives of Holiday Inn at the time, Bill Goforth and his wife Millie. They had taken us under their wing from the outset and supported us both personally and professionally. The week prior to the opening of the

Every night was New Year's Eve at Wink's— pictured with Wink and Sandy are friends Millie and Bill Goforth.

restaurant, they threw a big good luck party for us at their lovely home, inviting many friends who would become our best customers in coming months. Bill presented me that night with the following beautifully framed plaque, which read:

TOAST TO WINK

OH WINK! OH WINK!
We're tickled pink.
We think you've got a winner.
But we'll know for sure next week
After we've had our dinner.

OH WINK! OH WINK!
We pause to think
Of days before the glory.
A Jackson tyke, with broomstick mike
Begins our hero's story . . .

From there to dear old Jackson High
A quarterback and lefty.
You went to work for twenty-five bucks.
(In radioland—that's hefty!)

Then on to "WINK OF MARS PATROL."
(*Dance Party's* floors were packed.)
Then on L.A. and KHJ
Your "Deck of Cards" was stacked.

Then *WHAT'S THIS SONG?* came along,
Then *GAMBIT* — what a show!
And now you've bought a restaurant
With all your *tic-tac-dough*!

OH WINK! OH WINK!
We're tickled pink that Martindale's will be
A gathering place where friends like us
Can eat and drink for free!

Then there was Homer and Joyce Formby, at whose home in Germantown we were invited to stay during most every trip to Memphis. Sandy and I had made fast friends with this terrific twosome when Homer ("Nobody knows wood as good") was my guest while hosting the *Bob Braun Show* in Cincinnati in 1981. They were so special, and we still count them among our closest friends in life!

So you want to own a restaurant? I suggest you be a doctor, a lawyer, a teacher, a scientist, an astronaut, *ANYTHING* but the restaurant business. It's very time consuming — and sometimes, you're only as good as your last meal.

A Sad Ending

One final and sad thought to this chapter of my life. Less than ten years after we closed the doors to Wink Martindale's Restaurant, my partner

Wood finishing guru Homer Formby, and wife Joyce, opened their home to Wink and Sandy during numerous visits to Wink's restaurant.

and youngest brother David suffered a brain aneurysm in 1990. Although he was a good person of abnormally good health, this came suddenly and without warning. He lay in a comatose state at Madison County General Hospital in Jackson for about six months, before he died. He was only 47 and at the height of his career as one of Jackson's most prominent builders and civic leaders. He left his wife Lynn and two sons, Jeff and Rich, college graduates, married and parents themselves. Lynn remarried in 1997. We all miss David very much. But I know he would be proud of Lynn, and his boys. His legacy, through them, will live forever.

Chapter Six

WHOOPS!

Game Show's Embarrassing Moments

J ust as there were game shows on radio long before television came along, by the same token there were radio bloopers prior to those of the television variety. The first person to ever create a successful *business* out of human boners on radio, then television, was an enterprising guy named Kermit Schafer. During the thirties he began collecting slips-of-the-tongue that he heard when every show was *live.* Somebody asked him once if people became angry when he pointed out their mistakes. Kermit said, "For the most part their feelings are best summed up in the immortal words of Mark Twain, who said, 'I am never more tickled than when I laugh at myself!' "

One of the most famous of all radio bloopers came from the mouth of famous announcer Harry Von Zell: "Ladies and gentlemen, the President of the United States, Hoobert Heever!" One of my favorites happened when the announcer was in-

Kermit Schafer, who came up with the idea of marketing radio and television's most famous boners in a series of albums, *Pardon My Blooper!*

troducing the great banjoist Eddie Peabody: "Ladies and gentlemen, Mr. Eddie Playbody willl now *pee* for you!" Or how about the football play-by-play announcer who actually said, "He's at the 40 . . . the 50 . . . the 60 . . . *look at that sonofabitch run!*" Also the sportscaster who said, "Yankee catcher Yogi Berra was hit in the head by a pitched ball. X-Rays of the head showed nothing!"

Believe it or not, even on radio we had weathermen: "That's the weather from Anchorage. Now I'll take a *leak* out the window to see if it's freezing outside our studio." Here's a part of a local commercial: "And Friday night is poultry night. All ladies present will receive a free goose!" A newscaster said this within his lead story: "The collision of the two boats was due to the fog, which was thick as sea poop!" Another radio commercial that received extra-special attention: "Visit our coin-o-matic laundry. All ladies who drop off their clothing will receive prompt attention!" I'll bet they did!

Creating Special Moments

Obviously, even when professional comedians mis-spoke, they seldom did it on purpose. But arguably, some of our biggest radio laughs were "at," not "with," those committing goofs. But with the emergence of game shows on television, producers learned to create those *special moments* by providing celebrities with several possible "answers" to true-false, yes-no questions. This method of *creating* comedy made a mediocre show into a hit. Cases in point: Host Peter Marshall to Paul Lynde: "Paul, what's the one thing 'Dear Abby' says you should never do in bed?" From his familiar perch squarely in the center of the *Hollywood Squares*, Paul answers, "Point and laugh!" And the audience did just that!

The long-time "Master" of
Hollywood Squares,
Peter Marshall.

Monkey Business

Another time, another show, Peter asks: "Paul, will anything bring tears to a monkey's eyes?" Another example of why comic Lynde was paid the big bucks, he replies, "Learning that Tarzan 'swings' both ways!" Or how about this one: Peter: "Paul, can the puppies in a litter come from different daddies?" Without hesitation Paul fires back, "Why, that bitch!"

Peter Marshall was "Master" of the "Squares," but Paul Lynde was unquestionably, "The Master Square."

Hollywood Squares will go down in game show history alongside such long-running hits as *The Price Is Right, Let's Make A Deal, What's My Line? Password, I've Got A Secret, Concentration, You Bet Your Life*, and *Match Game,* among several other qualifiers, as TV's funniest. Producer Merrill Heatter introduced what would later become *Hollywood Squares*, as NBC's *People Will Talk* in 1963, an opinion show featuring 15 players and host Dennis James. The show didn't work, and following its cancellation by the network, Merrill took advantage of the show's final month on the air to tape an on-the-air pilot for another show, which he sold to CBS as *The Celebrity Game*, hosted by Carl Reiner. It was this show that gave Merrill, and partner Bob Quigley, the idea for a human *Tic-Tac-Toe*, piloted at CBS with Bert Parks as host, but rejected and picked up by NBC with host Peter Marshall. By 1971, *Squares* was television's highest rated game show and ran as originally formatted for 14-1/2 years. Not bad for a reject, huh?

In a touch of irony, Paul Lynde, who was without question the funniest of all the occupants in the coveted center square, was on neither the first *nor* the last show taped. Ernie Borgnine was in the center square on the first show, and George Gobel the last. But for countless shows in between, Paul gave the *Squares* viewers some of their biggest laughs! Peter: "According to the food editor of the *Dallas Morning News*,

Producers Merrill Heatter and Bob Quigley came up with the idea for a human *Tic-Tac-Toe* **game. Here we see their megabucks idea in action, including the three most popular celebs to play** *Hollywood Squares* **. . . Paul Lynde, Wally Cox and Charley Weaver.**

what's the best reason for pounding meat?" Paul: "Oh — loneliness!" Or, how about this one? Peter: "According to the book, *The Encyclopedia of Fairies*, who's generally better looking — a pixie, or a fairy?" Paul: "Looks aren't everything!" Then, in Paul's all-so-familiar style, he made his expected choice: "I'll go for the fairy!"

The loveable Charlie Weaver (from Mount Idy) was another long-time regular in the bottom-left square who gave us some of the most memorable retorts to Peter's questions. "When properly dressed in a kilt, what should a Scotsman tuck in his stocking?" Charlie: "Is he a very *big* Scotsman?" Or how about this one. "Charles, how many balls would you expect to find on a billiard table?" Charlie: "How many guys are playing?"

A "Very Brady" Answer

On the same subject, Peter's question to *The Brady Bunch* mother Florence Henderson was: "Will humming help your tennis game?" Florence: "Sure. It's suppose to take your mind off your . . . balls . . . or something like that!"

And remember gentleman George Gobel? He proved another perfect "square" for the show, for you never knew what to expect. "For $200— George — according to archaeologists, True or False? A 'pea' can last 5,000 years." George smiled and with that familiar slow drawl replied, in all seriousness, "Boy, sometimes it sure seems like it!"

Long-time actor/comedian Charlie Weaver really hit it big as the pride of Mount Idy on *Hollywood Squares.*

As a star of *M*A*S*H*, McLean Stephenson became a semi-regular on *Hollywood Squares*, because he, too, had the perfect sense of humor suited to the show. Peter: "In the *Bible*, McLean, what was so unusual about Balaam's ass?" McLean, always one to play the question to the hilt, paused, chuckled a bit and said, "Oh sure," as if to say, "Where am I suppose to go with *this* question?" Then he ad libbed, "Nice ass, Balaam!" The audience roared, not knowing what was to come. McLean then requested of Peter, "Could I call it a donkey now,

so we can be sure to get this part in?" Peter assured him that would be acceptable. So McLean explained, "Balaam's donkey was the one Joseph and Mary borrowed to go to Bethlehem to have their baby Jesus." To this the contestant agreed. But Peter said, "No, that's incorrect McLean. Balaam's ass could actually *talk*! A talking ass!" To which McLean blurted out, "Your ass it could talk!"

Celebrity Straight Man

Here's another award-winning Q&A between Peter Marshall and McLain Stephenson on *Squares*. Peter: "Listen carefully McLean. True or False? In 1912, the King of Denmark married the Queen of Norway. Today, one of their children is the King of Sweden and another is the Prince of Finland, and the third gives saxaphone lessons in Philadelphia." Never one to be thwarted, McLean's very serious answer was, "That sounds incredible, and people can laugh and snicker all they will. But what's *more* unique about what you said, Peter, is that one time, the King of Denmark *WAS* the Queen of Norway!" Never a dull moment when McLean sat in a cubicle.

Popular singer/actor John Davidson followed Peter Marshall as Host [Master] of the *Hollywood Squares.*

Peter Marshall, a seasoned performer on Broadway who fell into the job of "Master" of the *Hollywood Squares* almost by accident, was the perfect straight man for the celebrities. His timing was perfection in dealing with his stars. But most important was his innate sense of just how far to let them go with their remarks. Remember, the network Standards and Practices Departments were much stricter then than they are today. Another example of why: Peter, to comedian Marty Allen, "You're from Pittsburgh, right?" Marty answered in the affirmative. Peter then asked, "Okay. Tell me, what does a person from Philadelphia dunk his pretzel in?" Marty: "A girl from New Jersey!"

A favorite *Hollywood Square* Marty Allen with show's producers, Merrill Heatter and Bob Quigley.

Shaved by the Censors

Finally, Peter to John Davidson (who later became host of *Squares*): "John, traditionally, Japanese brides used to shave something off at the time of their marriage. What?" John, with a sort of smirk on his face, repeated the question to himself as if giving this unusual tradition deep thought. Then he said, "— Must be hair — off some part of the body . . . h-m-m-m — where could it be?" Then almost as a side comment, John said, "On the whole — I would say . . . "

Before even *he* realized what he'd said, the audience let him know in a heartbeat with their uproarous laughter. It was one of the funniest moments ever on *Hollywood Squares,* which, like most of the others printed here, never made it past the censors.

Canadian native Wayne Cox was the affable host of Wink's *2nd Honeymoon* on CBN.

We're Talking Money

Second Honeymoon was a family show, where kids of all ages, making up three different families, answered questions about their parents in an effort to win them a second honeymoon. It was my wife Sandy's idea, to show how much kids knew about their folks by virtue of having lived under the same roof for a number of years. But never in her wildest dreams did she foresee 7-year-old Kevin and brother 8-year-old Christopher in the following dialogue with host Wayne Cox.

Wayne: "Kids, Mom has just caught you flushing her expensive perfume down the toilet. She's threatened you with 'You're gonna get it when your father gets home!' What will your dad do when he gets home? Will your dad, 1) Give it to you, just like Mom said he would? 2) Yell at Mom for not punishing you when you should have been punished? 3) Dad won't do anything, 'cause he *never* does anything?" The older, and obviously wiser Christopher takes the lead with, "If it was expensive perfume (I know it is 'cause Mom always gets that stuff) . . . he would really give it to us." Host Wayne says, "Oooh — how does Dad 'really give it to ya' when he 'gives it to ya'?" The younger Kevin admits, "He yells at us!" Then Christopher goes a step further, saying, "He beats us!" Kevin disagrees. "He does not beat us!" But big brother

Chris will not be outdone, making the revelation on television that, "He does so! He gets out the belt, Kevin. Whack! Whack!" Kevin again disagrees, saying, "He would just ground us. He wouldn't *hit*

Host Wayne Cox and three families prepare to begin another episode of *2nd Honeymoon.*

us." Then Christopher, in an attempt to prove motivation, replied "Expensive perfume, Kevin! Money! We're talking money!" Kevin still wouldn't agree with his big brother. "Remember when we gave away his expensive aftershave? He didn't beat us—he just grounded us!" But Christopher, with the last word, fired back, "He beat *ME!*"

You can imagine the parents' reaction when they came back onstage and were confronted with Kevin and Christopher's eye-opening discussion about Dad's methods of handling dire situations on the homefront. Remember Art Linkletter's book, *Kid's Say the Darndest Things?* Well, believe it. I was there!

Come on . . . *Down!*

If you've heard about this one, stop me! For it is one of the most chronicled laughs in the history of game shows! To me, Bob Barker is the quintessential game show host. Nobody does it better. Perhaps that's because, in Bob's own words, "I set out to do what I am doing. I've never wanted to do anything else. What I do, the essence of it, is to make my living making other people funny. Ralph Edwards told me that I do game shows like Jack Benny did comedy. I have that kind of timing."

In all of Bob's 43 years on television, 28 as host of *The Price Is Right*, it is doubtful that talent, timing *or* minute planning could have

prevented what happened one day at CBS when announcer Johnny Olson was cued to tell the next contestant to "Come on down!" She did all right. In every sense of the word. A very attractive young woman wearing a skimpy, baby blue halter top, took Johnny at his word and literally flew out of her seat —as well as her halter top—and continued her run down the isle to greet the impeccable Mr. Barker. Un-

Bob Barker, the dean of game show hosts with 28 years at the helm of "The Price Is Right."

daunted, though uncovered, she simply completed a nip here and a tuck there and was ready to make her first bid! No problem. Bob, ever the pro, never skipped a beat.

The most famous announcer in game show history, Johnny Olson.

(Left to right) Henry Morgan, Bill Cullen, (host) Garry Moore, (on ladder) Bess Myerson, and Betsy Palmer trumpet the new days and time for their *I've Got a Secret* panel show on CBS.

On another occasion, when Johnny announced, "Come on down. You're the next player on *The Price Is Right*," not one but TWO people ran down the isle— they *both* had the exact same name.

One of the most popular and longest-running game shows, *I've Got A Secret*, was derived from the old parlor game "Secret, Secret, Who's Got the Secret." Each week, four celebrity panelists tried to determine the secret of each contestant, much like an attorney cross examining a witness. Each panelist had 30 seconds to quiz and then guess the secret. Contestants were awarded cash based on their ability to stump the panel, made up of people like Bill Cullen, Jayne Meadows, Henry Morgan, Betsy Palmer, Faye Emerson, Steve Allen and Bess Myerson. Incidentally, the first celebrity guest was Boris Karloff, whose secret was, "I am afraid of mice!"

How many of us remember the night that two brothers, one 9, the other 4, strode on stage for *I've Got A Secret,* sat down on either side of moderator Garry Moore, and, in turn, whispered their secrets in his ear. "I collected 40 different kinds of bugs for my school project," revealed the 9-year-old. Then added the little guy: "I ate them all." Their "secrets" were flashed on a screen out of sight of the panel. The studio audience roared! Predictably, the four panelists failed to guess the youngsters' secrets.

Big Blowhard

Then there was the contestant whose secret was that he could blow up and explode a full-sized inner tube using only his own lung power, in two minutes. But he refused to demonstrate before the show, because he was afraid he'd "blow himself out." Came the show and the contestant began to blow—and blow—and blow. After three minutes, Garry Moore urged him to give it up. After four minutes, the cameras cut away for a commercial, returning to him two minutes

Host Jack Bailey asks one of his thousands of television hopefuls, "Would *YOU* like to be *Queen for a Day?*"

later to find him red-faced and bug-eyed but still blowing away. Finally, 30 seconds before sign-off, and after nine full minutes of blowing, the tube exploded— with such force that the man was propelled several feet to the rear and landed flat on his back. Andy Griffith, guest celebrity that night, never got the chance to reveal his secret 'cause everybody on the show just sat back to watch what did eventually happen! But hey, the guy was in show biz for nine minutes!

Bob Eubanks, host of the long-running hit, *The Newlywed Game* on ABC and in first-run syndication.

Queen For a Day started on radio in 1945, and debuted on NBC Television 11 years later. Each day four or five women would plead their special case as to why one should be chosen "Queen." The show was a real tear-jerker, but there were some rare times when emcee Jack Bailey and the audience enjoyed a good laugh. Like when he asked one of the competing ladies what she wanted if selected *Queen For a Day.*

Sandy was working for Bob Eubank's *Concert Express*, when she and Wink were first dating.

With a straight face she said, "Twin beds more than anything else, because my doctor said I should take it easy!"

Bob Eubanks, the man who has asked more embarrassing questions than anyone else in the history of TV doesn't even crack a smile when asking one of his perennials, "Where's the strangest place you ever made whoopee?" Bob says, "That's a personal question. I don't answer personal questions!" Yet he's currently writing a book based on that very question to celebrities. I know

(Left) The lovely Arlene Francis and (right) publisher Bennett Cerf, make their entrances on *What's My Line?* long a Sunday night staple on CBS.

'cause he called Sandy and me just last week. We didn't have an answer either. But on *The Newlywed Game* one night, a husband shocked even Bob Eubanks, when he answered Bob's favorite question with the reply, "The butt, Bob!"

One of my idols when growing up hoping for a career in radio and television, was Arthur Godfrey—in my view the greatest natural salesman television has ever seen. But aside from that inherent talent, perhaps his memory was not always what it should have been, for there was the night Mr. Godfrey almost forgot. He had just showered and stretched out on his sofa to watch TV when the announcer said, "Stay tuned to *What's My Line?*" "Oh my God," said Godfrey, jumping up and reaching for his clothes. "I'm tonight's mystery guest!" He arrived just in time to make the show.

They Got Wind of It

What's My Line? was network television's longest-running game show with a broadcast run of over 17-1/2 years. Of course the concept was simple: four celebrities trying to guess the unusual occupation or product of guest contestants. There were some memorable moments on the show, like the night they guessed Frances, the Talking Mule. The show's staff had carefully wrapped her hoofs in burlap. But when the wind shifted, the secret was out! But how about the night no one guessed Bob Hope? It soon became obvious to the panel that the mystery guest was a comedian, but the *real* joke was on Hope when the quartet blithely named everybody *but* him. Bob's ego had been seriously damaged. He was furious, until it was obvious that the otherwise astute panel was doing it all in fun.

Speaking of fun, the show's final mystery guest was the moderator himself, John Charles Daly, who kept moving back and forth between two seats to answer the panel's questions. But perhaps one of the

Gene Rayburn with panelists Peggy Cass, Joanne Carson, Bennett Cerf and later host Wally Bruner get ready to play *What's My Line?*

most interesting of all the shows was the night the mystery guest was *such* a mystery the panel never even bothered to put on blindfolds. *Nobody* recognized the governor of Georgia, Jimmy Carter, in 1974, just one year before he ran for president. Finally, it seems that when a professional makes a pizza, he flips the dough into the air, twirling it as he does, so that it will spin out flat as it comes down. With an expert doing the flipping, it is rather a pretty thing to watch. With amateurs handling the dough it can be quite otherwise. During a panelist pizza-making lesson, Gene Rayburn flipped his dough so high it caught in the overhead studio lights and never did come down. Who knows, Gene's pizza dough may still be hanging up there from a 5kw spotlight in the upper reaches of Studio 8H at NBC.

"Gamey" Game Shows

Speaking of Gene, his proudest moments came as host of *The Match Game*, where two teams, each composed of a celebrity guest and two studio contestants, tried to match answers to a question for cash prizes. The fact is, *Hollywood Squares* and *Match Game* were two very similar shows, as both featured celebrities who cracked jokes, and both

A seemingly serious Dick Clark explains the rules of *The $10,000 Pyramid.*

featured contestants trying to guess how the celeb would respond. The show hit the air in 1962, went off the air in 1969, but returned in 1973 as a downright raucous, risque comedy game show. And in this format, Gene Rayburn was in his element, with celebrity regulars like Richard Dawson, Brett Somers, and Charles Nelson Reilly. Gene reveled in those risque moments provided by contestants, too. Case in point: "Time to meet another player now. It's with a great deal of pleasure we present Karen Lescoff." A fairly mundane introduction, right? But Gene's follow-up comment as the applause died down, provided one of the most used game show bloopers over the years. Rather than saying, "She has very pretty dimples, doesn't she?" Gene mis-spoke by saying, "She has very pretty nipples, doesn't she?" Donohue was so amused with this clip that when several of us appeared with him in a salute to game show hosts, Phil played that clip three times.

Actors Clifton Davis and Anita Gillette surround host Bill Cullen on the "$25,000 Pyramid."

There have been many famous moments on the various incarnations of *Pyramid*. But perhaps the most memorable one came on *$25,000 Pyramid*, starring Bill Cullen. Actress Anita Gillette went slightly overboard listing "Things that are stiff." Her answer was bleeped.

A Dollar Earned

On a less erotic note, Jack Benny, one of America's comedic treasures, had not one but two classic moments on two different game shows. As a gag, Jack guested on *The $64,000 Question,* hosted by his CBS compatriot Hal March. The format dictated that with every correct answer the contestant won a certain amount of money until the final level of $64,000 had been reached. Hal introduces "Mr. Thrift" to an adoring television audience of millions, instructing Jack how to play the game. When he learns a possible $64,000 jackpot is at stake he was beside himself! "Let's play . . . let's play . . . I'm losing money the longer we wait!" screamed Jack. When a new contestant was introduced, the first question was always extremely easy and was always worth—$1.00! Hal asks the first question; Jack answers correctly. Fine. We're off to a great start. When asked the required, "Do you want to stop now, keep your dollar, or continue to the next level?" Jack Benny (as only he could do) looked at the one dollar bill in his hand, then stared blankly into the camera while the audience was going wild, and predictably uttered the words, "I'll stop!" He proudly put the dollar in his pocket, threw his head back, and slowly walked off stage.

With a bank account that rivaled that of John D. Rockerfeller, comedian Jack Benny was known as being 39 and a "miser!"

Another memorable and classic Benny moment occurred on the set of the 1962 version of *Password*, hosted by the late Allen Ludden. Came time for Jack to give the clue to his contestant partner. The password was "Cheap"! Everybody in the audience was falling down with laughter. Jack stared at his fellow contestant, seemingly for an eternity—and finally gave his clue—"Me." The contestant *immediately* snapped back, "Miser"!

Elephant Drop

Long before Bob Barker took the reins of *The Price Is Right*, the irrepressible Bill Cullen hosted the show for nine years, 1956-1965.

Host Bill Cullen was one of the most glib and talented game show hosts in the history of television. But here he seems to be asking himself, "Where's the guy who thought it was a good idea to invite this elephant on *The Price Is Right*."

Like Bob, gamemeister Bill lived through a few anxious moments on the show as well. One of the *most* anxious came during 1958 when all the shows were aired LIVE. While contestants were bidding on a real live elephant, the pachyderm felt nature's call, answering that call in front of millions of television viewers. Elephant or no, when you gotta go, you gotta go.

Art James, host of *Say When!!* never again liked peanut butter after his disastrous live commercial on the show.

Goober Blooper

Art James hosted several classic shows over the years. Among them, *Concentration, Who, What or Where Game, Pay Cards!* and his first solid hit, Goodson-Todman's *Say When!!* in 1962, on CBS. It was during this LIVE taping of the show when Art's favorite blooper took place. While he was doing a commercial for Skippy Peanut Butter, Art was saying how easily it spread on bread and crackers. When he finished, he placed his knife back into the glass jar. It went right through the bottom of the jar. Seems the hot studio lights had turned the sponsor's product into liquid peanut lava! It went all over his hand, his arm, his leg and his shoes. But being the smooth talking host that he is, Art simply smiled, laughed at the situation, licked the peanut butter off his fingers and said, "The show must go on!" And it did.

We never knew what to expect when Jaye P. Morgan was a judge on Chuck Barris' *The Gong Show!*

A Jaye Exposé

Popular game show panelist/singer Jaye P. Morgan hit a high note with television viewers during an episode of Chuck Barris' *Gong Show* one night in 1977. You will recall that Chuck loved his celebrity judges to take an *active* role while the various acts were performing. Jaye P. loved to participate, but this particular night one of the acts must have really turned her on. Suddenly, without warning, she bared her breasts to the studio and television audience! It was never determined just why she did this—perhaps she was just proud! From that day forward, it seemed the show's ratings always showed a gain when Jaye P. Morgan was a judge.

Television's big dealer for many years, host / creator / producer Monty Hall on *Let's Make a Deal.*

During the Seventies, one of the most popular shows on the air was *Let's Make a Deal,* hosted to sheer perfection by its creator/emcee, Monty Hall. On this show, contestants wore outlandish outfits in the hope that they would catch Monty's eye as he searched for contestants on the trading floor. This day, Monty happened to choose a somewhat husky lady who ended up winning the "big deal of the day." She showed her pleasure and excitement by literally picking Monty up and giving him a big bear hug. In doing so, she did two things. She picked him up at least three feet off the ground — and she cracked one rib! Monty went on with the show, but it was the first and last time he ever let a lady award him with a bear hug, if he could avoid it.

Host Allen Ludden strikes that familiar pose, and tells Lucille Ball that the clue she just gave her contestant partner on *Password,* unfortunately, is unacceptable!

Gaffes and Laughs

I'll end by laughing at myself! When hosting a game show one must fight the tendency to lose concentration. Otherwise, disaster can be looming. Once when taping an episode of *Tic-Tac-Dough*, the category was "Famous Movies." I showed a contestant a picture of Roger Moore surrounded by a group of beautiful women. "Name this James Bond movie released in the summer of 1983," was my question. "In the summer of '83?" the contestant asked, making sure he heard me correctly. To which I replied, "Wrong. The name of the picture is 'Octopussy!'"

Through all the goofs and gaffes, turning bloopers into laughs, somehow we all have persevered. The hosts I've mentioned here, and some I haven't, have become part of the fabric of American television, as important to the instrument as rabbit ears, or the 19-inch screen. We are all part of a very special club — and proud of that membership.

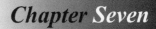

Chapter Seven

THE SANDY STORY
The Second Time Around

Following my divorce from Madelyn, I had strong misgivings and gross feelings of guilt. We had been together since high school days and eighteen years of marriage. We brought four children into the world, a bond we shall share for the rest of our lives. And though our marriage failed, we still remain friends to this day. For that I am very happy for it makes our relationship with the children so much more harmonious.

Madelyn remarried within about a year after our divorce became final. For me it would be almost five years before I would enter into my second marriage. Not surprisingly, the introduction to my future bride came about in a most unlikely manner, at a most unlikely place and in a somewhat unlikely way.

As sadly as 1971 had ended, 1972 would turn out to be a year I would never forget. I began the year living in the Villa Lorena apartments, two rooms, one frying pan, and a car. That was about it for me.

But things began to take a definite turn for the better when I won the position as mid-day deejay on the pride of Gene Autry's television and broadcasting empire in Los Angeles, KMPC. Just as twenty years before when I realized my dream of working at WHBQ in Memphis, I enjoyed a similar feeling. KMPC was one of the most popular addresses on the radio dial in the entire country. Known as the "Station Of The Stars," its stable included such popular personalities as morning man Dick Whittinghill, Geoff Edwards (later to host several game shows for Chuck Barris and Bob Stewart) and popular *Laugh-In* announcer Gary Owens, among others. It was another of my dreams come true in radio.

Sandy and Wink do the Twist in the KMPC parking lot during their *Pacific Ocean Park Dance Party Reunion* in 1978.

This would also be the year I won the job as host of *Gambit* on CBS. The show was a television version of the card game "blackjack," created

Wink and Sandy return to Gene Autry's Palm Springs Hotel, and the table where they met in 1971.

and produced by game show icons Merrill Heatter and Bob Quigley, the same team who would later give us the original *Hollywood Squares*, with the hysterically funny Paul Lynde, the native son of Mt. Idy, Charlie Weaver, and hosted by the master of the squares, Peter Marshall. *Gambit* enjoyed a run of almost five years before succumbing to its counterpart on NBC, *Wheel of Fortune*. But it would be just the first of several shows I had the pleasure of hosting for Heatter-Quigley Productions, namely *High Rollers, The Last Word,* and a later incarnation of *Gambit, Las Vegas Gambit,* from the Tropicana Hotel.

Bob Noah, Wink's *Gambit* producer, asks for quiet! "Genius at work."

Poolside "Action"

One Sunday in '72 our crack KMPC traffic reporter, Herb Green, allowed my buddy Mike Schmidt and me to hitch a ride with him to Palm Springs. I was scheduled to complete an industrial film for General Telephone that afternoon, but we arrived an hour early. So Mike and I killed some time by checking out the pool action at the Gene Autry Hotel.

As we walked by the hotel coffee shop, unknown to my friend and me, Teri Brown, a long time acquaintance of mine (and niece of bandleader Les Brown) was enjoying lunch with her friend, Sandy Ferra. Teri asked, "Wasn't that Wink Martindale who just walked by"? Sandy replied, "No. Wink Martindale's an older guy with a bunch of kids!" Obviously Teri turned out to be the more accurate of the two. Having

struck out at the pool, Mike and I walked into the coffee shop, saw these two lovely ladies and joined them at their table. The girls happened to be in the Springs as hostesses for an annual music business golf tournament.

Oddly enough I spent most of the time chatting with Teri while Mike talked to Sandy. About a week later Teri called Sandy and said, "You'll never guess who just called me for your phone

Sandy and Wink visit their favorite getaway— romantic Hawaii! Can you tell?

number. Wink Martindale!" Our first date was to have been a double with a *Dance Party* regular from my Pacific Ocean Park days Karen Samson, and her date TV newsman Bill Smith. While Sandy, Karen and I enjoyed our memorable evening together at the Chart House in Malibu, Bill got fogged in on Catalina Island and never did arrive. So I was left to pick up the check! But it was the beginning of a long and close friendship that flourishes to this day.

Maui Memories

Thus my plan to become an active member of the dating scene following my divorce came to a screeching halt. Sandy and I became almost inseparable. One would seldom be seen without the other. We went everywhere and did everything together. Our first trip as a team took us to Kapalua,

Mary Lou Ferra, the mom, casts an adoring eye at the bride, daughter Sandy.

Maui twenty-six years ago. And to this day Maui remains our number one destination when the subject of vacation time arises. At one time we owned a Golf Villa at Kapalua but after seven years, when our friends and business aquaintances enjoyed its use more than our average of two or three weeks per year, we decided to forego the condo for the more luxurious and enjoyable Four Seasons room service.

As our relationship together grew and became more and more serious I was happy to see that my children were drawn to Sandy. Naturally this was very important to me. In fact, over the years she and Madelyn have enjoyed a pleasant friendship as well.

During our entire dating period Sandy had worked as a talent coordinator for Bob Eubanks' *Concert Express* (the Bob Eubanks who hosted *Newlywed Game*). In addition to booking the Beatles' first tour in this country, Bob's company managed Merle Haggard, Barbara Mandrell, Dolly Parton and others. Before hitting superstardom, Dolly was introduced to Las Vegas the very first time by Sandy, who accompanied her.

Never Looked Back

It was during one of Sandy's business trips to Nashville for *Concert Express* that my loneliness got the best of me. I called Sandy and said, "When you get back home I'm going to see this doesn't happen again"! Without question it was my way of proposing. And we've never looked back.

We were married in a fabulous ceremony at Arcadia Presbyterian Church, August 2, 1975, with our dear friend, the Reverend Jack Longley officiating. (Ever since, the vanity plates on my car have been 2Aug75, while Sandy's have been Ms. Wink.) For our honeymoon we took a two week cruise to the Caribbean. We returned home to our first

Sandy and Wink made friends for life on their Caribbean Honeymoon cruise—Howard and Audrey Rosenberg, Beverly and Bob Chell.

house, a model home we had purchased in the Palisades Highlands of Pacific Palisades, complete with all the furniture, right down to the daily china on the kitchen table! Remember, I was starting with just a frying pan! We needed *everything.*

About three years later, and after beginning a seemingly successful and lengthy run of *Tic-Tac-Dough*, we sold our "dream house" (more like a doll house) in favor of a beautiful condominium, part of a gate-guarded complex called Century Hill, being built in Century City. Our friend Darrell

Howe took the reins and guided us through the decoration process, giving us a jewel of a condo in one of the nicest areas of Los Angeles, adjacent to Beverly Hills, Rodeo Drive, and all its shops. We felt we would live there forever. Until . . . .

During my first marriage the kids would always razz me about constantly being on the move. In truth I have always harbored a penchant to grow tired of

The cozy kitchen/den of Wink and Sandy's first home together in Pacific Palisades—1975.

the same residence. So, as regular as a clock, they would say, "Dad. Five years are up. When do we move?" Well, I thought I had grown out of that mode! Then came roughly five years in the Palisades home, five years in Century Hill, and wouldn't you know it! Along comes a friend of Darrell Howe's, Bill O'Connor, who had built several homes in a

Sandy feeds Wink a scallion in their Malibu kitchen.

valley of Malibu called Serra Retreat. The homes were much too large for our needs and much more expensive than I ever thought reasonable to pay for the right to lay your head on a pillow. But Mr. O'Connor made us an offer we couldn't refuse. So two million dollars and a big

Their vows having been repeated on their 10th anniversary, Wink says "Time to party!"

mortgage later, here we were: Sandy, Wink, our Yorkshire terrier Gambit, our two chihuahuas, Mr. Bumper and Miss Stumper, plus Gypsy, our cat.

Vows Renewed

For the most part we enjoyed our days under the mission at Malibu. Our fondest memories were of those times on weekends when all the kids, grandkids and friends would gather for swimming and tennis. Really special times! But the biggest and best memory of them all?

The celebration of our tenth wedding anniversary. This party was in the planning stage for over a year, and everybody had a ball. Over four hundred guests came to witness Sandy and me reaffirm our wedding vows that hot August night in 1985, including Reverend Jack Longley,who by now had left Arcadia Presbyterian church for a pastorate in San Jose.

Sandy had the house decorated to the nines, thanks to our long-time housekeeper and friend Naomi Suarez, and our

Rev. Jack Longley from San Jose officiated at "both" weddings—1975 and 1985.

flower power genius, Delores Cantu West. The backyard, gazebo and tennis court (carpeted for dinner) were a virtual cornucopia of color, thanks to Delores and our nursery god in heaven, the late Don McKenzie. After dinner and during dancing, Danny Thomas took the microphone and proceded to act as emcee for the evening, asking various celebrity friends to come up and offer either words or a song. Barry "The Voice" White sang Billy Joel's "Just The Way You Are" and brought down the house. Singer/impressionist extraordinaire Fred Travalena brought the past five presidents to life, and that was a killer! Especially his Richard Nixon!

The Five-Year Itch

About four years after that unforgettable celebration, almost predictably, it happened again. The realtor for actor George C. (*Patton*) Scott knocked on our door and asked if we would be interested in selling our house to George and his wife, actress Trish Van Devere. They had been planning to buy a home in Montecito, CA, near Santa Barbara, but decided it was a bit too far from LA., happened to see our home in Serra Retreat and made us another offer we couldn't refuse. Done deal! Besides the Malibu lifestyle had begun to get to us, with its perilous Pacific Coast Highway, which during summer months was so busy with beach traffic we were practically prisoners in our own home. Our time there had been fun, but the calendar showed our five years were up.

Naomi Suarez, Wink and Sandy's housekeeper for over 15 years, babysits the Chihuahuas in limo on the way to a TV appearance.

We settled into a comfortable apartment/ condo in Westwood for the next six years, all the while searching for a home that we both agreed would be our final purchase. Moving was a drag under the best of circumstances and already we had amassed enough junk (uh, possessions according to Sandy) to fill two private storage facilities (which we still have). Upon leaving Malibu we felt it best to give Gypsy a new home, but our puppy family, with Gambit and the five chi-

The Martindales are truly content in their English Tudor Calabasas home.

huahuas totaled six. So our quarters were a bit cramped. After a while they too became anxious to get more running room than just a concrete runway outside our kitchen!

Sadly little Gambit, our 14-year-old Silkie who was our pride and joy and probably had more airline miles to his credit than many people, passed on to doggie heaven before we found his new environs. Sandy insisted we have him cremated. He's still with us in spirit, and in a pretty urn in our home. A home that turned out to be in a lovely gate-guarded bedroom community called Mountain View Estates, Calabasas. Wherever we looked in our search for a new and permanent place to drop anchor, we kept going back to this place. Now after seven years, Sandy still says that when the white gates open and we drive through them, it's her earthly paradise akin to heaven.

Their silkie "Gambit" brightened Wink and Sandy's life for 14 years.

A Bit of Heaven

Our home was privately built, and unlike most of the other Mediterranan style homes where we live, it is the only English Tudor home in the community. And we love it. I'm well past my self imposed "five year rule" and see no reason to leave. Perhaps I have grown up in more ways that even I can imagine. As is often the case in this day and age our personal and business offices are combined at home which is nice. It means we hit the freeways for points outside our gates *only* when necessary. Lots to be said for that lifestyle. Call it having paid one's dues or whatever. I think at this time in our lives we deserve it!

In 1997 we converted one of our bedrooms into a radio studio so I might record my daily "Music Of Your Life" radio shows within the comfortable surroundings of

Sandy's Dad, Tony Ferra, enjoys a dance at his daughter's wedding.

home. All my life I had gone to a radio station to do my show. Now I could jump out of bed at 5 or 6 AM, and if it suited my fancy, could knock out an hour or two of my show, stop for breakfast, business calls, do an interview, discuss plans for the evening with Sandy — whatever, then jump back into the studio and complete the final third hour of my show. Without ever leaving the house. Life is good!

The Balance of My Life

The *Music of Your Life* is a 24-hour, seven-day-a-week radio network syndicated to almost 300 stations around the country and featuring music of the Forties, Fifties, Sixties, and Seventies. Frankly it's the only music I know . . . I remember . . . I understand, and can talk about with some measure of authority. Fortunately I retained my many interviews from 12 years at KMPC, and I frequently draw non-dated, biographical sound bytes from them, which I use to surround a song by a Neil Diamond or a Perry Como or a Peggy Lee or any one of hundreds of past guests.

I am often asked which I like better, radio or television. The truth is radio goes back to my roots. From my Sunday School teacher's first radio job at WPLI in Jackson, Tennessee, at age seventeen, seldom has there been a time when I was not engaged in producing a radio program for a radio employer. The financial rewards have been greater for me in television and the medium no doubt served to better and more quickly introduce me to the viewing public. But the truth is, one so complemented the other that I cannot imagine my professional life without both.

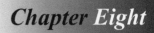

Chapter Eight

TALKING A GOOD GAME:

Conversations with . . .

O ne of the great residual benefits of my job in radio and television over the past 45 years has been the opportunity to meet
and speak with show business personalities that I would *never*
have met had I pursued any other line of work. And since music, in
various forms, has been so much a part of my life, I would like to share
with you some random moments from various conversations with
favorite people.

The Seventies came to be known as the "me" decade because people
"did their own thing." They "let it all hang out!" Men wore hair down
to their shoulders, women joined the work force in record numbers and
little girls joined The Little League. We scurried to see *The Godfather,*
while on Broadway, *A Chorus Line* sold out *forever*! On television *All
In The Family* was king of the small tube. VCRs and cable TV were
revolutionizing our viewing habits (and still are)!

Specifically, in 1972 Fischer played non-chess first, then beat
Spassky for the world title. Governor Wallace, of Alabama, was
almost assassinated. In Washington, DC, five men were arrested
for the infamous break-in at the Democratic National Committee
offices at the Watergate Hotel, and Congress considered the
Women's Rights Amendment.

Bette Midler—Changing Musical Taste

Bette Midler was feeling her oats as she hit the record charts the week of December 23, 1972, with a re-make of Bobby Freeman's "Do You Want to Dance," from her debut album *The Divine Miss M*. After that she made the Top Ten with her *second* single, a hit for the Andrews Sisters in 1941, "Boogie Woogie Bugle Boy," which was appropriate for this lady born in Patterson, New Jersey but raised in Hawaii, for she has always been a *student* of popular music. I found her philosophy most interesting as to why people desire constant change in their music from era to era and from decade to decade.

Bette: "I think it all works together. I think each thing gives the other thing a push. I think the best two examples of that, the examples that are most clear, would be Elvis Presley and The Beatles. Of course, Elvis got his thing, took his thing from other things that were going down. But he, himself, caused a great social change. From those changes we went into something else. Then the Beatles came and brought a change, forced a change. Then the music started changing, and life started changing. Things became free, and people were talking about love and peace and happiness, and all those things. It was like the first time that it had occurred to this nation. So that forced the music into another direction, too. I feel like I'm an historian sometimes, ya' know. Like I'm a big catalog of popular music. I can listen to almost any kind of popular music, and get the same feeling that people would get if they were listening to it back then."

Prior to her movie career, Bette Midler lets Wink know that "Miss M is *growing!*"

Ever since Bette Midler burst on the scene in '72 she's been compared to everybody from Tiny Tim to Mae West, from Barbra Streisand to Janis Joplin. But comparisons have never bothered Bette: "Well, I think people feel a necessity to pigeonhole me. They have to put a label on me, 'cause otherwise they wouldn't be happy. You know, they'd be uncomfortable. As long as they say 'she's this and she's that and the other thing,' then they can relax and enjoy it. But if they're sitting there trying to pick it all out, then they get nervous and agitated! It frustrates them. I try not to put labels on anyone because I feel a label limits you, ya' know. And a label does not allow you to grow. And honey, Miss M is *growing!*" Was she ever.

Eventually came hit movies like *Down and Out in Beverly Hills*, *The Rose*, and finally *Beaches* in 1989, for which she sang a song near the end of the film, a song that went to Number 1, won the Grammy for Song of the Year and Record of the Year. That song was "Wind Beneath My Wings."

The Glen Campbell Phenomenon

Instantaneous stardom is not unusual in rock 'n' roll ranks. But the way to the top in pop, and country and western music usually calls for many, many years of seasoning. Perhaps this accounts for the smooth showmanship of many first-rank popular and country artists. So when youthful Glen Campbell became a national favorite in 1967, he'd served an apprenticeship going back quite a ways. By the late Fifties Glen was ready for Hollywood, but was Hollywood ready for him? The answer, as he soon found out, was a resounding *YES*! His skill as a 12-string guitarist led to many offers for studio work. Glen: "I learned a

Glen Campbell, shown here during his stormy relationship with Tanya Tucker (to his left) and friends. Sandy and Wink Martindale (right).

great deal in the studios. One year, from the middle of '63 to the middle of '64, I kept track of the sessions I did; 586 recording sessions! Out of those, I think about three of 'em were hits.

"When the session work started, I didn't think there was that much money in the whole world, 'cause the first year I think I made something like 35 or 40 thousand dollars in the studios. I said that's unbelievable! When I did 'Strangers in the Night' with Sinatra, I was the end guitar player sitting within three feet of Frank. I was petrified 'cause I'd been such a big fan of his. He's just fantastic. And after running the song down two or three times, I knew it. I'd be looking at Frank, and everytime he'd look over toward me, I'd cut my eyes back to the music. Finally Frank said to Jimmy Bowen, who was producing the session, 'Who's the gay guitar player over there on the end? He keeps looking at me!' "

Real stardom for the young man from Delight, Arkansas arrived in 1967 on the wings of a song John Hartford had written, "Gentle On My Mind." Glen said, "The first time I heard it I was driving up Laurel Canyon. I got so involved in the words that I almost went over one of the curves there!" Later that same year Glen recorded a bona fide *national* hit, written by 21-year-old Jim Webb. "I was doing a session with the group called The Association at Western Studios, and they had a Johnny Rivers album on the wall they'd done about six months before that. I was lookin' at it and the title caught my eye, 'By the Time I Get to Phoenix.' I didn't know if it meant 'risin' from the ashes' or what!" He soon found out.

Glen Campbell has a natural feel for playing country and bluegrass music. "It was really

Pat, Shirley and all the Boone girls stopped by KMPC as Wink reviewed Pat's singing career.

something I grew up with, Wink, more than something I acquired. Actually I grew up with all kinds of music, 'cause when you play the joints . . . well, back in my early days back in Arkansas and Houston was strictly country stuff, then when I got to New Mexico and worked in my uncle's band, he played everything from 'Rose Room' to 'Tumbling Tumbleweeds' to 'Come To Jesus' in A-flat. Therefore, I got a pretty good lesson in all kinds of music." And that's where the training I guess, came from. That's why I like all kinds of music today. To me, we shouldn't segregate music. There's really just *two* kinds of music.

Good music, and bad music."

"Rhinstone Cowboy" has become more associated with Glen than "Phoenix," "Gentle On My Mind," or any of the early hits. "I love what the song said. The lines that hooked me on 'Rhinestone Cowboy' in the first verse said, 'there's *been* a load of compromising, on the road to my horizon.' The second verse says, 'there'll *be* a load of compromising, on the road to my horizon.' And so I accept that, and just try to get my compromises in order. Things I want to compromise with, things I can live with that are honest, that are right, that are good." Sadly, the story of Glen Campbell's compromises with drugs and alcohol, causing failed marriages and career damage, have been well documented in his own autobiography. But as a professed born-again Christian and with his present wife Kim as his guiding light, Glen has turned both his life and career around.

Henry Mancini's 20 Grammies!

He was the son of an Italian immigrant steelworker; raised in Aliquippa, Pennsylvania. The title for his biography, written in 1989, asked the question a songwriter for movies might predictably ask of the audience: *Did They Mention the Music?* Well, in the case of Henry Mancini, nominated eighteen times for an Academy Award, the answer was always a predictable, *"Yes!"* One of my most revered interviews was with this great composer, who gave us theme music for more than a dozen TV shows, scored more than 80 films and picked up 20 Grammys. I asked him why movie scores had changed so much since the

Wink and Henry Mancini during visit at KMPC.

days of "Laura," "My Foolish Heart," and "Gone With The Wind."

Henry: "Well the reason for the change is that in the early movies, there was a certain *total sound* of movie music that was almost directly out of Europe. They normally did not play the contemporary pictures with contemporary music of that period. They would have a kind of classical approach to it. Now, in a contemporary picture, everybody is so wise to what's going on around them."

Who would Henry Mancini name as the greatest composer of all-time? "As far as popular composers go, I think I would have to go with George Gershwin, and it's very unfortunate that he died when he did because I think he was really on the threshold of — he was just starting to go, you know — with all the things he had done. He was getting into bigger forms. By far, I would say he is the biggest of the popular writers."

Andy Williams, whose recording of Henry's "Moon River" sold millions of copies and be-

Andy Williams joins Wink in admiring Andy's award-winning LP "Moon River and Other Movie Themes."

came Andy's signature theme (as well as the name of his giant theatre complex in Branson, Missouri), calls Mancini "the greatest songwriter since Irving Berlin, and the nicest man I ever knew!" Everything began to jell for Henry Mancini the day he walked out of the Universal Studio's commissary and ran into producer Blake Edwards, who asked Hank if he'd be interested in scoring a television series called *Peter Gunn* (which he initially thought was to be a *Western*). Did the success of the series come as a surprise? "I knew we were on to something different by the various vibrations you get in Hollywood when something is happening good. It gets around and you hear from it, people will mention something. If they don't like something, they don't talk about it. They can find a million ways to avoid talking about a bad picture that your friend just did. I was assigned to "that thing" (*Peter Gunn*) and I just did it, I did it with the knowledge I had at the time. And it worked!"

The most humorous story I recall Henry telling me was about the time he went home to West Alaquippa for "Henry Mancini Day," long after his was a household name. Amid all the excitement surrounding him, he ran into an old classmate who said, "Hi Henry! It's good to see you after all this time. Where ya' been? Whatcha' been doin' lately?" Obviously the man hadn't listened to the radio or gone to a movie in a while! This prolific and innovative composer, arranger and conductor, who gave the world memorable, elegant music for its movies ranging from the *Pink Panther* comedies and cartoons to the classic about alcoholism, *Days of Wine and Roses*, died Tuesday, June 14, 1994, only four months after being diagnosed with pancreatic and liver cancer. We are less rich now, but the melodies will linger.

Neil Diamond and the "Diamond Rush"

On January 24, 1848, James W. Marshall discovered gold near Coloma, California. That discovery touched off what came to be known as the "Gold Rush." On that same date, 95 years later, in 1943, a man was born in Brooklyn's Coney Island section. That birth touched off what later might be known as the "Diamond Rush." The name "Diamond" is easy to remember by itself. But add the first name "Neil" and it becomes ingrained! I first saw the paradox we know as Neil Diamond in the early seventies at The Troubadour on Santa Monica Boulevard in Los Angeles, a small club famous for introducing future stars. You just knew he had the magic appeal of a superstar. Hit after hit followed. In the last few years he hasn't hit on that single which is attracting the *contemporary hit radio* station. And while album sales have tapered off, they don't explain why he is such a phenomenal concert draw. The widely held opinion for Neil's success is that he appeals to such a wide range of fans. It's not just women over 40, it's everybody 25 to 55. For his audience, there's no other artist like him. The only comparable performer is Barbra Streisand. As an admirer and a fan, I jumped at the chance to sit and talk to this somewhat "solitary man."

The Gift of a Guitar

Memories of his youth?

Neil: "Well, Coney Island has to be the most fantastic place in the world for a kid to grow up, 'cause it's all rides, it's all amusement with an enormous amusement center. It was at *that* time, and it was fantastic. It was always like Christmas. But we moved when I was about 10 to an area that was less than what Coney Island had been to me. It was a very rough, poor section of Brooklyn. We lived on top of a shop. Those were very tough years, when I was 10 to about 16 when I started to write."

His writing was enhanced when, on his 16th birthday, Neil Diamond received a life-altering present: "I got a guitar as a gift, and I started to play it. One of those nine-dollar models that 'eat' your fingers away and warp in about a week. I took lessons for a coupla' weeks, then the instructor made an error and taught me to play a chord progression, and I wrote my first song. I never went back to take lessons.

Australian lovely Olivia Newton-John paid Wink a visit to talk about her 1981 smash "Let's Get Physical."

I just wrote all the time after that." And that he did! Our pop culture is the richer for it.

Wink: "Were songs such as 'Brother Love's Traveling Salvation Show' that reflect knowledge of the deep South a result of playing concerts there?"

Neil: "Yeah, that was really the only exposure I had to the deep South, which left the strongest impression on me, because I had been a relatively sheltered person, living in New York. Never traveled anywhere. I enjoyed it though. I think it's a very passionate area. I mean their passions run high. They hate you and they love you. There are still all those social things that are going on down there, but I think they're coming out of it. The young people are coming out of it. The vibrations I get in the audiences down there among the kids is that they're not tied to their parents' generation as much. I think a lot of good things are gonna happen down there."

Unforgettable Nat "King" Cole!

It was titled *Nat "King" Cole: An Intimate Biography*, written by Nat's widow, Maria. When I received a call asking if I'd like to interview her, I jumped at the opportunity. Times changed, record audiences changed, other performers became stars and were forgotten, but Nat Cole continued steadily along year after year, hit after hit. He was loved as perhaps few singers were loved, by his fans and by his peers. Singer Joe Williams: "He was an integral part of my life. So when I sing a song like 'Nature Boy' I get a little misty. I hope that he's in me. Part of him is in me."

Los Angeles Dodger broadcaster Vin Scully: "I remember sitting on the floor of his suite with Jack Leonard in San Francisco. They were playing the latest album, I think it was *Wild Is Love*. I could not believe I was sitting with this genius and listening to this syrupy voice knowing that in a coupla' hours he would be at the ballpark screaming at an umpire."

Dick Clark: "I think Nat fit into the changing music scene of the fifties as well as any popular music artist, because it was then acceptable among young people to adore black performers (that is, the white listener). Nat was always accepted by both races. Kids loved his music, too."

Maria: "Nat and I were a team. We *really were* a team. What I didn't know, he knew, and what he didn't know, I knew. He was a very tolerant man, while I was not too tolerant. He was a very sweet man."

The story of Nat "King" Cole had begun with a skinny, four-year-old boy being pushed onto the stage of a Chicago theatre to play "Yes, We Have No Bananas" on the piano. It ended in a hospital room in Santa Monica, California, into which poured messages of prayer and hope from all over the world. In the 41-year interval between his first public performance and his death from cancer in 1963, Nat Cole, the minister's son, became a friend of presidents, a star of stage, screen, radio and television — truly the singing idol of much of the world.

Maria: "I read somewhere once that when you judge someone, you should weigh their accomplishments and then assess them. And I tell you, I feel that my husband, in his *field*, accomplished more than anyone in that field, as a human being. We all know, and I'm sure the records will certainly say, that he was a great, great artist. Good entertainer — a great jazz musician. I like to think that his accomplishments went way beyond that. As far as I'm concerned, he's in a class, in a different way in *his* field, with Ellington, with Jackie Robinson (it's sad that these people I mention are gone). But these were all great people, and I think Nat Cole belongs in that class. And he never would have stopped working. Nat was like Jack Benny. He would have just worked and worked, until — I think he would have even worked more than Frank (Sinatra) did because he loved the people. He wanted them to love him so much."

Wink realized a dream when he met Nat "King" Cole (with daughter Natalie) at a 1959 Hollywood movie premiere.

He Helped Us Fall in Love

Wink: "Maria, Nat died of lung cancer. Did he know, when he was hospitalized, how gravely ill he was?" "He never let anyone know if he did. He never said anything to me, except when they started giving him the cobalt treatments. I was in the room one day and he mentioned (this was when he still wasn't feeling too

Wink, with Nat's widow Maria, a friendship that began with Wink's reading of her book, *Nat "King" Cole: An Intimate Biography.*

badly) 'Hey Skees' (he called me 'Skees'). He said, 'Ya know, they've got something new they give you, something called cobalt.' I looked at him dumbfounded! I couldn't believe that Nat had never read anything about tumors, or cobalt treatments, or something of that sort. He just knew nothing about it whatsoever. And I don't think until the very end that he ever really accepted it. Then I think it was just a couple of days before his death that he stopped fighting. He used to go down to the chapel and pray, until he couldn't walk. And, even after he couldn't walk, the nurses said for awhile he would go down in his wheelchair until he just couldn't make it at all. A couple of days before he died, my sister had him in the wheelchair, and we took him out for a ride. When we came back, he was waiting for them to fix the room up for him, and he was looking out over the mountains; he just looked up at her and touched her hand and said, 'Turn me away.' "

When I concluded this three-day audiobiography, I received more calls and letters than for anything I had ever done during my radio career. I had grown up living, loving, and yes, even falling in love to the songs of Nat Cole. I had the pleasure of meeting this man only once. But I recall so well my feelings that night in the forecourt of Grauman's Chinese Theatre in Hollywood, the summer of 1959. I had shaken the hand of a true giant of the entertainment world, and I knew it.

I concluded my comments on the radio Special by stating, unequivocally, that if I ever came back in another life, and was given the gift of song, I would wish for a voice like Nat "King" Cole.

Manilow's Miracle

"If you want to know the truth, I don't consider myself a singer," Barry Manilow said. "I consider myself a musician. The singing is just a vehicle; that's why I don't like to classify myself as a 'ballad-eer' or an 'up-tempo' singer, because I don't consider myself a singer in the first place. The reason that I did this [began a singing career] was because I enjoyed making records, not because I wanted to become a singer or get up in front of 2,000 people and entertain. That was the only way, however, that I was going to be able to continue to make records. If I'd promise to go out on the road and perform the stuff, Clive Davis said he'd give me a record contract, and I wanted to be in the studio so badly that I thought, Okay, I'll go out on the road!" Not bad for a singer who didn't care to be a singer.

I can't help but think back to a telephone conversation I had with Barry Manilow right after "Mandy" and "It's A Miracle" had helped further solidify Barry's new found success as our "King of Pop." His third album had just been released, and he had high hopes that people would like this latest effort as much as they had the first two. While he had reservations, he mentioned the one title that would soon become the nation's number one hit and his trademark for all time.

Check the resemblance between Barry Manilow (right) and Doug Saleeby (of Hudson & Saleeby). Barry was visiting Wink's Memphis restaurant.

Barry: "Well, it's a combination of a few songs I've written and a few songs that I've found . . . that Clive Davis, the president of my record company found. I think the closest thing to a single is going to be a tune called "I Write the Songs," which I didn't write! It was written by Bruce Johnston of The Beachboys, and it's a real hot song." Needless to say, he was right.

Years of Hits from Tony Bennett

Wink: "Some singers survive for decades on a single hit record. That's happened time and time again. Few singers have come up with more than a dozen new standards. Crosby did it, Sinatra did it, Nat Cole did it, Fred Astaire did it in pictures, and of course Tony Bennett pulled it off. Some songs you were first to record. Others you brought back into circulation. It has to give you a good feeling to know your performance of certain songs have made standards of those songs."

Tony: "Oh, it definitely does. It's filled my heart and soul with good music. I just hope I can always keep doing this. It's something I love to do."

Wink: "Do you subscribe to the theory that a little voice exercising should be practiced every day?"

Tony: "Yes I do. I think that after you've had good training from a good teacher that you should do at least 20 minutes a day of woodshedding."

Wink: "You have enjoyed quite a resurgence in popularity, especially among the young people watching MTV on a regular basis. You have said that today's average teenager, given the chance to enjoy all kinds of music, will like your kind of song, as has been proven."

Wink and Roberta Flack are all smiles thanks to the success of her all-time favorite single, "First Time Ever I Saw Your Face."

Tony: "I just think that the advertisers kind of insist that to make a quick buck they're always insisting that this is *your* music. They still use the old Alan Freed disc-jockey attitude of sublimating the teenager's mind by saying this is your music, and there isn't any other kind of music except this for you. But actually the music business is full of all kinds great sounds — the hills are alive with the sound of music! There's all kinds of music, and the best of it is classical music. So there's a spectrum out there. I think it would be healthier for the whole music business, for every radio and television station and every record company, to advertise the fact that there's all kinds of music, instead of just *one type* of music."

Tony Bennett also said the non-creative people in our business oftentimes make the most influential decisions impacting an artist's life. "Well, it just seems to be the greed of society. I mean, it's a proven fact that when the *un*creative tell the creative what to do, it stops becoming art, and this becomes a heck of a problem because the producer should respect the artist and just say, well 'We have you Mr. Ellington, now please create for us.' "

Wink: "Are you enjoying the business as much as ever?" Tony: "Yes, I love it. I have an awful lot of fun. Most important, I love the public!" You know what? It shows!

Wink and Johnny Rivers remember the beginning of Johnny's career at the Sunset Strip's Whiskey A-Go-Go.

Ella Fitzgerald . . . in a Class by Herself

Her ear was said to be so exact that musicians could tune their instruments by her voice. Her phrasing close to perfection; her voice with a clarity of tone beyond compare. Her style so cogent that she was once called the "Hemingway of singers." She was one of a few in her field — Judy, Sammy, Frank, Elvis, recognizable by just her first name — ELLA. A 16-year-old Ella Fitzgerald first took the stage, not as a singer but as a dancer. She was gripped with such stage fright that her legs simply refused to function, and instead she sang a song titled "Judy." It won her a first prize, twenty-five dollars! Dancing's loss was our gain.

In 1956, while rock was beginning with a truckdriver from Memphis singing "Hound Dog"— Ike was beating Adlai, *again*, and while Grace Kelly was marrying Prince Ranier of Monaco in the show biz wedding of the century, Ella

The "first lady of song" Ella Fitzgerald (upper right) on the bandstand in Harlem's famous Savoy Ballroom singing with Chick Webb's band. Webb was her mentor.

was making a landmark album of show music, *Ella Fitzgerald Sings the Cole Porter Songbook*. It became such a colossal success that other songbooks followed in fast succession; those of Duke Ellington, Harold Arlen, Rodgers and Hart, Irving Berlin and George and Ira Gershwin. Bing Crosby once said of this first lady of song, "Man, woman, or child, Ella's the greatest."

"All the pictures you see on the walls here are those I feel are very close to me," Ella said as she gave me a guided tour of her home in Beverly Hills, ending with a "Wall of Fame" in her den.

Ella: "Down here we have Pearl Bailey, who I call Sis, and myself. And here's Frank. I love this picture, not the smiling Frank, but the one that sings. The pensive Frank Sinatra! Of course here is Miss Dinah Shore, and of course on top here, you see Nat."

Wink: "I notice Nat 'King' Cole has front and center position."

Ella: "Right!"

Wink: "Would you read the inscription for me?"

Ella: "To Ella, you are the greatest. Best of luck to you, always. Nat."

Wink: "And over here is a very famous actor."

Ella: "That's right, Cary Grant."

Wink: "Why Cary Grant, Ella?"

Ella: "I don't know. I just always admired him and when I met him he was so warm and so friendly that I just took to him. I always admired his work, and I never thought I would meet him person-to-person. Then I found out that he was a fan of mine. Everywhere we would play, even in Europe, he would come to see me. And this is Sassy, Sarah Vaughn. I love her. I love her."

I can honestly say that I was in total awe of this marvelous lady and her God-given talents. My visit to her home was another moment in time I shall remember with great love for the rest of my life.

Steve and Eydie — Together, Wherever

As Ella's dancing had led to singing, Sidney Leibowitz's piano accompanment work for his vocalist brother Bernie led to Sidney becoming a singer as well. He adopted the names of his nephews, *Steve* and *Lawrence*, and won first prize on *Arthur Godfrey's Talent Scouts*. In July 1953, while we were flocking to the movies to see *From Here To Eternity, Can-Can* on Broadway, and hearing everything from "Dragnet" to "Doggie in the Window" on radio, Steve Allen was picking a young Mr. Lawrence over 50 other applicants to be a regular performer on his local New York TV variety show, which evolved into the origi-

Steve and Eydie remind Wink it's a tough job he has, but somebody's gotta' do it!

nal *Tonight Show* on NBC. This is where Steve met Eydie Gorme, a meeting that led to the altar in 1957. Since their union those many years ago, Steve and Eydie have personified class and artistic genius through their records and live concerts.

Could they even *imagine* working alone again? Steve: "Wink it would be very difficult for us to go back working alone now because . . ." Eydie: "It would be dull!" Steve: "It's so much nicer when there's somebody there to bounce off. Like in Vegas, the clock is at the other end—we get to bed, like at six in the morning—I sleep a little later in the morning than Eydie, or go to the steam room and come back. Sometimes, the first time I will have seen her that day will be on stage, or in the dressing room. We really haven't had a chance to talk too much. She'll start talking to me on the stage like I'm the audience. I'll have to remind her sometimes, 'Could we discuss this later? We have a show to do!' And she'll say 'But I didn't see you.' And sometimes some funny things come outa that. It's much more enjoyable when there's somebody else there."

Eydie: "It's more like a job when you're alone. You're just out there doing your thing. When we're together it's a lot less like work. I really hate to say it, but we really enjoy it. It's really a lot of fun."

Anyone who has not seen this fabulous couple "do their thing," live on stage, is depriving him or herself of seeing a unique and talented act. They are without doubt, one-of-a-kind!

Vic Damone's "Elevator" Career

"I can't even remember saying, 'Well this is going to be my life. I'm going to make singing my profession.' It was only after hearing a Frank Sinatra record, while he was still with Tommy Dorsey, that I decided I'd like to sing."

The Damone family arrived in America shortly after the First World War. Vic was born Vito Farinola, June 12, 1928, and his career was another that followed a roller-coaster ride so common to show business. He was a star by nineteen, then went into eclipse for several years before making a comeback around 1960. He began as an usher at New York's famed Paramount Theatre, and when he was boosted to elevator operator, the move helped change his life.

A young and handsome Vic Damone, at the height of his career as one of America's premiere popular singers.

One day while between floors, Vic mustered enough intestinal fortitude to mention to an already famous barber-turned-singer that he, too, would like to pursue singing. Vic: "I said, 'Mr. Como, I would love your opinion. I think I can sing. I can't afford it, but I'm taking singing lessons. But I would like to sing for *you*, even if just a couple of bars. If I could sing for you, and if you could just tell me if I'm wasting my time. He said, 'Go ahead kid.' And he just sorta leaned back in the elevator and I started singing." And he's been singing ever since, with one of the purest singing voices of them all.

The year was 1962. The world mopped its brow when Khrushchev backed down and removed his missiles from Cuba. John Glenn went up for three orbits. James Meredith enrolled as the first African-American at

Veteran actor Carroll O'Connor with Wink.

Ole Miss. Marilyn Monroe took an overdose of sleeping pills. Albee's *Who's Afraid of Virginia Woolf* enthralled Broadway with four-letter words. TV hypochondriacs confirmed symptoms with *Dr. Kildare* and *Ben Casey*. The ex-Veep bade farewell to politics, telling newsmen, "You won't have Nixon to kick around anymore." The Twist took off like a tornado around the world. "Good-Luck Charm" by Elvis, his 17th number-one record, would be his *last* for 7-1/2 years! Singles sold at 98 cents and albums were $3.98 (mono) and $4.98 (stereo). New names on the charts were Peter, Paul and

Mary, the Beach Boys and Herb Alpert, whose "Lonely Bull" was recorded in his West Hollywood garage at a total cost of $65! It was the start of a billion-dollar record company.

"Mellow" Mathis

A New York statistician once reported that the music of Johnny Mathis was responsible for 1.5 million baby births during 1962. Johnny is listed as the #8 all-time best seller of albums. Thirty-one of his singles have hit the Top 40 and eighteen the Top 10. After releasing over 100 albums, he's earned 60 gold and platinum record awards.

Wink: "After all these years, does Johnny Mathis have to work up the enthusiasm and emotion it takes to perform as many concert dates as you do each year?"

Johnny: "Oh sure, Wink. I start thinking about my performance the minute my eyes open in the morning. And, physically, I do some exercises and what have you. I *don't* like to vocalize very much. In fact, I heard Beverly Sills, one of my favorite singers of all time, say that she didn't like to vocalize either. She just did some physical exercises, because there's an edge to your voice that you lose if you vocalize too much."

Wink and Johnny backstage at a '93 concert at Harrah's, Lake Tahoe.

Johnny and I clicked as friends when we first met in 1960. He never failed, whenever possible, to answer our call to appear on the *POP Dance Party*. When *Laugh-In* announcer Gary Owens and I were colleagues at KMPC in Los Angeles, Johnny invited us to his home for dinner, to prepare and serve one of his famous gourmet meals. He admitted to us that he was so nervous about feeding us something we'd like, he prepared *three* different entrees! Another one of those unforgettable evenings! To return the favor, right after Sandy and I were married in 1975, Johnny was one of our very first dinner guests. Like Johnny, Sandy was nervous about what to prepare for this gourmet. She even bought a beau-

Wink checks the mail from his "Most Popular Singer" contest on KMPC. (The winner . . . Johnny Mathis.)

tiful new tablecloth, and all the placecards read, "To Johnny, with love." My Italian bride's mom, Mary Lou, was enlisted to ensure that our pasta entree was "just right." Just before Johnny was to arrive, I noticed a small camera on the table by Sandy's plate, and I asked her about it. "You are not going to embarrass us by taking pictures!" But, sure enough, when Johnny arrived with our longtime mutual friends, George and Tess Russell, and he saw the picture-perfect table, his response was, "How beautiful! Before we mess it up, can't we take a picture of it?" Sandy looked at me, beaming. We took dozens of pictures that night, to my wife's delight. Incidentally, the dinner received rave reviews from our guests.

After all his years of success, Johnny told me he finally has total control of his life, and is happier than ever. "I get to do what I want to, when I want to, and I know I'm very fortunate to be able to say that. And I'm very grateful that this is the truth."

If any performer today deserves "living legend" status, it is Johnny Mathis. It's hard to believe that Johnny, who has been called by many, "The World's Greatest Living Romantic Singer," and his rich, velvet sound has been delighting listeners since 1957.

Kirk Douglas wrote: "Years ago, I heard Johnny sing 'It's Not For

Neil Sedaka celebrates with Wink his pop comeback, "Laughter In The Rain."

Me to Say' in a Greenwich Village night club. I loved his voice and hired him for a little movie, *Lizzie*, that my company was producing. He tried out three songs, and we picked 'It's Not For Me To Say.' The movie was a flop — the song and Johnny Mathis were a hit! He has been a big hit ever since. Congratulations!"

These have been but a few random comments from over 200 interviews: from Paul Anka to Neil Sedaka; from Roberta Flack to Olivia Newton-John; from the Righteous Brothers to Richard Rodgers — and countless artists in between. I feel fortunate to have shared a mike with many of the most outstanding performers of the past 50 years. They enriched my life.

Talking a Good Game

Chapter Nine

GIVING SOMETHING BACK

A Tradition of Caring

"**Winston, God gave you that wonderful voice. Why don't you think about becoming a preacher?**" That was a question I heard often from my mother. Of course, my reply was predictable. "Mother, one must receive a *calling* to enter the ministry." I'm not sure Mom ever really understood my reasoning, just as she never understood why I would want to leave Tennessee to pursue my career in California. But short of entering the ministry, and having been raised in a Christian home, I was taught that it was far better to give than to receive. Over the years, I have attempted to give of my time and energies to those charitable causes close to my heart. There is a word for this uniquely American tradition—volunteerism. This is an area I feel very strongly about.

Volunteerism had its roots in the bucket brigades, barn raisings, and quilting bees that characterized community life in the colonies. It grew into organized societies of every size and purpose. Today volunteerism is bigger than our ancestors ever dreamed it could be. As many as five-million volunteer organizations exist in the United States alone. A Gallup poll showed that half of all American adults and teens practice some form of volunteerism. The commitment even stretches *beyond* our borders into a troubled world. Without question, we all can feel a certain pride in our voluntary efforts. But improving our society entails a lot more than pride in past accomplishments. Only participation can make the real difference in our lives. That has always been my belief, and I have tried to hold fast to it.

Why do we support causes we believe in? Cynics would have us believe that the most important reason is to save taxes. And, while that is certainly a good reason, those who have studied charitable motivations tell us that other reasons take precedence: *Commitment to a particular cause.* Albert Schweitzer is an outstanding example of this. His reverence for life

Brothers David and Kenneth Pose with Wink and his Mom on the porch of their homeplace on Burkett Street in Jackson,

caused him to give up a promising theological, medical, and musical career in Europe to become a medical missionary in the jungles of Africa. *Desire to share.* We like to give something back, and let others participate in our good fortune. In so doing, we deservedly gain recognition. *Personal satisfaction.* This reason involves the pure enjoyment of helping others, magnified by the heart-warming gratitude of those who have benefitted. These are the primary reasons we give so generously of our time, our talents, and our money.

Leo, Cokey, Wink, Jr., Sandy and Wink Martindale and a St. Jude official in front of the original St. Jude Hospital entrance.

Personally, *my* main influences and motives for helping others could be traced back to my upbringing. I was witness to my mom always reaching out to others, often doing without, herself, in her efforts to assist those in need. Then as I reached a certain celebrity status and was asked to participate in various and sundry charitable causes, I quickly found it necessary to balance my work schedule with the time left to take part in those charity endeavors closest to my heart; St. Jude Children's Research Hospital in Memphis, Tennessee, and the West Tennessee Cerebral Palsy Center in my hometown, Jackson, Tennessee. In truth, the fact that both of these facilities are located in my home state is unrelated to Sandy's and my association with them. First, St. Jude Hospital.

A Prayer and a Promise

St. Jude Children's Research Hospital was the result of a promise founder Danny Thomas made to St. Jude, Saint of Impossible Causes, during his years of struggle to carve a place for himself as a comic and singer. His promise was simple, and made on a night in Chicago when he was desperately in need of a job to put food on the table for him and wife, Rosemarie. Danny prayed, "St. Jude, I promise that if you help me in this time of need, I will build a shrine in your name to aid all of humanity." Danny got that job, and the rest, as they say, is history.

St. Jude Children's Research Hospital is the only childhood cancer research center designated as such by the National Cancer Institute. It is the first and the largest institution established for the sole purpose of conducting basic and clinical research in catastrophic childhood diseases. The hospital is non-sectarian, interracial, and is open to all patients whose diseases are under study at the institution. Patients meeting these criteria are admitted regardless of their ability to pay. Since its opening in 1962, more than 13,000 children from across the United States and from 49 foreign countries have come to St. Jude seeking help and hope. Because of breakthroughs at St. Jude, great strides have been made in improving childhood cancer survival rates since the early 1960s. In 1962, 95% of children with some form of cancer died. Currently, the survival rate has climbed to almost 60% for all cancers; and for leukemia patients, it has risen to 73%.

St. Jude is sometimes called the hospital without walls because children all over the world benefit from knowledge gained there. Since the hospital's founding, the St. Jude staff has been committed to a policy of sharing with all physicians and scientists their basic and clinical research findings and accomplishments. For this reason alone, any gift of time or money is more than a gift to *one* hospital—it extends far beyond the hospital's walls, helping children the world over.

Sandy and I first fell in love with St. Jude Hospital in the mid-Seventies when we met Danny Thomas during our annual KMPC "radiothons" benefitting the hospital. Then when the annual summertime St. Jude benefit Gala became one of the *events* of the season, we actively participated in helping make those bigger and better each year. These Gala Evenings began with a fund-raising dinner for St. Jude at the Century Plaza

Danny's business partner Ron Jacobs produced, and Wink hosted, a "$100,000 Walkthrough of St. Jude Hospital."

Hotel in 1979, an idea of Danny's wife, Rosemarie. In addition to a featured star performer, someone also came up with the idea of a live, on-stage auction. A sound idea! However, when Sammy Davis, Jr. and I, acting as auctioneers, began describing the items and opening the bidding, there were few, *or no bidders*! So the two of us, to save face and avoid embarrassment, began bidding *ourselves*. At the end of the evening, Sammy and Wink had bought 90% of the items, running up a tremendous credit charge in the process — and 95% of the purchases, we couldn't even recall! Three things resulted from that disasterous auction: 1) St. Jude never again held a "live" auction, resorting only to the "silent" variety. 2) I promised myself I would never again agree to hosting *any* kind of auction. 3) Danny met with Sammy and me the next day at his home and exonerated us from buying anything we didn't really want.

While at Danny's house that day, (we were in the midst of a prolonged gasoline shortage), Sandy and I happened to pull up in front of the statue of St. Jude, alongside the circular driveway. When told that we'd just made it to the house, being low on gas, Danny informed us that St. Jude could perform miracles — but he would **not** fill our gas tank!

Our participation accelerated to the point where we were added to the Los Angeles Board of Directors for the hospital, a position

we both held for several years. I was also honored to have been
appointed a member of the St. Jude National Advisory Council from
1988 through 1991.

Miracles Cost Money

It was during this period
that Danny honored me by asking that I host a "$100,000
Walkthrough" of the hospital,
the purpose of which was to
show just how rapidly the sum
of $100,000 was spent in the
day-to-day operation of the
hospital. Danny's business
partner Ron Jacobs flew with
us to Memphis and produced
this eye-opening one-hour Special that was effectively used
for several years in raising

Danny presents to Wink a framed picture
of St. Jude Children's Research Hospital,
which was signed by all the doctor's of the
world-renowned facility.

funds on the St. Jude Telethons. To see the hospital "at work" was
enlightening as well as inspiring. We learned of a young girl who was
battling acute lymphocytic leukemia (ALL), the most common form of
childhood cancer. The girl had been miraculously cured, and when she
grew to adulthood, her greatest desire was to be married in the St. Jude
hospital auditorium. She wanted her *new life* to begin where her *young
life* had been saved.

Though I had been raised a Methodist, Sandy was of the Catholic
faith, and on many occasions we both found ourselves praying to St.
Jude for help and guidance in our lives. One such occasion found the
odds solidly against me becoming host of a show I wanted very badly,
Las Vegas Gambit, the 1981 NBC version of a "21" game I had originally hosted on CBS in the early Seventies. This particular day, we
stopped at church to pray to St. Jude on our way to an LA St. Jude
Board meeting. Immediately afterwards, while driving to the meeting, we received a phone call from my agent informing me that I *had*
the job. Then at the meeting, what happens? As an expression of
appreciation, Danny presents Sandy and me with a plaque and a framed
picture of the hospital autographed by all the doctors, with the famous
statue of St. Jude standing watch at the entrance to St. Jude Children's

Research Hospital! Needless to say, our connection to Danny and St. Jude Hospital was, and is, a deep and sincere one.

Golden Galas

I would like to mention a few of the more memorable of the Summer Gala's that have become so much a part of the fundraising arm of the hospital, and a social event held for all the right reasons.

The Gala held Saturday evening of August 30, 1986 was special for *two* reasons. First and foremost, it was the 7th annual event for the benefit of this world class children's research center. Secondly,

Sandy poses with Danny during one of his many visits to Wink's restaurant in Memphis.

Danny and Rosemarie were celebrating their 50th wedding anniversary! In honor of that milestone in their lives—joining them to celebrate their golden years was an "Array of Golden Stars"— their incomparable (son-in-law) Phil Donahue acted as emcee, along with singers Rosemary Clooney, Peggy Lee, Tony Martin, The McGuire Sisters, Helen O'Connell, Kay Starr, and comedians Jan Murray and Bob Newhart. It was truly a night when the stars came out and shone brightly on this marvelous humanitarian duo.

The following year marked the 25th anniversary of the hospital, the only one of its kind on earth. And once again the giant ballroom of the Century Plaza Hotel was packed in celebration of this God-

St. Jude supporter Rosie Clooney was a featured star for the 1986 St. Jude Gala.

given milestone. Talk about God-given—The "Daddy" of all show business, George Burns, gave of his time and comedic talents as the St. Jude Superstar. And, you know George—he insisted on bringing *the girls* along—the legendary Peggy Lee and Helen O'Connell. The date was September 5, 1987, an evening of evenings in the annals of St. Jude Children's Research Hospital.

The "Daddy" of show biz, George Burns, featured star of 1987's St. Jude Gala.

We still have Rosie's letter announcing the Gala for Saturday, August 20, 1988. It was extremely noteworthy. "How do you keep the music playing?" was the theme, inspired by guest Superstar Tony Bennett's exciting version of the new hit song. The lyrics were paraphrased as follows: "How do you keep the research going? How do you make it last? How do you keep their lives from fading too fast?" The answer, of course, was all of us who care for suffering children all over the world stricken with catastrophic dis-

Wink and Sandy Martindale visit with St. Jude Hospital medical director Dr. Albert Mauer during the making of Wink's "$100,000 Walkthrough."

eases, and now a new and devastating one AIDS had begun to strike children, newborns, and those yet to be born. So this St. Jude Gala struck a chord like none before or since.

Triple Your Pleasure

The 10th annual St. Jude Gala, August 12, 1989, was

The 10th Annual St. Jude Gala featured the "Living Legends of Comedy"—Sid Caesar, Danny, and Milton Berle (pictured above between Sandy and Wink).

thrice blessed with the help of The Living Legends of Comedy — Milton Berle, Sid Caesar and of course, Danny Thomas, truly "A Gala Night!" These three master showmen had been touring the country together for months with spectacular success, and, to no one's surprise this Gala was one of the most successful of them all in raising the funds necessary to save the lives of children suffering from cancer, leukemia, cyclecell anemia, neuroblastoma and of course, the most recent scourge to raise its ugly head—AIDS in children.

Eydie Gorme and Steve Lawrence sing "Alone Together," (except for Wink in the background).

Sandy and I have attended, and sold tickets to almost every Gala since that first one in 1979. They all were, and are, so very *special*. I must mention one more as another shining example of the love and esteem the Superstars in show business held for Danny and Rosie, and St. Jude hospital in Memphis. Remember, all these stars through the years have performed gratis. And on this night, Saturday, July 21, 1990, the St. Jude faithful were treated to a marvelous evening called "Steve and Eydie: Alone Together." Combining their many hits with a generous sprinkling of standards by Rodgers and Hammerstein, Cole Porter and George Gershwin, with the help of rear-screen projection, they featured a retrospective of the great days of big-bands. Steve Lawrence and Eydie Gorme, truly "one-of-a-kind!"

Your invitation to the 1990 St. Jude Gala starring Steve Lawrence and Eydie Gorme.

St. Jude — "St. Thomas"

There are so many memories of our attachment to Danny and his shrine to St. Jude for children. We were only one couple among hundreds and hundreds doing what we could to further the work of his world-renowned hospital in Memphis. But he made everyone feel as though the hospital would somehow not survive, but for our efforts. He was truly extraordinary, with an extraordinary memory. For example, in 1988 Sandy and I were guests on a short-lived game show called *Relatively Speaking* hosted by comedian John Byner. We luckily won a complete kitchen and contributed it to the St. Jude chapter in Spring Hill, Florida, where a house was being built, to be sold with proceeds going to the hospital. Though the house raised only $40,000 for St. Jude, Danny spoke many times of our small gesture as a valuable contribution and splendid example to others of support for the hospital. This from a man who ran a worldwide fund-raising effort netting multi-millions of dollars every year for St.

St. Jude founder Danny Thomas became one of Wink's dearest friends.

Jude hospital.

The untimely death of Danny Thomas, February 6, 1991, in Beverly Hills at the age of 79, was a tragic blow to his many friends and his countless fans. Not to mention the hospital he founded.

Mike ("Austin Powers") Myers and wife lend their strong support to a St. Jude Gala.

St. Jude Children's Research Hospital is financially secure in continuing its work as one of the world's premier medical facilities into the next century. The imprint this man made on human society is a legacy that is incalculable. Personally, we think of Danny almost daily. His smile, his stories, his infectious laugh, the ever-present cigar — are pictures indelibly etched in our memory. Like the night of our 10th wedding anniversary party in Malibu, 1985. After dinner, without even being asked, Danny took the microphone and became emcee for the evening, introducing various guests, beginning with his wife Rosemarie. He asked Barry White to sing a song, and appropriately, Barry chose Billy Joel's "Just the Way You Are." Fred Travalena did his famous Richard Nixon impression. It was an expression of love and caring that so typified Danny.

Of Love and Friendship

The night of the St. Jude Gala in 1990, in expressing his appreciation to Steve Lawrence and Eydie Gorme for their incredible performance, Danny recited some words that impressed Sandy so much that she later requested a copy. He wrote out in longhand these words she cherishes to this day, and reprinted here:

> "Sandy, beloved—When you hear that I am breathing my last, come to me; be not tearful, only smile; smile that the lenses of my eyes might photograph you—and as my lids are closed, I will take only your picture into eternity.

> P.S. Don't let Wink see this!

> Love, Danny.

Our feeling for Danny Thomas is best expressed in this poem.

Friendship:

Friendship is a priceless gift,
that cannot be bought or sold.
Its value is far greater
than a mountain of gold.
For gold is cold and useless,
it neither can see nor hear
and in times of trouble, it is
powerless to cheer.

It has no ears to listen, it has no
heart to understand.
It cannot bring comfort, or reach
out with a helping hand.
So when you ask for a gift, be
thankful if you receive
not diamonds, not pearls, but
instead the love of a real true friend.
—author unknown

Upon his death, Danny wished to be entombed at the hospital that had meant life to so many, St. Jude Children's Research Hospital. How do we part with a man who gave so much to so many? Who laughed with us, worked with us, and loved us. Who felt a never-ending drive to shine his light upon the world—and to make it last forever. How do we part with this man? We remember!

Man of Music

Over the years, I have gladly given of my time and whatever talents I may possess, to further the work of many charitable causes. Included among my *personal* favorite events, however, was an annual Celebrity Banquet and Softball Game staged by award-winning songwriter/producer David Foster to raise funds for families of children requiring organ transplants. A native of Victoria, British Columbia, Canada, David has become the premiere man-of-music in every sense of the word, having produced the *Bodyguard* album, fastest and biggest selling soundtrack in history, including Whitney Houston's "I Will Always Love You." Add to that his recent work

Crack record producer David Foster seems to be in a smile contest with Wink.

with Barbra Streisand, Michael Bolton, Natalie Cole ("Unforgettable") among many other pop superstars, and one might be surprised to discover that even with an endless schedule of rehearsals, record sessions, concerts, composing, a wife and eight children, David still finds time to give something back.

Some Time in Your Life

Another activity I find most rewarding is visiting the Los Angeles

In 1985, Lambuth College confers an Honorary Doctorate degree on Jackson's Wink Martindale.

Mission once or twice a year. It is imperative that there be concern for the hungry and homeless men, women and children in our society. To dish up food for those less fortunate than we is an experience everyone should experience at some time in their life. Sharing and caring with those who, for whatever reason, have so little is an unforgettable feeling.

While hosting *Tic-Tac-Dough* for seven years, it was my pleasure to visit Philadelphia on many promotional trips. Among the nation's top ABC network affiliates, WPVI (which carried our show), also produced an annual Variety Club telethon, hosted by Monty Hall. Though local in geographical terms, this is still one of the most professionally produced telethons—network or otherwise—that I have ever seen. Each year some of the biggest network stars can be counted on to take part in this two-day fund raising event that never fails to raise millions of dollars for the charitable work of Variety Clubs International. Art Moore, then head of promotion and publicity for WPVI, is still one of my dearest friends in the industry as a result of our working relationship with *Tic-Tac-Dough* and the telethon. Today Art is director of programming for WABC in New York, and Executive Producer of *Live! With Regis and Kathie Lee.*

Wink's agent Fred Wostbrock (far left), Sandy, Ray Conniff, Jerry Vale and Buddy Hackett serve up food for the homeless at L. A. Mission.

Bittersweet Memories

Other than my work with St. Jude Children's Research Hospital, my only other *long-term* commitment to a charitable organization was to the West Tennessee Cerebral Palsy Center in my hometown, Jackson, Tennessee. It was an unforgettable association that began almost accidentally— and ended 10 years later in what might be described as somewhat bittersweet. While watching television one cold, winter night in 1977, I received a surprise call from a friend in

Host Monty Hall is joined by singers Pearl Bailey and Jack Jones for the giant annual Philadelphia Variety Club Telethon.

Jackson whom I hadn't heard from in years. He explained that the local CP Center was not receiving adequate funds (approximately $25,000) from the National Cerebral Palsy telethon to maintain the Center—and would I consider coming back to emcee a local telethon? I accepted for several reasons: the plight of the CP Center; my love for children disadvantaged with cerebral palsy; my longstanding friendship with Jean McCoy (who ran the Center at the time); plus, this would afford me the opportunity to do something for others in the town in which I had grown up and enjoyed my first days in radio.

Following that first telethon, I was "hooked." I fell in love with those kids, the Center, and all it represented. I offered to come back the following year, which I did. One year led to another, then another, and the fund-raiser became the *Wink Martindale Cerebral Palsy Telethon.* Natu-

Los Angeles news personality Bill Smith and wife Karen gave Wink and Sandy a helping hand for several years during Wink's Telethons.

rally I was honored to have my name attached to it, but I also felt a greater and greater sense of responsibility to produce a better and better show. In my view, the more professionally entertaining the show, the bigger the audience watching the show. And more viewers would just naturally translate into more pledges and donations.

Ed Lojeski traveled from L.A. to Jackson every year to conduct the Telethon orchestra.

From year two, I began putting "the arm" on as many performing friends as I could to set aside a weekend in March to fly to Jackson and participate. They all knew the term CP, but few knew there was a Jackson, Tennessee. When I would mention it was strictly a local telethon seen within a 100-mile radius at best, many times I would receive blank stares.

But after a promise of true Southern hospitality, red carpet treatment, an excellent orchestra of professional Nashville musicians to play their arrangements, and fun beyond words, people like The Lettermen, Toni Tennille, Foster Brooks, Fred Travalena, Jerry Vale, Maureen McGovern, Frankie Avalon, Mel Carter and Pia Zadora, to name a few, would consent to make the trip—many more than once. Ed Lojeski, a longtime friend, came every year to handle all the music charts, rehearsals and most of the conducting. L.A. sound expert Andy Waterman would fly back to assure network quality sound for television. KTLA, Los Angeles' news personality Bill Smith and my brother-in-law Jack King, a director with KMOX in St. Louis, would volunteer their directorial services for the long and sometimes grueling two days.

Wink with singer/impersonator Fred Travalena, who performed five consecutive years at the CP Telethon.

Naturally, all the Los Angeles participants would expect, and receive, first-class air transportation to Memphis, where they would be picked up and driven the remaining 85 miles to their weekend home away from home, the Holiday Inn. Naturally, to transport and lodge those from L.A. was much more expensive than a *drive* would be for a singer from Nashville, a scant 100 miles away. But with rare exceptions, like Minnie Pearl, John Hartford, Shelley West and David Frizzell, getting artists to commit to a local telethon from Music City U.S.A. was next to impossible. Without question Nashville stars would have been a far greater draw than any ten singers I might bring from California.

Wink performs a favorite narrative "To a Sleeping Beauty" to a beautiful young lady served by the West Tennessee CP Center.

A Momentary Disappointment

This fact was brought home and proven beyond question in 1982 when Johnny Mathis consented to give a summer concert at the Jackson Coliseum to benefit the Cerebral Palsy Center. A disappointing crowd of no more than 2,000 attended— for an entertainer who fills venues around the world performing to SRO audiences. As I walked out on stage to introduce Johnny

Hudson and Saleeby harmonize during rehearsals with "Little" Peggy March.

that night, I cried shamelessly. The lack of response to this golden opportunity was an embarrassment that haunts me to this day, a disappointment only in the sense that this sensational evening of classic popular entertainment could have reaped great financial rewards for the Center.

Jacksonian Carl ("Blue Suede Shoes") Perkins never failed to plan his schedule so that particular weekend could be spent at home. He would sing a song or two and verbalize his always effective appeals for the local Cerebral Palsy Center. Thanks to telethon chairman Bob

Singer Pia Zadora, shown here with Wink and young daughter Kady, created quite a stir when her private jet landed at the Jackson airport.

Arrington, a master of organization and detail, along with Jimmy Exum, Dick Arrington, Hilliard Murphy and longtime friend of the CP Center "Cousin Tuny"— and by *combining* our professionals with many local bands, singers, quartets and an army of local volunteers — we formed a teriffic team successful in mounting a first-rate television program that we all could be proud of, and one that seemed to draw an appreciative and better than average home audience.

During the 1986 CP Telethon, Wink's longtime friends (and neighbors) KingWorld President Michael King, and wife Barbara flew to Jackson, answered phones and surprised Wink with a check from the King family in the amount $25,000 for the Center.

Earlier, I used the word *bittersweet* to describe how my 10-year association with the telethon ended.

What proved to be my tenth and final CP Telethon in March, 1988, had barely ended when a local television talk show host named Bill Way, and some of his callers, described a litany of items portraying my use of the telethon as mainly self-serving. The callers were vindictive, inaccurate and showed a total disregard for what our primary purpose had been for the ten years I had been involved.

For two years I had been vocal in my opposition to the outmoded

In 1982, Johnny Mathis (between Sandy and Wink) gave a live concert in Jackson to benefit the CP Center.

telethon form as the Center's primary means of financially operating the Center. I felt a full-time professional fundraiser contracted to the Center was a viable answer. To continue to rely on a telethon was unrealistic and financially unsound considering the state of the economy. I also realized that while the telethon was receiving more financial support than ever in terms of local businesses and individual pledges, the cost of producing the show had grown beyond the ability of the community to support it.

In June of 1988, I wrote the Center officials expressing my views and in effect, resigning from further involvement in the show, "To continue attempting to bring talent and personnel from California was ridiculous, time-consuming, and most certainly too expensive. Nashville is the answer. Sandy and I thank you for the opportunity to have served the Center these past ten years. We wish for it, and its precious children Godspeed and nothing but continued success."

Then on Wednesday, November 23rd, the local paper's front-page headline read:

TELETHON CROSSES OUT WINK MARTINDALE
Cerebral Palsy Center Can't Afford Celebrity

The "loveable lush," comedian Foster Brooks, also proves his way with a song in this picture from one of five telethons in which he participated.

It was this sub-headline that cut the deepest personally, for while the words showed the writer was ignorant of the facts, those few words had been written to sound as though

I had received something other than gratitude from the parents and children served by the Center. This led me to purchase a full page ad in the paper to set the record straight as to how and why I first was asked to host the telethon, and how pride of participation and the cause for which the telethon served led me to be involved for 10 years. Whatever the writer's motives, the slant of her story was immature and unprofessional in its approach, and hopefully has long since been forgotten.

Mel Carter proved a big Telethon favorite singing his hits "Hold Me, Thrill Me, Kiss Me," "Band of Gold," and "All of a Sudden My Heart Sings."

This unfortunate episode, has certainly not affected my quest to help others whenever possible. My *tradition of caring* is stronger than ever, as is my love for the West Tennessee Cerebral Palsy Center and the precious children served by it. Several years ago I was honored to have been asked by the 700 Club's Pat

Singer John Adair, Wink and Sandy are joined by the cast and crew to wrap another CP Telethon in Jackson.

Robertson to co-host with Carol Lawrence, *Wings of Hope*, a one-hour television special for Operation Blessing to raise funds and awareness for a revolutionary new outreach, responding to the desperate needs of hurting men, women, and children around the globe.

Longtime favorite from the Lawrence Welk Show, ragtime pianist/singer Joanne Castle, was a Telethon favorite.

Operation Blessing launched the "Medical Strike Force" plane, a Lockheed L-1011,

OPERATION BLESSING

equipped with the latest medical technology. The Medical Strike Force can quickly respond and save lives in any area of the world when moments count.

Toni Tennille sings one of her many A&M hits, "Love Will Keep Us Together" during the 1984 CP Telethon.

Giving Something Back

Chapter Ten

THE NEW MILLENNIUM . . .

What Next?

T he Nineties might well have been termed "the decade of talk." Television ran the gamut. Whatever we as view- ers desired to talk about or hear discussed, television gave it to us. For better or worse. From *Oprah* to *Jerry Springer.* From *Jenny Jones* to *Howard Stern.* From *Judge Judy* to *Divorce Court.* Et cetera. Et cetera.

During this period I was asked time and time again, "Will game shows ever be back?" My answer was always the same. No matter how popular the genre, be it the talk show, the situation comedy, the *Movie of the Week*, the sports event, the audience can always be won over with a show, game, whatever, that is enter- taining, enjoyable to watch and compelling. Call it what you will, such a game/quiz show finally came along in 1999 that

Regis Philbin asks America, "Who Wants to Be a Millionaire?"

was right for its time. A time when the public had grown tired of talk, talk, talk. *Who Wants To Be a Millionaire?* hosted by Regis Philbin on ABC, turned television on its ear during a summer of discontent, and repeat after repeat shows.

The show gave away over $1.4 million during its two-week run and the summer blockbuster won its time period and improved upon its lead—in all 13 nights on the air. In fact its final airing Sunday night averaged an 8.7 Nielsen rating in adults 18-49, 22.4 million viewers and a 14 rating and 22 share in households, making it the most-watched program of the week. ABC had taken a chance, and hit the jackpot! Needless to say it returned in the fall, amid speculation by the skeptics that the overwhelming success of *Millionaire* was due to its weak competition of tired summer re-runs. Once again those skeptics failed to recognize that the show was entertaining, enjoyable to watch, and compelling! By the end of its second run during November, the show had beaten all its competition and had given away over five million dollars!

Follower Frenzy

Television has always been a world of fast-followers. The success of *Millionaire* triggered a frenzy around Hollywood, with game shows being pitched at every network. Even before this breakthrough show, ABC had been considering a current events show *Have I Got News for You?* and CBS was planning to remake the classic *What's My Line?* It was the second summer in a row ABC had experimented with alternative first-run fare. The summer of '98 they clicked with the combination improv/game show *Whose Line Is It Anyway?* which, like *Millionaire*, was an adaptation of a successful British series.

Games have always been a staple of television, and they were popular with listeners to radio in the Forties and Fifties. *Stop The Music* with Bert Parks kept the nation glued to their radios on Sunday nights. Our business is a cyclical one. What goes around, comes around. Remember the Seventies? And the long running series of *Pyramid* shows, *Tic-Tac-Dough, The Joker's Wild, Family Feud, Match Game,* and the original *Hollywood Squares*? Even doctors take a sabbatical. Why not game shows, and their viewers? Let us bear in mind that in addition to *The Price Is Right* on CBS, the two highest rated shows in first-run syndication for many years were GAMES — *Wheel of Fortune* and *Jeopardy!* Game shows never really left us. Perhaps, just perhaps, it was the *producers* of game shows who continued to develop ideas and concepts that were just fair to mediocre.

Game Show Network

For those who enjoy the freshness of the new with the classics of the past, Sony began delivering the 24-hour Game Show Network in 1993. With the multichannel universe and the expansion of the information superhighway, the network was a natural. In addition to those I have already mentioned, now we could again enjoy *The Newlywed Game, I've Got a Secret, To Tell the Truth, Password, The Dating Game, Card Sharks,* even *The Gong Show!* And many more.

Additionally, the key factor in the convergence of TV, telecommunications and multimedia was wrapped up in one word: Interactivity. Game Show Network was among the first to produce shows that were viewer friendly. My partner, Bill Hillier, and I, were the first to produce inherently interactive programming in 1993 when the shows *Trivial Pursuit, Boggle* and *Shuffle* premiered on The Family Channel giving the viewers at home the chance to play real-time by using their touch-tone telephones and compete for great prizes. These games and our method of play-along were covered in an earlier chapter.

But it was Game Show Network that took the available technology to another level offering the American public the benefits of a dynamic program service, the best of game shows plus a taste of the whole new world of interactivity.

Family Channel President Tim Robertson, Wink and partner Bill Hillier cut the cake signifying the kick off of *Trivial Pursuit* game block in 1993.

The Weaving of the Web

With the emergence of the worldwide internet and WebTV came the inevitable. Games, games, and more games. Personally, I am delighted to be actively involved with a new and popular game channel on the internet. As spokesperson, host, and producer for this channel we created the kick-off show *I-Road Cracks,* where internet contestants use their street smarts to play "the funniest game show on wheels!" Described as the high speed, action-packed, grand prix of internet game shows, it helped to drive the internet game player into the next millennium!

It is abundantly clear that many media companies large and small recognize the need, and promise, of viewer friendly games on the internet. Not the least of which is Sony. It has long featured a series of gameshows online, including online editions of *Jeopardy!, Wheel of Fortune* and *The Dating Game.* They have continued to push the interactive versions of the shows with an extensive marketing campaign.

Fans of *Wheel* and *Jeopardy!* can now play along with show contestants. Where will it all end? More importantly, just imagine how exciting games on the internet transferred to television will be in years to come! And television game shows using home viewers as contestants interactively competing against in-studio players? Just around the corner!

My Guiding Light

Shifting from the future to the past, among my most vivid child-

The Garden Tomb in Jerusalem, possibly the site of Jesus Tomb. On the door reads "He is not here—for He is risen."

hood memories are those of my Mother sitting under the light of a dim lamp in our living room reading the *Bible* each night. When she had read it cover to cover, it was back to Genesis again. I asked her once how many times she had read the *Bible.* She couldn't tell me. She had long since lost count. I mention this because I was anything *but* a student of the *Bible* as a kid growing up. Sunday school, church, and grudgingly, Vacation Bible School was about it for me. But recently, as Sandy and I were touring the Holy Land, I felt more than once that Mother was holding my hand and leading me gently through this unique and beautiful land, rich with a variety of historical, archaeological, and religious sites. Sites that my Mom knew so well. Not from being there, but through the word pictures painted by those hundreds and hundreds of nightly visits to faraway lands where her precious *Bible* had been written thousands of years before.

The Mount of Beatitudes north of the Sea of Galilee, where Jesus gave the Sermon on the Mount.

We'll Be Back

As an on-air personality on *Music of Your Life*, Sandy and I, in the year 2000, will pay a return visit to the Holy Land, hosting hundreds of my listeners who desire to experience the special thrill of walking

The Silver Star in the Church of the Nativity designates the spot where, as tradition has it, Jesus was born.

the hills where Abraham roamed four-thousand years ago. It was in these regions that Jesus, the Son of God was born. Here He grew in wisdom and stature. Here He was crucified. Here God raised Him from the dead. This first trip was more or less a familiarization tour. Days we shall never forget. Days we look forward to repeating.

From the Mount of Olives to the tomb of King David, who reigned here three thousand years ago, we walked along the Via Dolorosa to the Church of the Holy Sepulchre—then to Bethlehem and the Church of Nativity and Manger Square. We drove to Jericho, the oldest city in the world, through the Jordan Valley to Tiberias, stopping at Nazareth to visit the Church of the Annunciation. To take a boat ride across the Sea of Galilee and visit Capernaum and see the ancient synagogue where Jesus taught, and to visit Tabgha, where Jesus fed the 5000, onto the Mount of Beatitudes, the site of the Sermon on the Mount, was like

Wink and Sandy in an amphitheatre of Beth Shean, one of the oldest cities in the Holy Land.

taking a trip back through the ages.

We visited the Dead Sea, lowest point on Earth, and stopped at Qumran to visit the site where the Dead Sea Scrolls were found. Then we went on to Massada and the ancient fortress where the Zealots made their last stand against the Romans before committing mass suicide in 73 A.D.

A Tiny Land of Biblical Giants

Perhaps you can sense now just why I felt my Mother's presence in all these Holy places. Before going there friend after friend would say to us, "Visiting those lands will change your life." I didn't understand the full meaning of their words. Until we were actually there.

Like my Mom, many of you may simply experience this land of promise in beautiful pictures, Biblical and otherwise. But if it is ever possible
for you to visit this little land that is so large in biblical history, do so.

Believe me when I tell you—*it will change your life forever!*

Retire from What?

As for me, at this writing, I hope to continue being active in this
business I chose to be a part of as a young boy in Jackson, Tennessee
many years ago. As a radio and television performer, and as a producer of shows, I have watched as many of my peers have come and
gone. Personally I love to compete in this arena. Occasionally someone will mention the word retirement to me and my retort is always
the same: "Retire from what?" If I ever reach the point in my life
where I do not truly have fun and enjoy what I do, then I'll walk off
into the sunset. But I love the joy of developing ideas and concepts
into shows with the hope of sharing them with you on the air. And
although it is common knowledge that youth reigns in our business
and the powers that be are always searching for "fresh faces," there is
much to be said for age and the experience of the last show, and the
show before that, and the show before that.

When ABC decided to put *Who Wants To Be a Millionaire?* on the
air in prime time, they argued and fought against Regis Philbin as
host, ignoring his high profile popularity on most ABC affiliates carrying *Live! With Regis & Kathie Lee.* But Regis insisted he had never
before asked ABC for a favor. He wanted to host this show! Finally,
combined with his fervor and his agents at William Morris, Regis got
his way and handled the hosting of *Millionaires* in superb fashion,
making himself, the Morris Agency and especially the *suits* at ABC
look like geniuses!

God, Country, Mom, and Apple Pie

The world of games has been fun and fascinating for me, but not my
entire focus. "Deck of Cards" emergence as a public favorite in 1959 led
me to record several narrative albums over the years, even a song or two
thrown in! 1999 marked the fortieth anniversary of my surprising entry
into the exciting world of records, an anniversary marked by the release of
this book's counterpart, which was a CD entitled *Winking at Life.*

Though "Deck of Cards" was fiction, I realized how much people
identified with strong stories. So my partner and good friend, Rick
Quintana, pulled together my collection of favorite stories, poems and

vignettes covering God, country, mom, and apple pie and had them richly arranged with choir and orchestra by talented Nashville producer/arranger Steve Peppos. They are released on our own Century Hill record label, and the result showed more dramatically than I could have ever imagined, the power of the spoken word.

"Dear Teacher" was a father's note sent to his daughter's first teacher. "Working Man's Prayer" honored the common man's daily grind. Stories about the Pledge of Allegiance, Mother's Day, legendary slugger "Casey at the Bat," a newly recorded version of "Deck of Cards," plus an intriguing story that asks: Would you be ready to share your every day TV, reading and social habits, "If Jesus Came to Your House"?

As I mentioned earlier in this book, I was raised in a Christian home. But neither do I carry my religion on my sleeve, nor do I try to impose my beliefs on others. On the other hand, I would feel remiss not to use whatever celebrity I may possess in an effort to convey my feeling about a growing sense of moral bankruptcy in certain areas of our society today. Perhaps you would agree that the old days of common respect for your neighbors, women, God and country has all but died. One only has to visit his neighborhood theater or tune in one of many popular radio or television talk shows, soaps or situation comedies to witness first hand examples of the new levels to which our industry has sunk in the name of the almighty dollar. With the amount of sex, violence, and killing just for the sake of "dramatic effect" on the large and small screen, is it any wonder we have the rage and mental sickness seen among our young people in the past few years?

The Family Hour?

Please do not misunderstand. I consider myself anything but a *prude!* But when a mom and dad cannot risk gathering their brood around the TV set without first checking a show's rating, who's to blame? The actors, the writers, the viewers, or perhaps the programming gurus who make the decisions to allow or disallow a questionable word or phrase to be used. Whatever happened to that misnomer called *the family hour*? Whatever happened to that Federal agency in Washington that protected the listener/viewer from filthy language? Not just common swear words but disgusting, embarrassing smut and talk about bodily functions and sexual acts coupled with the images of equal trashiness.

The FCC (Federal Communications Commission) used to put the fear of God into those of us who even *thought about* swearing on the air, much less *saying* what we were thinking. But modern day radio and television is reaping millions and setting new levels of filth for folks to live *DOWN* to.

Where does it end? Unfortunately the new 21st Century bodes no better. Only worse. Until those who yell from the rooftops, as in that famous scene from the movie *Network,* "I'm mad as hell and I'm not going to take it anymore," *AND MEAN IT!* Only

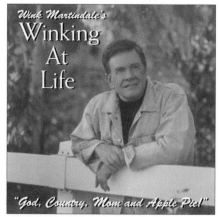

Wink Martindale's
Winking At Life

"God, Country, Mom and Apple Pie!"

Wink's new CD of favorite narratives touches on God, Country, Mom and Apple Pie.

when a grass roots effort takes such a large and powerful stand that the largest of advertisers (and we know who they are) feels the pinch right where it hurts — bottom-line profits — will a turn for the better begin to emerge. *Winking at Life,* the CD series, is intended as a modest effort at trying to create a little equity on the playing field.

With all that in mind, I'll see ya on the tube. By the way, thanks for taking the time to read my story.

The New Millennium

INDEX